T0373672

Countering Cyber Sabotage

Countering Cyber Sabotage

Introducing Consequence-Driven, Cyber-Informed Engineering (CCE)

Andrew A. Bochman and Sarah Freeman

CRC Press
Taylor & Francis Group
Boca Raton London New York

CRC Press is an imprint of the
Taylor & Francis Group, an **informa** business

First edition published 2021
by CRC Press
2 Park Square, Milton Park, Abingdon, Oxon OX14 4RN

and by CRC Press
6000 Broken Sound Parkway NW, Suite 300,
Boca Raton, FL 33487-2742

CRC Press is an imprint of Informa UK Limited

Library of Congress Cataloging-in-Publication Data
Names: Bochman, Andrew A., author. | Freeman, Sarah, author.
Title: Countering cyber sabotage: introducing consequence-driven,
cyber-informed engineering/Andrew A. Bochman and Sarah Freeman.
Description: Boca Raton, FL: CRC Press, 2021. |
Includes bibliographical references and index.
Identifiers: LCCN 2020032432 (print) | LCCN 2020032433 (ebook) |
ISBN 9780367491154 (hardback) | ISBN 9781003130826 (ebook)
Subjects: LCSH: Computer security–United States. |
Computer crimes–United States–Prevention. | Automation–Security measures. |
Infrastructure (Economics)–United States–Protection. |
National security–United States.
Classification: LCC QA76.9.A25 B596 2021 (print) |
LCC QA76.9.A25 (ebook) | DDC 005.8–dc23
LC record available at https://lccn.loc.gov/2020032432
LC ebook record available at https://lccn.loc.gov/2020032433

ISBN: 978-0-367-49115-4 (hbk)
ISBN: 978-1-003-13082-6 (ebk)

Typeset in Palatino
by Newgen Publishing UK

CONTENTS

CONTENTS

FOREWORD
BY MICHAEL J. ASSANTE

It is time to recognize how traditional engineering practices have fully absorbed cyber technology across the full engineering lifecycle. We must do more to fully understand our most critical systems, how they were built, how they work, on what they depend, and how they can be mistakenly operated. With this knowledge we need to make next generation designs demonstrably more secure. For many engineers, and the managers who employ them, this will require a series of conceptual leaps as the behavior of software is completely unlike the laws of physics in which they have until recently placed their full trust.

The aerospace sector provides a few recent instructive examples. The 2018 and 2019 Boeing 737 Max crashes revealed, catastrophically, erroneous assumptions about how software would compensate for observed flaws in engineered design. Earlier, other assumptions encoded in an overreliance on software doomed an AirBus A400M, prompting me to write this at the time:

> This tragic accident reminds us of the nature of cyber and its ability to achieve scales that often surprise us. The safety basis for the aircraft failed to analyze a scenario involving software problems for more than one engine. There are numerous process safety efforts that also failed to account for software errors or malware conditions in many places at once (horizontal susceptibility) throughout the world's power systems, chemical plants, and transportation systems.[1]

Safety use case assumptions coded in software that are effective in individual systems can quickly break down when software links multiple systems. These risks exist separately from what can go wrong when an adversary enters the picture.

Although we are already well down the road to total dependency on digital systems, there remains much to be discovered about how engineers have come to trust software to fill gaps in first principles engineering.[2] We must achieve and promulgate a much deeper understanding of the cyber contents of critical physical systems and the potential conflicts within them, including the processes used to create, operate, and maintain them.

This isn't just a recommendation; there's a warning here related to what is occurring in infrastructures around the world. Nation-states are leveraging substantial technical capabilities to put and hold critical infrastructure at risk, with ever-increasing cyberattacks against target (or victim) countries. While that's happening at the state-on-state level, companies are also being caught in the crossfire. Where infrastructure providers (e.g., energy, water, communications) used to focus emergency planning on assaults from Mother Nature, they've now become pawns in a geopolitical chess match. It's been demonstrated that strikes on them can and will be used as shots across the bow, to deter military mobilization, to punch back, or to send whatever message one country feels like it needs to communicate to another, with all others watching.

That's where we find ourselves. It's not Tom Clancy, it's not marketing, and it's not hyperbole. If you take what we've seen and heard as intentions, this is an iterative, unending, defensive call-to-arms. You must strive to understand your most vital systems more deeply than you ever have. This is one of the main tenets of consequence-driven, cyber-informed engineering (CCE), as is the need to identify potential paths of entry and closely monitor potential adversary activities in your supply chain and subcontractors, as well as network paths of entry, egress, and maneuver. This level of understanding is needed to achieve the earliest of warnings and tripwires, so you can move in ways that minimize consequences, work through attacks, recover fully, and get ready to do it again.

Cyberattacks like these have been going on beneath the surface for years, but cyber was used with more restraint as an instrument of projected international power and intimidation. Today the genie is out of the bottle and there's no going back. In this new world, critical infrastructure providers find themselves among the most attractive targets, not because of who they are but because of the essential services they provide and to whom they provide them.

Something I want to be sure to get across is that by understanding your most essential processes and systems deeply enough, you have a very good chance of minimizing the worst consequences during an event. Not only that, but you may be able to stall longer campaigns aimed at you. Those who lack the requisite level of understanding hand adversaries repeated opportunities to access and re-access their networks and systems.

What was the origin of CCE? For me, in the wake of the 9/11 attacks, it was when a series of government-sponsored experiments exposed the fact that very creative cyberattacks against complex infrastructure systems could be surprisingly effective and highly destructive. In ways reminiscent of General Billy Mitchell's post World War I demonstration which showed, in the face of nearly universal skepticism, that aircraft could sink large-surface combatants, we quickly came to understand that as a nation, we were living with a huge, unacknowledged Achilles Heel.

Initially the "blue team" cyber guys attempted to hold the line. However, due to the high level of "red team" attacker knowledge and skill, they were simply and repeatedly overrun. We quickly realized these challenges could only be solved by non-cyber people like engineers. Engineers could stop attackers in their tracks because they understood physics and processes in ways attackers could not. This series of games ultimately helped us uncover the concept that former Secretary of the Navy Richard Danzig would name "going beyond cyber."

At the time I was collaborating with Richard as he urged everyone to step back and look at what cyber means to our society: It brings manifold, transformative benefits to every sector, but it also brings complexity, dependency, and civilizational risks that we're not even close to understanding. He called this situation, "Surviving on a Diet of Poisoned Fruit." As with the paper, Andy and I wrote projecting trouble for Megacities in 2025, CCE-like thinking will be necessary to even begin to deal with the overwhelming and increasing technological complexities and interdependencies, to help cities and nations continue to function and prosper with more than a modicum of safety.

The folks who design, integrate, and operate the future systems that will undergird civilization, if they can adopt a CCE mindset, hold the keys to preventing or limiting the worst things that can happen by digital means. Organizations will have to achieve and maintain new levels of cyber-physical mastery. In the purely physical world, the time has now passed, when master technicians, like industrial electricians and boiler techs, really understood their machines. The challenge for us collectively is how to develop and expand the ranks of cyber-informed engineers to face off against increasingly well-resourced and adaptive adversaries. We'll be getting some help from improvements to modeling tools, and we're starting to see software systems capable of understanding and improving other software. But with more and more levels of abstraction and complexity forming on the horizon, we're going to need a large cadre of cyber-informed engineers to keep us tethered to ground truths, to design systems that are inherently more secure, and in the end, to help defend what matters most.

Michael J. Assante
Alta, Wyoming

SIDEBAR: THE DAY THIS FOREWORD WAS RECORDED

While in 2018 he had pledged to write a foreword, events related to the return of cancer (his second bout) rendered that impossible. Not to mention the fact that whether from his home or one of many hospital rooms in Seattle, Washington and Jackson, Wyoming, Mike continued to share guidance and friendship with his colleagues at the SANS Security Institute and others around the world. But by May 2019 it had become obvious that his time was quite short, so I told him then not to worry about writing anything; I felt I had enough notes from our many previous conversations and collaborations that I could construct a serviceable one that would get his points across. Very quickly, by mid-June and as doctors were telling him his runway was being measured in weeks not months, it was time to say our final goodbye.

Many long-time friends and colleagues streamed to the Assante's beautiful home in Alta Wyoming—a home that Mike himself had designed with input from his wife Christine and their three children—the first half of that month.

I didn't want to stay too long; he was clearly tired, weak, in pain, tethered to a 50-foot oxygen lead and resting on a couch with his feet elevated. Still, and in all encounters prior, his sense of humor was fully intact, even as it drifted ever darker. As we started talking, I gave him an update on the book and sought to put him at ease (as he always put those at ease around him). I said I had already assembled what seemed to be a good working draft of a foreword, his foreword. To that he nodded, and then this happened: He started talking CCE origins.

Even when his body was in the worst condition during this long cruel descent, his mind had stayed super sharp, and his dedication to the national security mission remained fully evident. Chris elbowed me saying "hey, you should record this," and so I scrambled for my phone and did just that. Mike went for about ten minutes with occasional interjections and questions from me.

After we said what turned out to be our final goodbyes, I drove back to my hotel room in Idaho Falls and immediately started transcribing what I'd captured. Two and a half weeks later he was gone. The foreword to this book is the spirit of what Mike relayed to me that day.

Figure 0.1

MICHAEL J. ASSANTE—A BRIEF BIOGRAPHY

In 2019, the Idaho National Laboratory (INL) marked its 70th anniversary and the passing of INL alum Michael Assante. At age 48, Mike lost his battle to leukemia and left behind his wife and three children, and a large community of national defense and cyber practitioners who looked to him as a visionary leader. And if they were lucky enough to know him well, as a friend.

Born and raised in Brooklyn, he was clearly driven to be different at an early age, leading his younger brother on mock military "missions" in their big city neighborhood. He attended Miami University in Ohio as a political science major with an interest in stoic philosophers. This interest led him to studying ancient infrastructures and the research for his groundbreaking paper comparing Rome's dependencies of an engineering marvel—a massive network of aqueducts—and how this led to their ultimate vulnerability.

After graduation, he was commissioned to the US Navy where he performed missions that caught the attention of prominent US security officials. These same officials turned to Mike for immediate post 9/11 national security threat insights. After Mike retired from the Navy, he become one of the first (and the youngest) Chief Security Officers in the nation at one of the largest electric utilities in the United States. In 2005, Mike joined INL and around the same time was asked by SANS Cybersecurity Training Institute President and founder Alan Paller to develop an Industrial Control System (ICS) security training program.

While at INL, Mike and his family embraced the rugged high-mountain-west culture and with influence from seasoned colleagues, Mike emerged an avid hunter, fisherman, and photographer. He had become a full-fledged modern mountain man.

In 2007, Mike played a leading role in making the Aurora vulnerability test happen at INL. Garnering support from several federal departments and Congress, this highly prescient demonstration proved what until then had only been theory, that large industrial machines could be destroyed by cyber means and that increased efforts were needed to prevent serious consequences. Although unrelated, the experiment had

Figure 0.2

global implications the next month, with the first documented nation-state-level cyberattack on a US NATO partner country. Sometime later, media outlets reported that Russia had launched a targeted cyber campaign against Estonia's government and business websites.

The world has seen an escalation of cyberattacks against critical infrastructure ever since, and in many cases, including the several attacks on the Ukrainian power grid, Mike packed his bags and flew in to help figure out what happened, to help the victims whose systems were attacked, and document for others the lessons that might help protect everyone else.

He did so much in his brief span at INL that he was the only candidate qualified to fill an extraordinary new position for the nation, one created just for him in late 2008. As the first Chief Security Officer for the North American Electricity Reliability Commission (NERC), Mike made several bold moves to ensure the security and reliability of the nation's electric power, including overseeing the launch of the first (and still only) mandatory cybersecurity standards for a critical infrastructure sector: the NERC Critical Infrastructure Protection Standards (NERC CIPS) aimed at protecting the US grid from cyberattack.

In 2009, during congressional testimony before the US House of Representatives Committee on Homeland Security, Mike stressed the need to secure the electric grid from cyber and physical attacks. His visionary leadership is in full evidence as he explains the roots of one of the most promising new programs for INL and for the nation, one whose lineage can be traced directly to him: the CCE methodology. Responding to a question from a Congressman about preventing cyberattacks, Mike said:

> I don't think we should put our full faith in preventing attacks. It is very important that we also address investments in being able to categorize them, observe them, and respond to them, and minimize their consequences in the system.

As his family, countless friends, colleagues, and students mourn the loss of this visionary researcher and his far-too-early passing, there is also ample cause to celebrate the many high-impact accomplishments he had during his truly remarkable life. In his final days, Mike wrote a goodbye letter to the industrial control systems community. He said:

> As a good Navy man, I relinquish the watch to your capable hands. Watch over each other and care for one another. The world is beautiful, and the right principles and values are worth fighting

for. Know I am smiling right now. Your friend in this life and your vanguard for the next!

Figure 0.3

NOTES

1 "Airbus Says Software Configuration Error to Blame for Crash." SANS Newsbites. Volume VXII, Issue 43. June 1, 2015. www.sans.org/newsletters/newsbites/xvii/43

2 Maggie Lynch. The first principles of engineering are foundational propositions and assumptions that cannot be inferred from any other theory. From "'The rules of the game': Applying first principles of engineering to manufacturing." www.in-pharmatechnologist.com/Article/2018/11/16/The-rules-of-the-game-Applying-first-principles-of-engineering-to-manufacturing

PREFACE

The situation we find ourselves in today in the realm of cybersecurity is not much different than the one the software world faced in 1994, except that without a significant shift in strategy, the consequences for citizens and civilizations are likely to be much more dire.

Prior to the release of the first edition of *The Capability Maturity Model: Guidelines for Improving the Software Process* by Carnegie Mellon's Software Engineering Institute (SEI) just as the personal computer era was getting underway circa 1994, the world of software development was, to be generous, a complete goat rope.[3] Project scoping with any degree of precision or confidence for any semi-complex platform or application was impossible. Project success was the exception, not the norm. To put it another way, outside of the National Aeronautics and Space Agency (NASA) or certain organizations in the US Department of Defense (DoD), software development was about as far from an engineering discipline as one could possibly imagine.

SEI's authors sought to bring order to the chaos and in so doing, help software development teams and the projects they undertook on behalf of all manner of end-user organizations begin to gain a semblance of order, predictability, and efficiency. While improvement has continued, a quarter century later and with very many lessons learned, pairing the word "engineering" in the context of software development, as in "software engineering," still strains the credulity of many.

As the Acknowledgments section illustrates, this book has multiple champions, many contributors, and more than a few sources of inspiration. But one important factor shaping its construction was guidance from my boss at INL, Zach Tudor, to pattern it at least partly after a SEI's seminal work that has shaped technology ever since. Sarah Freeman and I have attempted to do just that.

There are in fact a number of security maturity models, frameworks, and standards, all intended to encourage behaviors that improve security posture and reduce the frequency or impact of successful attacks. Perhaps most relevant from the CCE perspective is the Department of Energy's Cybersecurity Capability Maturity Model or C2M2, brought into being in the early 2010s by Samara Moore, Jason (J.D.) Christopher, and a slew of government and industry experts (and recently revised).[4]

Maturity models are helpful for bridging the gap between objective and subjective methods of performance measurement. And since no one has yet been able to define what a fully secure computer is, let alone a fully secure organization, (or how we would recognize either if we saw one), gauging security by inference is what we have to settle on for now. C2M2, like the maturity model for software before it, is subjective as it doesn't measure the actual strength of cyber defense. By inference we mean that what's being measured are a cluster of observable behaviors which have been found to have some degree of efficacy in detecting and/or thwarting cyberattacks. However, due to the massive complexity of modern, highly networked digital systems, even an organization that is assessed to have achieved high levels of maturity across the board in its security program may find itself compromised, with sensitive data stolen or encrypted, or worse, with attacks that reach deep into the operational side of the house to disrupt industrial processes or destroy long lead-time-to-replace capital equipment.

As was discussed five years ago in "The Case for Simplicity in Energy Infrastructure,"[5] the levels of complexity and dependency we've now accepted have created a situation where current approaches to cyber defense are incapable of stopping well-resourced, targeted attackers from creating potentially catastrophic results. *Countering Cyber Sabotage* introduces not a maturity model, but a new methodology to help critical infrastructure owners, operators, and their security practitioners defend their absolutely most important functions and processes against the most capable cyber adversaries.

From a national security perspective, it is not just the damage to the military, the economy, or national critical functions (NCFs) that is of concern but also the civilization-disrupting second- and third-order effects from prolonged regional blackouts, transportation stoppages, water and wastewater issues, etc. CCE uniquely begins with the assumption that well-resourced, adaptive adversaries have already taken up residence, performed extensive reconnaissance, remain undetected, and are preparing their cyber-physical attack. Having captured credentials and elevated privileges, they are "living off the land"[6] in target organizations' networks and systems, including industrial control systems, and preparing to leverage functionality intended solely for trusted operators. Our most important infrastructure elements are designed and rigorously tested to be resilient in the face of equipment failure and operator mistakes but at present have no defense against intentional mis-operation.

Where other cybersecurity standards and methodologies recommend the addition of more digital technology solutions to detect and/or block attacks, CCE often advises the use of non-digital fail-safes, engineered backstops, and other out-of-band techniques to put the highest consequence, processes, functions, and systems beyond the reach of distant digital adversaries. Now, with support from the US Departments of Energy, Homeland Security, and Defense, a number of successful engagements under its belt, with other companies, inspired by what they've learned from previously published materials, implementing CCE with excellent results, and with numerous inquiries from around the world, the Idaho National Lab has decided that it is time to reveal the methodology in greater detail to a wider audience.

Here's a quick run-through of what's coming up:

CHAPTER 1: RUNNING TO STAND STILL AND STILL FALLING BEHIND

Every year while we may be improving slightly, the gap between attacker and defender capabilities is widening. The folly of continuing down the same well-trodden incremental improvement path we've constructed over the past few decades is now plain for all to see. More and more money spent on new cybersecurity products and services, with hard-to-measure-but-low-percentage-of risk "transferred" via the emerging cybersecurity insurance market. Sadly, insurance isn't the escape hatch it seemed it might become.[7] Those who've been in the fight for a few years will find this a compelling resource to share with their mentees. But for the far too many who still turn to hope and hygiene to address these challenges, this opening serves as a cold dash of reality. Things are not getting better; quite the contrary, and Chapter 1 will prepare initially skeptical or ambivalent readers forge on with far keener eyes.

CHAPTER 2: RESTORING TRUST: CYBER-INFORMED ENGINEERING

With a decent grounding in the methodology now achieved, this final chapter gives motivated individuals, entities, government oversight bodies, engineering safety and security services providers, and other critical infrastructure security stakeholders some initial tools to get started. The two-day introductory ACCELERATE training course is described, and on the tools front, we provide a look into the checklists available to everyone who goes through ACCELERATE. Beyond tools and training, this final chapter explores other ways CCE is starting to take hold in cybersecurity policy, with looks at how countries outside the United States are adopting key elements. Lastly, we look to the future, previewing likely updates and improvements to the methodology, tools, and training, and lay out a vision for a network of training and delivery partners who will help bring significant scale to this most urgent enterprise.

CHAPTER 3: BEYOND HOPE AND HYGIENE: INTRODUCING CONSEQUENCE-DRIVEN, CYBER-INFORMED ENGINEERING

This chapter serves as a transition from higher level, business case and policy-oriented material to the more detailed treatment of the nuts and bolts of the CCE methodology that follows in Chapters 4 through 8. It begins with an introduction to the culture from which it sprang: the intensive engineering-safety environment at the INL. It then provides a short study on related cyber risk management frameworks, standards, and methodologies, pointing out what's the same, what's similar, and what's different with CCE. Finally, it reveals that while CCE may look at first like a roadmap for engineering-centric cybersecurity assessments, its true intent is organization-wide conversion to a new way of thinking about strategic cyber risk.

CHAPTER 4: PRE-ENGAGEMENT PREPARATION

The objective of these pre-engagement activities is to ensure reliable lines of communication are opened; that the right folks are identified and oriented; that scoping, expectations, data handling and protection strategies, and that related preparation activities—the types of things that could bog down an entity lead CCE engagement if not dealt with up front—are executed in ways that build trust in the team and the proposed tasks and timelines.

CHAPTER 5: PHASE 1: CONSEQUENCE
PRIORITIZATION

The demanding work that happens in Phase 1 sets CCE apart from alternate methodologies, in that it never seeks to discover or protect the whole enterprise but rather zeros in on the comparative handful of most vital processes and functions on which the success of the company or military organization hinges entirely. The question is posed: What would kill your company? Or its military analog: What would kill your mission? It is also predicated on acknowledging that the adversaries, most likely, have already gained credentials and are resident in the entity organization's networks and systems. As CCE can typically accommodate only a limited number of high-consequence events (HCEs) in its first pass, the work of the three phases that follow is entirely bounded by what is selected, and what's intentionally put out of scope, in Phase 1. The chapter concludes with a segue into preparations for Phase 2.

CHAPTER 6: PHASE 2: SYSTEM-OF-SYSTEMS ANALYSIS

This phase seeks to illuminate the entire technological and human process playing field adversaries will study, navigate, and leverage to reach their targets. For background, please note that few if any utilities, or other industrial companies of significant size, maintain a current, comprehensive, and detailed list of their equipment, including electromechanical machines, computer hardware, software, communications, services, and the human and technical processes that support all of this. One thing is clear, as much as we used to like to say no one knows your systems and processes better than you do, in many instances, that may no longer be true. Advanced adversaries have repeatedly shown ability to break in, gather credentials, "live off the land," and loiter in targeted networks and systems for months and even years prior to detection. Sometimes they've even purchased the same systems, so they can dissect and inspect them at their leisure. Suffice it to say, a conservative asset owner should assume they're already in, and they've been in for a while. During which time, and supplemented by other forms of information they've collected, they form a detailed map of networks, systems, and processes. In order to thwart them, asset owners and operators need knowledge that's at least as good as theirs, and preferably superior. That is the work of Phase 2.

CHAPTER 7: PHASE 3: CONSEQUENCE-BASED TARGETING

This phase mirrors the process by which nation-state adversaries convert objectives of commanding officers into ready-to-launch attack plans. Threat intelligence has an important role to play in this phase, whether it be provided by government or commercial sources. Up to this point, exposure to CCE concepts has suggested that this engineering-centric defensive methodology is focused on consequences and prioritization. But here the operative word is targeting, and in this phase, we're going to turn the tables and become the most feared, most capable adversary, and devise the attacks that would take your organization out for good. Using the information collected and summarized in Phase 2, the team identifies the shortest, highest confidence paths that attackers would take to cause the HCEs identified in Phase 1.

CHAPTER 8: PHASE 4: MITIGATIONS AND PROTECTIONS

After spending the previous phases in a largely offensive mindset, this final phase makes a decisive pivot to defense. Whereas most current cybersecurity tools (e.g., firewalls, intrusion detection systems, secure coding techniques, security incident and event management systems, etc.), standards, and frameworks demonstrate their effectiveness via non-deterministic (i.e., probability-based) methods, the recommendations will include protective measures that are verifiably effective via deterministic methods. In other words, cyber-physical safeguards can be counted on to block the progress of an attack or, failing that, keep the high-value target safe from damage or destruction. Or limit the damage enough to allow restoration and continued operation even if in a degraded state. Or at the very least, provide ample early earning, so defenders can swing into motion to disrupt the attackers before they reach their goals.

CHAPTER 9: CCE FUTURES: TRAINING, TOOLS, AND WHAT COMES NEXT

With a decent grounding in the methodology now achieved, this final chapter gives motivated individuals, entities, government oversight bodies, engineering safety and security services providers, and other critical infrastructure security stakeholders some initial tools to get started. The two-day introductory ACCELERATE training course is described, and on the tools front, we provide a look into the worksheets and checklists available to everyone who goes through ACCELERATE. Beyond tools and training, this final chapter explores other ways CCE is starting to take hold in cybersecurity policy, with looks at how countries outside the United States are adopting key elements. Lastly, we look to the future, previewing likely updates and improvements to the methodology, tools, and training, and lay out a vision for a network of training and delivery partners who will help bring significant scale to this most urgent enterprise.

APPENDIX A: CASE STUDY: BALTAVIAN SUBSTATION POWER OUTAGE

We've included a detailed case study that takes readers through CCE's four phases applied to a hypothetical scenario in a fictional country. As a prelude, Appendix A begins with a brief recounting of the December 2015 and 2016 real-world, cyber-enabled sabotage attacks on Ukraine's electric infrastructure.

APPENDIX B: CCE PHASE CHECKLISTS

Here you'll find four rudimentary Q&A checklists to help your team begin to understand what CCE applied to a particular organization—perhaps YOUR organization—would look like.

It remains to be seen whether humanity will collectively come to grips with the uncertainties and risks we've accepted via complex, connected, and highly interdependent software systems at the heart of our most important infrastructures. We at INL hope that CCE may mark the very beginning of a full acknowledgment of those risks, as well as a return to leveraging proven engineering practices to better protect those things that matter most.

NOTES

3 "A confusing, disorganized situation often attributed to or marked by human error." https://en.wiktionary.org/wiki/goat_rope

4 "The Cybersecurity Capability Maturity Model, version 2.0." The US Dept of Energy. June 2019. www.energy.gov/sites/prod/files/2019/08/f65/C2M2%20 v2.0%2006202019%20DOE%20for%20Comment.pdf

5 "The Case for Simplicity in Energy Infrastructure." The Center for Strategic and International Studies. October 2015. www.csis.org/analysis/ case-simplicity-energy-infrastructure

6 Mark Goudie. "Going Beyond Malware." May 7, 2019. www.crowdstrike.com/ blog/going-beyond-malware-the-rise-of-living-off-the-land-attacks/

7 "Big Companies Thought Insurance Covered a Cyberattack. They May Be Wrong." The New York Times. April 15, 2019. www.nytimes.com/2019/04/ 15/technology/cyberinsurance-notpetya-attack.html

AUTHOR BIO

Andrew A. Bochman is the Senior Grid Strategist for Idaho National Laboratory's National and Homeland Security directorate. In this role, Mr. Bochman provides strategic guidance on topics at the intersection of grid security and resilience to INL leadership as well as senior US and international government and industry leaders.

A frequent speaker, writer, and trainer, Mr. Bochman has provided analysis on electric grid and energy sector infrastructure security actions, standards, and gaps to the Department of Energy, Department of Defense, Federal Energy Regulatory Commission (FERC), North American Electric Reliability Corporation (NERC), National Institute of Standards and Technology (NIST), National Association of Regulatory Utility Commissioners (NARUC), the Electricity Subsector Coordinating Council (ESCC), and most of the US state utility commissions. Teaming with DOE, NARUC, USAID, and international partners, he has cyber-trained grid operators, and is a cybersecurity subject matter expert listed with the US State Department Speakers Bureau.

Mr. Bochman has testified before the US Senate Energy and Natural Resources Committee on energy infrastructure cybersecurity issues and before FERC on the security readiness of smart grid cybersecurity standards. He has also held recurring conversations on grid security matters with the Senate Select Committee on Intelligence (SSCI) and the National Security Council (NSC). Prior to joining INL, he was the Global Energy & Utilities Security Lead at IBM and a Senior Advisor at the Chertoff Group in Washington, DC.

Mr. Bochman earned a Bachelor of Science degree from the US Air Force Academy and a Master of Arts degree from the Harvard University Extension School.

Sarah Freeman is an Industrial Control Systems (ICS) cyber security analyst at Idaho National Laboratory (INL), where she provides US government partners and private sector entities with actionable cyber threat intelligence, developing innovative security solutions for the critical infrastructure within the US.

At Idaho National Laboratory, Ms. Freeman pursues innovative threat analysis and cyber defense approaches, most recently Consequence-driven, Cyber-informed Engineering (CCE). As Principle Investigator on a laboratory discretionary research, her current research is focused on new signatures and structured methods for cyber adversary characterization. Following the December 2015 electric grid attacks, Ms. Freeman partici-pated in the DOE-sponsored training for Ukrainian asset owners in May 2016. She has also researched the Ukrainian 2015 and 2016 cyber-attacks and the Trisis/Hatman incident.

Ms. Freeman earned a Bachelor of Arts from Grinnell College and a master's in security and intelligence studies from the University of Pittsburgh.

INTRODUCTION

The story of INL's methodology—consequence-driven, cyber-informed engineering (CCE)—begins in 1986 when Clifford Stoll, an astrophysicist-in-training at Lawrence Berkley National Lab in California, senses someone else was in his computer, so to speak, and begins a hunt that leads to the identification of a hacker operating out of West Germany. This marks the first documented cyberattack over information technology (IT) infrastructure and over ensuing years, a flood of sometimes sophisticated, often pedestrian, and eventually automated attacks followed.[1]

The following two decades witnessed the birth and expansion of what is now a well over $100 billion (USD) global IT-focused cybersecurity tool and service industry. Over this same period, nothing malicious and substantial had yet happened in the operational technology (OT) world: no Stuxnet attack on Iran's nuclear centrifuges, no Russian attacks Ukraine's electric infrastructure, no attacks on the safety system of a Saudi Arabian petrochemical plant. It seemed to most people running large industrial processes like power plants, oil refineries, water and wastewater treatment facilities, natural gas pipelines, and other processes built around industrial control systems, that because their equipment and their networking protocols were so esoteric and systems were protected by a type of islanding referred to as "air gaps," that they were immune to the troubles facing their colleagues in IT.

One person who doubted the immunity of OT systems to malicious, targeted cyberattacks was Mike Assante. The boyish, fiercely patriotic political science major was raised in Brooklyn and, as a decorated intel officer in the US Navy, exposed to the modern tools of war including cyber weapons. He was educated on the physics of electric grid operations at one of the largest US power utilities during his time as Chief Security Officer at American Electric Power. Assante had seen enough to know the OT world would not be spared. From his experience in post 9/11 cyber red-teaming, he knew there was no reason to consider increasingly networked and automated industrial machines invulnerable. When his career took him to INL, home to the foremost experts on securing nuclear power plants and other critical infrastructure elements, he judged was time to reveal the truth, and he acted.

On a cold winter morning in 2017, before some highly skeptical senior leaders from government and industry, Mike Assante began a demonstration he had devised. Though highly confident, the 32-year-old trailblazer's reputation was on the line as many of these important people had traveled long distances to this secluded desert site in Idaho. In addition, the experiment was costing taxpayers well over one-million dollars, so the pressure for results was high.

Drawn from interviews he did with Mike, Journalist Andy Greenberg has the best account of what happened that day:[2]

> The test director read out the time: it was 11:33 am. He checked with a safety engineer that the area around the … diesel generator was clear of bystanders. The he sent the go-ahead to one of the cybersecurity researchers at the national lab's office in Idaho Falls to begin the attack. Like any real digital sabotage, this one would be performed from miles away, over the internet. The test's simulated hacker responded by pushing roughly thirty lines of code from his machine to the protective relay connected to the bus-sized diesel generator.

In less than a second, the machine began to tear itself apart. One mile away, in a protective enclosure, the observers watched as …

> The giant machine shook with a sudden, terrible violence, emitting a sound like a deep crack of a whip.

Before a minute had passed, parts were flying, smoke rose high into the air, and the generator was destroyed. The experiment showed how relays could be intentionally mis-operated to bring about the destruction of what they were supposed to protect. The textbook proof-of-concept for the potential cyber-enabled sabotage of OT systems had arrived, and the earliest pieces of a new engineering-oriented approach to cyber defense of critical infrastructure began to form in Mike's mind.

Conceived in aftermath of 9/11 and Aurora, one of the more demanding and differentiating elements of CCE is that it never seeks to discover or protect the whole enterprise but rather zeros in on the comparative handful of most vital processes and functions on which the success of the company or military organization hinges entirely. The question is posed to CEOs: What would kill your company? Or stated to military leaders, what would you target to kill your mission?

Mike recognized a potential threat where skeptical or naive others did not and strove mightily to alert us. Now, with support from the US Departments of Energy, Homeland Security, and Defense, a number of successful critical infrastructure and military engagements under its belt, with other companies, inspired by what they've learned from previously published materials, implementing CCE with excellent results, and with numerous inquiries from around the world, the Idaho National Lab has decided that it is time to reveal the methodology in greater detail to a wider audience.

A FEW WORDS ON SABOTAGE

The type of sabotage that prompted the CCE methodology, and against which this book seeks to introduce practical protections, is most accurately called cyber-enabled sabotage. However, the editors have chosen to reduce the term to cyber sabotage as the title simply couldn't bear another hyphen. But no matter how it's phrased, improving one's posture vs. the 5 D's of cyber sabotage—Disrupt, Deny, Degrade, Destroy, or Deceive—must become a central element of all critical infrastructure organizations' cyber security programs from now on.[3]

To find details on sabotage of industrial processes or modern-day military capabilities in open-source literature is not an easy task. One of the first resources to pop up is the now declassified OSS Field Manual #3 on "Simple Sabotage," published in 1944 and declassified in the 1970s. Because it is on the "simpler" end of the sabotage spectrum (vs. the more spectacular high-tech tools we see in many thrillers), the means it commended approximately 75 years ago do not draw attention to themselves:

> *Where destruction is involved, the weapons of the citizen-saboteur are salt, nails, candles, pebbles, thread, or any other materials he might normally be expected to possess as a householder or as a worker in his particular occupation. His arsenal is the kitchen shelf, the trash pile, his own usual kit of tools and supplies. The targets of his sabotage are usually objects to which he has normal and inconspicuous access in everyday life.[4]*

Today while all those substances remain fair game for gumming up gears (and to this laundry list we could recommend the addition of more modern everyday items like mylar balloons and laser pointers), we would add the now completely ubiquitous and therefore mundane laptop or cell phone.

I was struck recently when reading about sabotage in World War II and the Allied countries several bold and eventually successful attempts to slow or stop Hitler's efforts to build the first atomic bomb by halting the production of deuterium (heavy water) made by a company called Norsk Hydro in Norway. Many readers of this book will have first heard of this company from reports on how it was hit by ransomware in 2019, how the large aluminum producer, a descendant of the earlier company, struggled with the loss of access to customer order data when its IT systems became unusable, and the efforts it undertook to get fully back up and running. The WWII attacks were clearly sabotage by physical means, while the targeted ransomware attack's objective was cyber-enabled extortion. Nevertheless, in this historical echo the experience endured by the modern-day company was very much the same: a crippling attack that disrupted its ability to perform its primary mission. And in this example one can see a linkage where preparing to defend against the very worst adversaries by identifying an organization's most essential processes and functions, and then protecting them in ways that go beyond standard cyber hygiene, would also make the organization more resilient in the face of the merely very bad adversaries.

Before we became as dependent on digital systems as we are today, adversaries like the Soviet Union's irregular Spetsnaz soldiers were prepared to infiltrate target countries and, through physical means, bring destruction to "targets of decisive importance: nuclear weapons sites, command and control points, civilian broadcasting stations, power plants, air artillery units and critical POL and ammunition supply points."[5]

But by whatever means, sabotage of the kind we seek to address in this book is conducted by nation-states on nation-states or terrorist groups-on-nation-states, or attacks on nation-states by the proxies of others. The goal is to weaken or cripple a state by targeting its critical infrastructures with short-term disruptive or long-term destructive attacks by employing the cyber and communications tools at the disposal of top-tier attackers. The NATO Review puts it this way in 2016:

> *Cyber-enabled sabotage can have important physical ramifications, especially when infrastructures such as energy or transportation networks are targeted or where data is manipulated to confuse the target and undermine command and control decision making.*[6]

Saboteurs typically try to conceal their identities, and the use of advanced cyber-based tactics, Techniques, and procedures has, to date, made attribution one of the most difficult tasks confronting those assigned to investigate attacks. Author Michael Head calls out the subterranean, opaque groups similar to those we've seen in the coordinated cyberattacks on Ukrainian infrastructure sponsored by Russia:

> *In war, the word [sabotage] is used to describe the activity of an individual or group not associated with the military of the parties at war, such as a foreign agent or an indigenous supporter, in particular when actions result in the destruction or damaging of a productive or vital facility, such as equipment, factories, dams, public services, storage plants or logistic routes.*[7]

A more modern instance of cyber-enabled emerged in 2015 and 2016 with the attacks that brought blackouts to Kiev and surrounding areas, conducted during a hot war in Eastern Ukraine, and the groups that orchestrated them have since been well documented by a number of authors and researchers[8] and can best be characterized as sabotage.

You won't see the word sabotage often in the pages that follow, but whether the aim of the attacker is destruction or paralyzing long-term disruption, it is precisely the type of cyber threat CCE prepares us to confront. There is a universe of bad actors out there, from angsty pre-teen hackers to a wide range of criminals, ill-tempered political activists, and information warfare specialists, with some of the latter now joined by their artificial intelligence (AI) analogs. But it's the most capable, whose aim is to destroy critical infrastructures using full spectrum tactics (e.g., direct cyber vectors, myriad software and hardware supply chain manipulation methods, social engineering, etc.), who are the antagonists in this book.

The legendary strategist Sun Tzu advises to "know the enemy and know yourself." When you hear us say that in order to win this fight one needs to think like the adversary, we mean to convey that we know them, and during certain parts of the CCE process, we intentionally try to think like them. And if all goes well, in pursuit of protecting what must not fail, you will benefit by better understanding and thinking like them too. And in so doing, become so much stronger a defender.

SABOTAGE, SURVEILLANCE, AND SUPPLY CHAIN RISK

Supply chain insecurity has emerged as one of the biggest concerns on the minds of critical infrastructure owners, operators and defenders. In the past few years we've come to realize that adversaries could add potentially damaging, but often very difficult to detect, new elements or modifications to the software or hardware components used to manage important infrastructure. Sometimes the purpose is mere surveillance, and many have already condoned monitoring of workplace and homelife behaviors through products like Facebook and phones, not to mention the entire universe of products prepended with the word "smart": electric meters, industrial turbines, cars, TVs, home assistants, etc. Somehow we have grown used to mass surveillance in ways, until recently, only Orwell imagined.

At the same time, we seek as much integrity as we can get in the products we trust to support critical business and military functions, and we have ample reason to be paranoid. In spite of this paranoia, almost all complex products, hardware and software, include parts and code made in more than one country.[9] In the arena of cyber protection for the bulk North American power grid, NERC created a new mandatory protection standard forcing electric utilities to examine and actively manage cyber risks in their supply chain.[10] The fictional future-war novel *Ghost Fleet* does an excellent job illustrating this type of risk, when, as one reviewer noted: "the anti-missile technology on board the Joint Strike Fighter, sabotaged by replacement parts, turns the plane's missile-evasion system into a missile-attraction system."[11]

Suffice to say, in the twenty-first-century global economy, it is virtually impossible to build anything more complex than a power drill in one place with high confidence that none of its constituent parts has been touched or modified by a third party. In fact, even a drill may be corrupted if the machines used to fabricate it include software. If they do, and in fact they probably do, tools coming off that assembly line could be altered in ways their owners wouldn't like one bit. Extrapolate this to the types of systems that make and manage electricity, deliver clean water, run manufacturing plants assembling cars and mixing chemicals, and you see where this is leading with our current approaches to cybersecurity. We now present a better way.

NOTES

1 Cliff Stoll. The Cuckoo's Egg: Tracking a Spy Through the Maze of Computer Espionage. Doubleday. 1989.
2 Andy Greenberg, *Sandworm*. Doubleday. 2019, pp. 69–70.
3 AFLCMC/HNJG, "Broad Agency Announcement (BAA ESC 12-0011): Cyberspace Warfare Operations Capabilities (CWOC) Technology

Concept Demonstrations," August 22, 2012. Available at: www.fbo.gov/utils/view?id=48a4eeb344432c3c87df0594068dc0ce.

4   "Field Manual (No. 3) on Simple Sabotage." January 17, 1944. The Office of Strategic Services, 1944. www.gutenberg.org/files/26184/page-images/26184-images.pdf
5   Captain Stephen C. Danckert. "Spetsnaz Reconsidered." Army Logistician. November–December 1990 issue, p. 36.
6   Neil Robinson. "NATO: Changing Gear on Cyber Defense." The NATO Review. June 8, 2016. www.nato.int/docu/review/articles/2016/06/08/nato-changing-gear-on-cyber-defence/index.html
7   Michael Head. *Crimes Against the State: From Treason to Terrorism.* 2011. www.amazon.com/Crimes-Against-State-Treason-Terrorism/dp/0754678199
8   In particular by Andy Greenberg, in his book comprehensively documenting the activities and approaches of the group many refer to as Sandworm.
9   In the US, Chinese communications equipment provider Huawei and cybersecurity software maker Kaspersky based in Russia are blacklisted out of concerns for the potential surveillance and sabotage they might enable.
10 CIP-013-1—Cyber Security—Supply Chain Risk Management. www.nerc.com/pa/Stand/Reliability%20Standards/CIP-013-1.pdf
11 Chris Zappone. "Ghost Fleet: World War III techno-thriller shows Australia's worst nightmare." The Sydney Morning Herald. August 24, 2015. www.smh.com.au/entertainment/books/ghost-fleet-world-war-iii-technothriller-shows-australias-worst-nightmare-20150822-gj5fp2.html.

1

RUNNING TO STAND STILL AND STILL FALLING BEHIND

We have a lot of bright people working on this problem, but the faster we go, the more behind we get. We don't seem to be getting ahead of it.[1]

—General Michael Hayden

The wellspring of risk is dependence.[2]

—Dan Geer

If the nation went to war today, in a cyberwar, we would lose. We're the most vulnerable. We're the most connected. We have the most to lose.[3]

—Mike McConnell

"I CAN DEAL WITH DISRUPTION; I CAN'T HANDLE DESTRUCTION"

The complete statement was "I can deal with disruption; what I can't handle is destruction of long lead-time-to-replace capital equipment." These words were spoken by the CEO of Florida Power & Light, one of the largest US electric utilities, in his 2018 Consequence-Driven

1

Cyber-Informed Engineering (CCE) brief to Congressional staffers.[4] Situated in the path of some of the largest hurricanes every year, his company, Florida Power & Light (FP&L), is more than ready for large-scale, multiday weather-induced disruptions. Stockpiles of essential parts and equipment, employees trained in restoration, plus well-established mutual assistance programs with other regional utilities are standing by to get the power back on fast even after enduring Mother Nature's worst.

It's another matter entirely when the adversary is planning cyberattacks that target energy companies' most important, long-lead-time-to-replace capital equipment, for example, the concurrent destruction of multiple combined cycle generators; natural gas distribution lines; or ultrahigh voltage transformers; or widespread destruction of thousands of geographically dispersed, digital protective relays, which could shut a utility down for months while waiting on the supply chain before rolling trucks to the site of each relay. In other sectors like water and wastewater treatment, massive pumps that would take months or years to replace are must what not fail, and therefore, make for the most prized targets.

While the struggle to protect the entire enterprise will continue to challenge Chief Information Security Officers (CISOs) for the foreseeable future, what's needed now is a way to take a highly specific subset of all systems, the things upon which infrastructure companies most depend, the adversaries' most desirable targets, off table.

IMPLICATIONS FOR CRITICAL INFRASTRUCTURE AND NATIONAL SECURITY

It's one thing for a restaurant, a lawn service, or a nail salon to be dependent on digital systems; it's quite another for some of the most important companies and government organizations in the nation to put themselves in that position. No matter how you define critical infrastructure, be it by sector[5] or by critical national function,[6] there is far more at stake than the well-being of the organization. In the private sector, downstream dependencies on electricity, water, and communications services often greatly eclipse mainly the economic, military, or societal value of the individual company, its employees, or its investors.

Consider what happens in a local or regional blackout. Almost everything, except what's powered by fuel still in the tank, stops in its tracks. Hospitals, military bases, and companies with the wherewithal to have backup power strategies can maintain essential operations for a few days or hours. Cell phones keep working until their batteries are depleted, and cell towers either stop transmitting or run a while longer on backup diesel generators. The macro effects are that offices and houses go dark and production lines stop midstream. More tangible effects are felt when passengers are trapped in elevators, traffic lights blink out, food spoils in warming home and grocery store refrigerators.

Here's what ex-Mossad director X Pardo said about victim hopes that governments will come to the rescue if and when cyberattacks create large-scale infrastructure effects:

> Faith that governments—including the U.S.—can respond to attacks in a timely and effective way may also be misplaced. I just say—God forbid—that on a hot summer day, [after a] cyberattack, pressure [in] the water pipelines in California will drop to zero. Thinking that the federal government will assist, solve the problem—it's not even a dream.[7]

Of the 16 critical infrastructure sectors monitored by the Department of Homeland Security (DHS), most rely to a great degree on the reliable functioning of Industrial Control Systems (ICS). And some of those that at first glance don't appear as reliant, like Financial Services, depend heavily on other sectors that do. Many ICS suppliers serve multiple sectors. For example, General Electric turbines propel jetliners and power cities. Caterpillar diesel generators provide emergency backup power to commercial and government facilities as well as to ships and submarines. Whether called ICS, operational technology (OT), or cyber-physical systems, it is thoroughly documented that the technologies that support industrial processes are highly susceptible to exploration and exploitation by parties interested in targeting them.

Goodbye to Full Manual: Automating Critical Infrastructure

It used to be machines did the one or several things they were designed to do, and the principal concerns for owners and operators were about how to operate them safely and keep them running as long as possible with scheduled maintenance. For example, think farm tractors, steam engines, diesel-powered backhoes, and coal-fired power plants. Bad things could happen when some part of them broke down from wear or a material defect, but from today's perspective, the upside was that with rare exceptions, they couldn't be made to perform tasks diametrically opposed to what their designers intended. And they especially couldn't be made to perform other tasks by distant humans.

As the saying goes, that was then, this is now. We've become quite accustomed to digital machines running the show, in factories and farms, in cockpits, and increasingly, in cars. The "Second Machine Age," "Industry 4.0," and the "Industrial Internet of Things (IIoT)" signal a full-on, buzzword-filled embrace of digital automation.[8] Unpredictable and error-prone human operators are replaced with programmable and reprogrammable machines that perform tasks much more quickly, efficiently, and without error and require neither paychecks nor benefits. Automation's business benefits are so clear, and the business case for it is so compelling that economists are warning that despite the likelihood that some jobs are being created to support the advance of automation, an unprecedented wave of job losses in a number of low- and middle- skilled job categories is likely to ensue.[9]

As human decision-makers are replaced with algorithms, efficiency advantages are offset occasionally by automation-induced catastrophes[10] that give some momentary pause. And even though sometimes it initially appears otherwise, the vast majority of these accidents are not the result of malicious bad actors but rather engineering design decisions that took humans so far out of the loop that there was no way for them to take back control when needed. The trend seems unstoppable and largely unnoticed.

Water sector engineering subject matter expert (SME) Daniel Groves sometimes teases his clients into examining their massive dependence on automation by daring them to consider going one full day without it. Here's how he describes the typical reactions:

> I call it "A Day without SCADA." Many operators indicate that they are not sure if they could run their systems without SCADA. Over the last few decades, as automation improved in reliability and was designed into all their systems, utilities began cutting back on their operator workforce. For example, a 50 million gallons per day (MGD) water treatment facility without SCADA may have had up to 3 full time operators 24 hours per day. After automation was implemented, these facilities may be operated by the SCADA system with oversight from a remote location, with only one operator and maintenance staff on hand during the day shift only. In this "lean" configuration of staffing, if the SCADA system suddenly became unavailable, they could keep things running by relying on on-call staff and required overtime, or even

4

perhaps mutual aid from a nearby utility. However, the load on their staff would become unbearable if the outage dragged on for days and weeks.

Other utilities have indicated that they have a regularly scheduled "Day without SCADA" as an operations activity at least annually. Management views these exercises as excellent training opportunities to verify that operators know how to run the plants in a manual fashion. However, these utilities indicate that running these exercises are a significant burden that no one looks forward to and can create operational issues.

Another key element in the equation are vendor systems. Many vendor systems (Reverse Osmosis, for example) are very complex and are not designed to be run without the automation. Several water utility operators have indicated that if the automation system became unavailable for a vendor system, they would not be able to run them. This is especially concerning as more and more utilities implement advance water treatment systems.[11]

Like the oft-referenced frog in boiling water, they hadn't realized the slow and steady ways their organizations had become so dependent on automation. You might say we're asleep at the wheel (or in the cockpit, or in the control center). The fact is we're no longer even at the wheel we're sleeping at.

Another water sector example comes in the form of so-called Magmeters.[12] A magmeter is a magnetic flow meter whose job is to measure the quantity of liquid flowing through a pipe, and the telemetry readings it provides signal control systems to either speed or slow the flow.

They can be bought and configured in one of two primary modes: with attached displays indicating what the sensors are sensing, or "headless," meaning they transmit the readings to a control system where the data feeds applications and may be viewed by an operator at an Human-Machine Interface (HMI) (see Figure 1.1). The problem with headless approach is that if attackers gain access to the control system they can interrupt and/or modify the magmeter data to prompt the operators to take potentially disruptive or destructive actions.

Of course, a major downside to automation, in fact the one that's one of the main catalysts that prompted the development of CCE, is how it can be manipulated by attackers to cause disruption to critical processes and/or destruction of critical equipment that's not easily or quickly replaced.

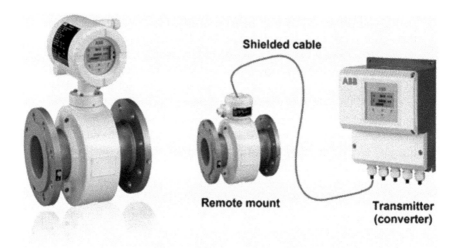

Figure 1.1   Headed and Headless Magmeters.[58] (Source: Used with permission ABB, Inc. https://new.abb.com/products/measurement-products).

WHAT IT MEANS TO BE A FULL DIGITALLY DEPENDENT IN AN INSECURE-BY-DESIGN WORLD

The triumph of digital over analog communications is now almost complete. In most of the world, no enterprise, from the smallest boutique to the largest global corporation, can proclaim itself free of worry about the reliability of the digital systems that it uses to:

- Execute core functions: make products and/or deliver services
- Communicate with partners and customers
- Pay its bills including payroll
- Heat, cool, ventilate, and light its buildings
- Transport its products and receive its shipments
- Operate its machinery
- Accept payments from customers

Whether the cause is malware or maintenance, it is by now a familiar occurrence for office workers to be sent home when the application(s) they use are down. Many are of no value without their IT tether. But there are indeed worse things than losing a day's work. When system failures occur in operational environments, employees can be sent to the hospital or the morgue.

Race to the Bottom

The United States has moved more quickly than most other nations to code, connect, and automate every aspect of our world. And we are now on the cusp of taking this to its logical conclusion with automation, artificial intelligence (AI), and the so-called Internet of Everything. Many believe that since so many good things have come from the embrace of digital technology so far, putting even more tech in our business and personal lives will be even better. That may be possible, but it is now readily apparent that we are in denial about what will inevitably go wrong. Or rather I should say, what is going wrong already:

1 We are becoming so dependent on technology that many Americans, especially younger ones who've never known life without portable computer devices and ubiquitous Internet access, are failing to learn once basic skills, such as competence in basic mathematics and map reading.[13]

2 Dependencies are tolerable as long as they are understood and everything generally works … They're not and it doesn't. For example, interdependencies in infrastructure are poorly understood by senior government and business leaders (e.g., natural gas is moved by compressors through pipelines to reach electricity generation plants, electricity drives pumps that move water, water is required to produce steam and cool natural gas turbines in electricity generation plants. None of this works without functioning communications and financial markets. Loss of any of these produces loss of all … and more).[14]

3 Cyber attackers have the capability to selectively alter, disrupt, or destroy systems now essential for operating the United States economy and defending the nation (e.g., stock markets, banking systems, water systems, electricity, telecommunications systems, fuel systems, etc.).[15][16]

We are in denial to the extent we fail to fully acknowledge our dependencies and our adversaries' ability to exploit them. For the few in government and private sector leadership positions who understand and appreciate the precarious situation we are in, the biggest problem is they don't yet have much clarity, let alone a workable plan, on how to meet these challenges.

Some note that there haven't been many attacks on ICS systems in critical infrastructure, wondering why there haven't been more prolonged blackouts, more explosions at chemical plants or refineries, more trouble with pumps moving water or compressors boosting the pressure of natural gas pipelines. They seem to have a point, compared to the daily drumbeat of cybersecurity troubles reported in IT and business environments. But if it seems like all has been well in industrial spaces, a perusal of the partial list of ICS cyber incidents compiled by Idaho National Laboratory (INL) and DHS' Critical Infrastructure Security Agency (CISA),[17] or in Joe Weiss's more comprehensive database on ICS incidents (some malicious, some not),[18] will quickly disabuse readers that all is well, safe, and secure outside of IT.

Insecure-by-Design

One would assume that if humans consciously allowed themselves to become fully dependent on highly connected, software-centric digital systems (especially in critical infrastructure applications where the stakes are so high), then everyone, particularly suppliers and asset owners/ operators, would demand systems that could be locked down tight. One might also assume that while Internet Godfather Vint Cerf and others have noted that we simply cannot write bug-free code,[19] every possible effort would be made to make life as difficult as possible for cyber attackers ... that by now we would have developed proven methods to keep hackers out of the most critical systems. Yet just the opposite is true.

Dale Peterson, one of the most respected if sometimes polarizing observers of the OT Security space, is credited as having coined the term "Insecure-by-Design." Here's how he explains it:

> Our definition of "Insecure by Design" would not cover a lack of security coding practices, using vulnerable libraries, poor QA, lack of fuzz testing, threat modeling, etc. Those are real deficiencies that can lead to bugs and exploitable vulnerabilities. They are not however the vendor consciously deciding to add features that allow an attacker with logical access to take complete control of the controller or application.
>
> A PLC (programmable logic circuit) is Insecure by Design when an attacker can use documented features to achieve his goals. Examples include:
>
> • Write requests with no authentication that allow an attacker to use protocol features to alter a process

- Unauthenticated firmware and ladder logic upload. This can turn the PLC into an attack platform and change the under-lying process a la Stuxnet.
- Open administrative command shells, documented hard coded support accounts …[20]

While the operational world has demonstrated plenty of vulnerabilities an attacker can use to work their way in to an industrial network or system, in most cases no malicious code is required. To achieve access and elevated privileges, attackers need not do much beyond gaining credentials (i.e., login and password) of an authorized user. Phishing and spear phishing, not to mention social engineering, have shown them-selves to be highly effective; high confidence and low risk means to gain credentials. After that, adversaries are as free to use applications and data, and maneuver among and across networks, as the employees whose identities they've assumed. This practice, for attackers, red teamers, and pen testers, is often called "living off the land"[21] and, by leveraging already installed tools and services to run legitimate processes, makes it more difficult for intrusion detection and other cybersecurity tools to detect that bad actors have gained access to internal networks, systems, and/or data.

A STRATEGY BASED ON HOPE AND HYGIENE

As the saying often attributed to Vince Lombardi goes, "hope is not a strategy." Yet many rely on hope as a central element to their cyber strategy: As in, they hope that attackers strike elsewhere and that if and when they hit home or close to home, their defenses will hold. These defenses are comprised of layers of people, process, and technology that form what is often called cyber hygiene best practices. As in, do these things well and thoroughly and without error and forever, and you'll be more secure than if you didn't. Ask how security is measured and you'll find nothing empirical, only maturity models and compliance regimes, which at best can be considered "security by inference."

Though some will chafe at this definition, "cyber hygiene" in this text will stand for doing everything cybersecurity experts in government and industry recommend we do, constantly, comprehensively, and without error, across the enterprise. This means expending maximal effort to adhere to dozens of cybersecurity best practices and maintain compliance with an ever-expanding body of relevant cyber standards.

In an ideal world, cybersecurity awareness and the actions it propels would make and keep us secure.[22] In reality, we are at best treading water. As legendary coach John Wooden cautioned, "Don't mistake activity with achievement."[23] We spend evermore money on products and services, endure time-stealing trainings, travel to conferences and trade shows, report material incidents and initiatives to the Securities and Exchange Commission (SEC) in 10Ks and 10Qs, and share our experiences with Cyber Information Sharing and Analysis Centers (ISACs) and sometimes with government "partners." Yet while some things have changed, the overall picture remains the same, and if anything, is darkening.

It takes some effort to practice personal hygiene, yet the time it takes to wash our hands and brush our teeth—demonstrated by fewer colds and cavities—has generally proven to be worth it. But cyber hygiene—the sum total of all current security compliance regimes and best practices—is another matter. Said one water sector expert, "Hygiene is so much work and mistakes can undo a lot of it."[24] Michael Assante puts its benefits and limitations this way: "Cyber hygiene is helpful for warding off online ankle biters. But it registers as barely a speed bump for sophisticated attackers aiming at particular targets."[25]

It seems the Atlantic Council's most pessimistic "Cyber Clockwork Orange"[26] future is upon us. Alarms are now blaring so frequently we've grown accustomed to tuning them out. Each day more sensitive information is lost or published to the public web; more intellectual property and state secrets end up in the hands of those of whom we are most wary. Money is being stolen, directly and via downtime. And some attacks, like ones targeting the last lines of defense in oil and natural gas, chemical plants, and the safety systems, are getting dangerously close to killing people.[27]

We've reached broad awareness of the problem, but the saturation of cyber breach and data loss news, combined with incessant marketing messages from cybersecurity vendors, has dulled the senses. No matter how "seriously" we take cybersecurity, or how many "wake-up calls" we endure, most of us know our organizations, as well as those we depend upon, are highly vulnerable today and will remain that way tomorrow. And they are especially so, if targeted by skilled cyber attackers, many of whom have shown a strong inclination to go after energy and other critical infrastructures.

The Hollow Promise of Cyber-insurance

Aware that despite their best efforts, they are likely to suffer damage and losses from successful cyberattacks, many organizations are now attempting to "transfer" some of their risk via payment of cyber-insurance premiums. During the first few years of ransomware, this approach seemed helpful, as the insurance companies often covered the full amount of the ransom, if not the losses from downtime due to loss of access to data and applications, or the recovery costs of returning IT operations back to their pre-attack state. Unfortunately, this pattern only reinforced the business model that propels even more and more costly ransomware attacks. Eventually the insurance companies will have to reduce their payouts, increase their premiums, and/or include exclusions for these types of attacks.

But when it comes to higher impact attacks like 2017's NotPetya, delivered via semi-targeted ransomware, this still largely untested type of insurance may return nothing to its buyers. It came as a surprise when large cyber-insurers declined to cover losses from NotPetya, and some of the victims who had the biggest losses found themselves in court.[28] According to Ariel Levite, a senior fellow at the Carnegie Endowment for International Peace, many companies are "running a huge risk that cyber-insurance in the future will be worthless."[29] It seems that when the stakes are highest and nation-state hackers may be linked to an attack, cyber-insurance may prove to be of little worth.

Experts Speak Out on Hygiene

Commenting on what he's seen at the world's largest annual cybersecurity expo, the RSA conference in San Francisco, Dr. Eugene Spafford, said:

> Sadly, the lack of foundations for the people at most of the booths mirrored t he lack of a solid foundation for the products. There are some good, useful products and services present on the market. But the vast majority are intended to apply band-aids … on top of broken software and hardware that was never adequately designed for security. Each time one of those band-aids fails, another company springs up to slap another on over the top …. No one is really attacking the poor underlying assumptions and broken architectures …. The industry is primarily based on selling the illusion that vendors' products can—in the right combination and with enough money spent—completely protect target

11

systems …. People would rather believe they can find a unicorn to grant them immortality rather than hear the dreary truth that they will die someday, and probably sooner than they expect.[30]

Echoing the term military industrial complex that attempted to capture the government agencies and commercial businesses perpetuating and benefiting from the global arms business, the term cybersecurity industrial complex[31] emerged to suggest something similar growing in the digital domain as far back as the early aughts. As with the defense industrial complex, the risks associated with cyber adversaries are never fully (and oftentimes not even partially) mitigated but if enough money is spent, one can potentially access the latest technology "solution." The motivation for this behavior is to show oversight bodies and stakeholders that the company is leaning forward on cybersecurity, when in fact, they are treading water at best.

In his book for industrial engineers, ICS analyst and author Ralph Langner addresses the lack of certainty the embrace of autonomy has given us: "Modern control systems and automation equipment, with their increasingly more complex integration and interrelations, are no longer fully understood—not even in nuclear power plants."[32] He says this in the opening pages and then dispenses with the term "cyber risk" altogether as an unhelpful concept for professionals seeking to achieve and maintain reliable control. It is not possible to fully secure systems whose basic processes are not fully understood.

And then there's Tim Roxey, former Constellation Energy nuclear energy risk analyst and former chief security officer for North American Electricity Reliability Commission (NERC), a frequent advisor to the White House on critical infrastructure cybersecurity matters. When asked to recall how his views on cyber hygiene tools and best practices have shifted over the years, his take was as sobering as it was simple:

1 With the arrival of the first antivirus (AV) products circa 2002—**Some is good**.
2 As AV matured, and new tool categories appeared (e.g., firewalls, IDS, SIEM, deep packet inspection, secure application development tools, etc.) up to about 2010—**More is better**.
3 Over the last decade however, as even more categories have appeared (see the list in the following section) and management's burden and costs have gone through the roof, we arrived at where we remain in 2020—**Too much is not enough**.

It's not hard to draw comparisons to the experience of drug addiction. Consider the escalation of the number and type of cyber tools an organization needs to buy and deploy to call itself secure and the quantity of increasing drug dose addicts required to achieve the effects they seek. Both share a spiraling sense of dependency, without any clear understanding of whether the relationship can ever be reined in.

According to Roxey, the key turning point that led us to the current "too much is not enough" condition was the monetization of hacking, transforming cyberattack activities from an outlet for small-time troublemakers and insular miscreants, too big—and then very big—business.[33] With ever-increasing complexity and the waves of new technology now breaking on our shores, he sees a potentially dystopian future.[34]

The Most Optimistic Take

More optimistic views also emerge. Fear, uncertainty, and doubt (FUD) has been used by sales and marketing professionals to motivate behaviors and move products since the first charlatans peddled cure-alls to the afflicted in ancient town squares. And no area of the modern economy has seen it used more broadly or more effectively than in the promotion of cybersecurity wares.

Amidst the sea of FUD promulgated by security product and services providers, and many analysts and other experts, one voice consistently pushes back. It belongs to Rob M. Lee, USAFA graduate and USAF veteran, now not only one of SANS Institute's top OT cybersecurity instructors but also CEO of the OT security company he founded. For the past half-dozen years or so, Rob has been declaring, to all in our community who would listen, that "defense is doable" and that what's required first is to "build a defensible architecture." He leavens that with the caution that "you don't just get to declare they are defended … if I have a defensible environment it means I have the architecture and technology in place to do defense, but it's the human component that makes it defended."[35] It's left unspoken in Rob's messaging how much faithful adherence to his guidance defends one's organization fully from top-tier saboteur-attackers that are well-funded, highly skilled, patient, and capable of preparing and delivering highly destructive payloads. But given his expertise and experience, Rob's enthusiasm definitely serves to buttress those defenders whose confidence in what they're doing understandably may waver from time to time.

Declining (or Unknowable) Returns on Increasing
Security Investments

The security research firm, the Ponemon Institute, released a report mid-2019[36] that painted an unsettling picture on the efficacy of current approaches to cybersecurity and the programs and products on which many companies rely in their attempts to achieve it. One statement from the accompanying press release sums it up: "Organizations are investing heavily in cybersecurity technologies, but their IT teams are unsure if these tools are working." Some salient findings were:

- 53% of IT security leaders don't know if their cybersecurity tools are working, despite investing $18.4M on average each year.
- 58% of companies will be increasing their IT security budget by an average of 14 percent in the next year.
- 53% of IT experts admit they don't know how well the cybersecurity tools they've deployed are working.
- 63% of respondents said they have observed a security control reporting it had blocked an attack when it actually failed to do so.
- Companies deploy on average 47 different cybersecurity solutions and technologies.
- 75% of respondents say their IT security team is unable to respond to security incidents within one day.

A Deep Ocean of Security Solutions

If you are a chief security officer (CSO)—or chief information security officer (CISO)—of a company of any size, you are likely besieged by companies wanting to sell you software and services that will save you. In a Q42019 update, investment bank and analysis firm Momentum Cyber lists dozens or even hundreds of products in EACH of the following categories:[37]

- Network and Infrastructure Security
- Web Security
- Endpoint Security
- Application Security
- Management Security Services (MSSP)
- Data Security
- Mobile Security
- Risk and Compliance
- Security Operations and Incident Response

- Security Analytics
- Threat Intelligence
- IoT Security
- Messaging Security
- Identify and Access Management
- Digital Risk Management
- Security Consulting and Services
- Blockchain
- Fraud and Transaction Security
- Cloud Security

Each one of these companies will pledge to either completely protect your company from all cyber badness, increase the visibility of your weak points, reduce you and your staff's workload, or help you demonstrate your compliance to standards and guidelines to internal and/or external oversight. CSOs and CISOs receive sales inquiries from at least a handful of companies in each of these categories. How could anyone be expected to vet them, identify the ones that best fit needs on every access point, deployment, configuration, integration, and patch and maintain these products? Don't forget the requirement and cost to provide initial and refresher train training to security and other pertinent employees.

Don't Stop Now

Given all that, one might conclude, as plenty have upon hearing this critique, that since:

- The performance of it is so fraught
- The defenses it builds are so permeable
- Metrics to measure its effectiveness still elude us
- It's expensive and getting more so every year

cyber hygiene is a waste of time and money. That is not the case.

If companies with experienced CISOs and competent cybersecurity teams stop their activities cold tomorrow, the day after would see them overrun with all manner of malware roaming the internet. Their applications would slow, and data would be more easily siphoned away or scrambled and made unusable via ransomware, of which there have been hundreds of different strains observed over the past half-dozen years or so.[38]

Given the enormous growth in the amount of bandwidth (and therefore the amount of data to manage and secure) and the number of endpoints, it's likely that the CISO's job is only going to become more difficult with the advent of AI, IoT, and 5G. Some say AI will arrive soon to save the day[39], but those who turn to it with hope may be ignoring its equally vast potential to aid those on offense.[40]

CONGRESS ASKS A GOOD QUESTION

On October 21, 2015 in Washington DC, Representative Eric Swalwell of California asked four experts the following question during a House Science Committee, Energy Subcommittee Hearing on Grid Security:

> Would you be surprised if a US city was blacked out by cyber means tomorrow?

He was met by chorus of "yes," from all but one of the four witnesses on the stand that day. Those who could not imagine an event like this included the Chief Information Officer (CIO) of large Midwest utility First Energy, the Government Accountability Office's cyber lead, and the Vice-President (VP) in charge of grid security at the Electric Power Research Institute. Only Mr. Brent Stacy, Associate Lab Director of INL's National and Homeland Security Directorate, thought it possible and said so.

Having worked closely with and for Brent since I joined the lab the prior year, his answer didn't surprise me one bit. There had been recent indications that such a scenario was possible if not likely in the proximate future. These included:

- Snohomish County Public Utility Demo—Billy Rios and his (red) team quickly reached ICS and could have shut down operations.[41]
- Black Energy 2 (and later, Black Energy 3)—While not designed primarily to target ICS, new modules had been released in the wild by Russia-based Sandworm team that assisted in gaining access to and data from IT systems containing information helpful for targeting ICS-related systems like HMIs.[42]

Note, the congressman didn't say "black out the grid"; phrasing used by some of his colleagues in previous inquiries, which has been generally taken to mean black out the entire country. By limiting the impact to a city, he signaled that this attack would only have to penetrate cyber defenses associated with utilities operating the lower voltage distribution grid, not the more heavily defended high-voltage transmission assets that fall under the purview of Federal Energy Regulatory Commission (FERC) and North American Electric Reliability Corporation's (NERC)' mandatory cybersecurity standards, the Critical Infrastructure Protection standards, or CIPs.[43]

Another aspect of Representative Swalwell's question worth considering relates to the modernization effort that began in the early 2000's soon after. When the Obama administration found the economy poised to go over a cliff as a result of the subprime mortgage crisis, one of the several tools it used to try and keep it on firm ground was called the Smart Grid Investment Program (SGIP). Managed by Department of Energy (DOE), the SGIP was essentially a $4 billion bucket of money that would reward US utilities with matching funds for purchasing certain kinds of new equipment, and they especially selected to buy many thousands or in some cases millions of digital "smart meters."

Beginning in 2009 and continuing over the next few years, digital smart meters and other new digital hardware and software falling under the smart grid heading, like smart inverters and smart grid applications providers, were often supplied by new companies, which in many cases were new entrants to the sector. The first smart meters, software-powered, networked computing devices that attached to the sides of houses and office buildings, hit the market with little-to-no security functionality. Digital synchro phasors[44] on high-voltage transmission lines notwithstanding, the smart grid technologies that utilities rushed to acquire incented by the SGIP, generally landed in lower voltage distribution environments[45] 90% of the time.

It's for these reasons that Brent's answer made the most sense. In hindsight, we agreed that the best answer, allowing for the fact that it would have been a first, would have been, "Yes, but not very surprised." As it was, Brent's answer proved prescient, as just two months later the world witnessed cyber-induced blackouts in Ukraine on December 23, 2015. Four distribution utilities were penetrated by Black Energy,[46] three of these were ultimately targeted in coordinated attacks, and hundreds of thousands lost power for several hours before it could be restored.[47] Fortunately the Ukrainian utilities still had the ability to revert to more manual, if less efficient modes of operation. Due to our much greater reliance on automation, similar attacks on US distribution utilities would likely cause a much more prolonged blackout.

THOUGHTS AND QUESTIONS

Until now most of the responses to address rising cybersecurity risks have involved:

- New cyber hygiene technologies, iterations of existing ones, and more money allocated to their purchase and maintenance
- Larger IT security staffs to manage all of the above
- Recurring (usually annual) cybersecurity training for all employees, particularly to warn them about the risk of phishing and spear phishing
- In certain sectors—nuclear power and electricity—substantial efforts to achieve and demonstrate compliance with mandatory cybersecurity standards
- Early investigations into the potential for transferring some amount of risk via cyber-insurance policies

Given what you knew before you even picked up this book, and whatever was new to you if anything so far in these pages, what would you say we should do to address these challenges … as nations, as organizations, and as individuals? Is there something new we should try, or would you recommend continuing along paths similar to those already carved out, but with much more energy and focus? What would you recommend to your boss? What if you are the boss, how do you begin to know whose guidance you can follow with confidence? If you can't trust your systems, can you at least trust your people?

SIDEBAR: EARLY CCE ORIGINS—PART I

THE BIRTH OF CORPORATE AWARENESS OF THE SUSCEPTIBILITY OF INDUSTRIAL SYSTEMS TO CYBER ATTACKS: AN INTERVIEW WITH ICS SECURITY EXPERT ERIC BYRES

In 1989, Clifford Stoll, an astronomer at the Lawrence Berkeley Lab just outside Oakland California, published the Cuckoo's Egg,[48] documenting what is widely believed to be the first successful cyberattack. Leveraging an early form of email, the attacker took advantage of the trust model built into the embryonic Internet, a trust model that is still very much intact today. A few years later ICS

Security expert Eric Byers is believed to have witnessed one of the very first attacks[49] in an industrial environment … a paper mill.

I asked Eric to speak about those times and here's what he told me:

Byres:

"The security of industrial systems became an interest of mine sometime around 1996 when a 'hack' of a Foxboro DCS by an employee caused a lot of problems for a pulp and paper client I had been consulting to (on serial communications design trouble-shooting, not security of course). I subsequently wrote up that incident as part of an article for the International Society of Automation's (ISA's) *InTech Magazine*. Here's an excerpt:

> *Often the hacker is not an outsider with malicious intent but an employee doing something he or she shouldn't. A good example of this type of problem occurred this spring in a large East Coast paper mill. The mill had just completed an upgrade of its paper machine, during which a number of engineers had been brought in from head office to assist with DCS commissioning. Everyone on the DCS commissioning team knew the passwords for the control system computers and when the project was completed, no one bothered to change them.*
>
> *Trouble started about a month later when one of the head-office engineers decided he needed a good data source for an expert system experiment he was running. Using the company's wide area network (WAN), he was able to dial into the mill network from the corporate headquarters several hundred miles away. Once into the mill's business LAN, he was able to connect to the DCS through a link originally set-up to allow mill supervisors to view operators screens from their offices. He then loaded a small program onto one of the DCS graphics stations (a UNIX machine). This program asked all DCS devices to dump their data back to him once every five minutes.*
>
> *All this would have worked fine, except that the engineer's new task would occasionally overload one of the DCS to PLC communications gateways, and it would stop reading the PLC data. This, of course, caused the machine operators great panic as they lost control of the motors controlled by the PLCs. Soon the electrical department was busy troubleshooting the PLCs. Meanwhile the head-office engineer had left the company to work for a competitor.*
>
> *Eventually the problem was solved by an eagle-eyed mill engineer who noticed that the problems always occurred at intervals that were at*

multiple of five minutes. Suspecting that it might be software induced, he started to inspect all the tasks running on the DCS computers and found the offending task. Of course, by then the lost production in the mill had been substantial.[50]

"After that I started getting exploratory calls from other pulp and paper and chemical companies about security and decided to write a peer-reviewed paper on the subject. [And not long after that], Marty Edwards and I were both working for an Emerson LBP in Canada and we started to do some basic security design as part of DCS network design. Marty will also tell you that I delighted in sending him off to troubleshoot data highways in sour gas plants in Northern BC in the middle of winter where the temperature was -40C.

We both left the Emerson LBL in late 1999, with Marty heading to Potlach Pulp and Paper and me going to the British Columbia Institute of Technology (BCIT). I didn't have industrial security in mind for my academic research at that time, but rather was planning to do Quality of Service (QoS) and latency research for ICS communications. But that all changed on September 11, 2001. Suddenly I was getting calls from government agencies and major oil companies interested in security research. Our little team of two researchers grew to 14 by the time I left BCIT in 2006. The reason was simple—if you did a literature search for 'security' and 'SCADA' or 'automation' or 'process control' in 2001 you would find papers by Joe Weiss and myself—that was all there was. It actually really bothered me at the time as academics are supposed to reference other academic work and I struggled to find much. One company even paid me to do a formal literature review. I eventually convinced some other academics in electrical engineering to start doing research on the topic, but I don't think anything meaningful was published until 2004.

The years from 2002 to 2005 were wild. Funding came in from BP, Cisco, Exxon, Chevron, INL, Kraft Foods and even a few security agencies I shouldn't name. We grew our research budget to over a million a year. We were getting a lot of papers published then. Dr. Dan Hoffman published 'Worlds in Collision: Ethernet on the Plant Floor' at the ISA Emerging Technologies Conference in Chicago, October 2002. Then Justin Lowe and I published 'The Myths and Facts behind Cyber Security Risks for Industrial Control Systems,' at the VDE 2004 Congress, in Berlin in October 2004. It turned out to be one of my most referenced papers in the academic world.

I believe that Joe Weiss was the first person to run a conference on the subject of 'SCADA Security'. It was in Vancouver in the summer of 2002 and Joe and I teamed up—Joe ran the conference and BCIT ran tours of my research operations…. BCIT decided to run its own event in 2003 (and 2004). I think it was called the International Symposium on Industrial Cyber Security. ISA also ran an early ICS Security conference in Pittsburg—I think that was in late 2002, 4 months after Joe's event.

By 2005, BCIT leadership was encouraging us to start to commercialize the considerable collection of intellectual property we were amassing in our research. So in 2006 Joann and I left BCIT and formed three companies in a period of four months; WurldTech, Byres Research and Tofino Security. We soon left WurldTech and focused on Tofino Security. Tofino released its first firewall in January 2006 and struggled along until Stuxnet appeared in 2010. After that Joann and I never looked back."

SIDEBAR: EARLY CCE ORIGINS—PART 2

THE BIRTH OF NATIONAL AWARENESS OF THE SUSCEPTIBILITY OF INDUSTRIAL SYSTEMS TO CYBER ATTACKS: AN INTERVIEW WITH ICS SECURITY EXPERT MICHAEL ASSANTE

Where Eric Byers was witness to what was going on in the field (and at paper mills, factory floors, chemical plants, etc.), former Navy intelligence officer Mike Assante had a bird's eye view on developments in Washington. Here's what he told me, largely in the form of a timeline of activities revealing the growing awareness of the potential for catastrophic harm not just to individual companies, but to the country itself.

Assante:

"The true cyber control and industrial security awareness started with a terrorism assessment under President George H.W. Bush and carried over to a PDD-63 work. The USG began its initial explorations under the Department of Commerce. Joe Weiss was there then and the FBI NIPC pursued it as well. The first organized conferences included a small handful of individuals, and INL was one of the first organizations to partner with [the SANS cybersecurity institute] and collect papers and speakers to launch the inaugural ICS Summit.

Here's a sketch of early events and responses to them that reveal the evolution of the national security mindset on potentially catastrophic cyber-physical risks:

THE RONALD REAGAN AND GEORGE H.W. BUSH YEARS: 1981–1989 AND 1989–1993

These terror events and others, and commentary around them prompted an uptick in awareness:

- 1982 Siberian gas pipeline explosion alleged to result from CIA cyber operations[51]
- 1983 Beirut barracks bombings
- 1990 Shining Path guerillas in Peru destroyed transmission lines[52]
- 1991 Cyber expert Winn Schwartau warns Congress of a coming 'Digital Pearl Harbor'[53]
- 1993 World Trade Center truck bombing

Earliest Federal level terror assessments began in the wake of these events. They examined various infrastructure elements like gas pipelines, but also included IT and communications assets like control centers and data centers, but primarily through a physical security, not cybersecurity, lens. The results were consumed by the national security community, which used imagination to extrapolate to the potential for larger terrorist attacks in future.

BILL CLINTON YEARS AND GEORGE H.W. BUSH YEARS: 1993–2003

Informed by information and guidance that flowed from preceding efforts, USG bureaucracy began to swing into action. Here are some of the milestones:

- 1998 Presidential Policy Directive 63 (PPD-63): 'Protecting America's Critical Infrastructures' was signed into law. Among other clauses, then-POTUS Clinton stated 'I intend that the United States will take all necessary measures to swiftly eliminate any significant vulnerability to both physical and cyberattacks on our critical infrastructures, including especially our cyber systems.'[54]

- 1998 (circa) Terror assessments continued but began to include cyber elements
- 2001 Hearing just weeks after the 9/11 attack: the Senate Committee on Government Affairs convened to try and ascertain which department or agencies were charged with critical infrastructure protection.[55]
- 2002 Alison Silverstein (at DOE and later, FERC) made first cyber notice of public record (NOPR) which became an urgent Standards Authorization Request (SAR) directing the electric sector 'do something' about its cyber risks[56]
- 2003 Silverstein also led Inquiries into the August 14, 2003 Northeast blackout and made sure it included a cyber investigation. But discovered DOE didn't have the capability to protect the information gathered. Nevertheless, interviews continued and soon it was ascertained that utilities had no means to investigate anything related to cyber on their systems
- 2003–2004 There was an unusual finding by NERC that remote terminal units (RTUs) kept turning off seemingly on their own and no one could pinpoint a root cause. This stuck out as strange, and made clear that no one at the time knew what was going on behind the front panel."[57]

NOTES

1 "What Lies Beneath a Cyber Breach." *OEM Magazine* online. July 9, 2018. www.oemmagazine.org/technology/machine-design-management/article/13274847/what-lies-beneath-a-cyber-breach.
2 David Geer. "A Rubicon." Hoover Institute. 2018. www.hoover.org/sites/default/files/research/docs/geer_webreadypdfupdated2.pdf.
3 Mike McConnell, the former director of National Intelligence, 2011 Senate Testimony, cited in Kim Zetter's *Countdown to Zero Day: Stuxnet and the Launch of the World's First Digital Weapon.*
4 Speaking to House staffers in DC. January 29, 2018.
5 "Critical Infrastructure Sectors." U.S. Department of Homeland Security web page, accessed January 3, 2020. www.dhs.gov/cisa/critical-infrastructure-sectors.

6   "National Critical Functions." U.S. Department of Homeland Security web page, accessed January 3, 2020. www.dhs.gov/cisa/national-critical-functions-set.

7   Olivia Gazis. "Ex-Mossad Director Says Cyberattacks Pose Biggest Threat to Free World." CBS News. May 22, 2019. www.cbsnews.com/news/ex-mossad-director-says-cyber-poses-biggest-threat-to-free-world/.

8   Andrew McAfee and Erik Brynjolfsson. *The Second Machine Age: Work, Progress and Prosperity in a Time of Brilliant Technologies.* W. W. Norton & Company, New York, New York. January 2016.

9   Paul Davidson. "Automation Could Kill 73 Million U.S. Jobs by 2030." *USA Today*. November 28, 2017. www.usatoday.com/story/money/2017/11/29/automation-could-kill-73-million-u-s-jobs-2030/899878001/.

10 Examples: Boeing 737 Max MCAS autopilot and earlier Airbus crash from engines turning off, both referenced in foreword.

11 Daniel Groves. In conversation. April 23, 2019.

12 Great example: Headless vs. Headed Magmeter example. Headless version has no display, so flow readings are only accessible via control system. More background on this from West Yost's Daniel Groves as well.

13 David Krakauer, President, and William H. Miller, Professor of Complex Systems at the Santa Fe Institute, call technologies that obviate the need for human mastery of once-common skills: competitive cognitive artifacts. On Sam Harris podcast (transcript). November 13, 2016. https://samharris.org/complexity-stupidity/.

14 David Geer. "A Rubicon." Hoover Institute. 2018. www.hoover.org/sites/default/files/research/docs/geer_webreadypdfupdated2.pdf.

15 Kate Fazzini. "China and Russia Could Disrupt US Energy Infrastructure, Intelligence Report Warns on Heels of Huawei Indictments." CNBC. January 29, 2019. www.cnbc.com/2019/01/29/china-russia-could-disrupt-us-infra-structure-with-cyber-attacks-odni.html.

16 The DoD has said this openly and plainly. "Defense Science Board Task Force on Cyber Deterrence." February 2017. Page 2. www.armed-services.senate.gov/imo/media/doc/DSB%20CD%20Report%202017-02-27-17_v18_Final-Cleared%20Security%20Review.pdf.

17 Kevin Hemsley and Ron Fisher, "A History of Cyber Incidents and Threats Involving Industrial Control Systems" in *Critical Infrastructure Protection XII*, Springer 2018, pp. 215–242.

18 Joe Weiss. "Databases for Actual Control System Cyber Incidents Exist—and They Are Important for Many Reasons." November 18, 2019. www.controlglobal.com/blogs/unfettered/databases-for-actual-control-system-cyber-incidents-exist-and-they-are-important-for-many-reasons/.

19 Vint Cerf speaking the University of Virginia School of Engineering on cyber-physical systems at a Cybersecurity Workshop. May 1, 2019.

20 Dale Peterson. "Insecure By Design / Secure By Design." The Dale Peterson Blog. November 4, 2013. https://dale-peterson.com/2013/11/04/insecure-by-design-secure-by-design/.

21 "What is Living off the Land?" Symantec's Security Response. October 3, 2018. https://medium.com/threat-intel/what-is-living-off-the-land-ca0c2e932931.

22 Secure—aspirational when used in the context of cybersecurity. Think of it as freedom for humans and digital devices to perform tasks without interruption or interference.

23 David Brim. "John Wooden Lessons for Life, Sport and Business." June 5, 2010. www.davidbrim.com/john-wooden-lessons/.

24 Gus Serino, in conversation. February 2019.

25 Michael Assante, in conversation. July 2018.

26 "Risk Nexus." The Atlantic Council. September 2015. Page 19. https://publications.atlanticcouncil.org/cyberrisks/.

27 Blake Sobczak. "The Inside Story of the World's Most Dangerous Malware." March 7, 2019. www.eenews.net/stories/1060123327.

28 Kieren McCarthy. "Cyber-Insurance Shock: Zurich Refuses to Foot NotPetya Bill—and Claims It's an Act of War." The Register. January 11, 2019. www.theregister.co.uk/2019/01/11/notpetya_insurance_claim/.

29 Adam Satariano and Nicole Perlroth. "Big Companies Thought Insurance Covered a Cyberattack. They May Be Wrong." *New York Times.* April 15, 2019. www.nytimes.com/2019/04/15/technology/cyberinsurance-notpetya-attack.html.

30 Eugene Spafford. "The RSA 2019 Conference." March 07, 2019. www.cerias.purdue.edu/site/blog/post/the_rsa_2019_conference.

31 Bruce Sterling. "The Cybersecurity Industrial Complex." *Wired Magazine* (online). January 1, 2003. www.wired.com/2003/01/the-cybersecurity-industrial-complex/.

32 Ralph Langner. *Robust Control System Networks*, Momentum Press, New York, p. 7, 2012.

33 Tim Roxey via interview August 4, 2017.

34 "The Case for Simplicity in Energy Infrastructure." Roxey, Assante, Bochman. CSIS, October 30, 2015. https://csis-prod.s3.amazonaws.com/s3fs-public/legacy_files/files/publication/151030_Assante_SimplicityEnergyInfrastructure_Web.pdf.

35 Robert M. Lee, Twitter post, June 21, 2018. https://twitter.com/RobertMLee/status/1009783411022626822.

36 "The Cybersecurity Illusion: The Emperor Has No Clothes." Ponemon Institute Research Report, July 2019. https://i.crn.com/sites/default/files/ckfinderimages/userfiles/images/crn/custom/2019/AttackIQ_REPORT_Ponemon.pdf.

37 Momentum Cyber web page, accessed January 3, 2020. https://momentumcyber.com/docs/CYBERscape.pdf.

38 "Ransomware." New Jersey Cybersecurity and Communications Integration Cell, accessed January 2, 2020. www.cyber.nj.gov/threat-profiles/ransomware/.

39   Naveen Joshi. "Can AI Become Our New Cybersecurity Sheriff?" February 4, 2019. www.forbes.com/sites/cognitiveworld/2019/02/04/can-ai-become-our-new-cybersecurity-sheriff/#f339d1936a8e.

40   "The Next Paradigm Shift: AI-Driven Cyber-Attacks." Darktrace white paper and web page, accessed January 3, 2020. https://pdfs.semanticscholar.org/6b18/6268d00e891f3ed282544ac5833c01a2891c.pdf.

41   Peter Behr. "Friendly Hackers Break into a Utility and Make a Point." EENews.com, accessed October 6, 2015. www.eenews.net/stories/1060025871.

42   "Black Energy." August 10, 2017. New Jersey Cybersecurity and Communications Integration Cell (NJCCIC). www.cyber.nj.gov/about.

43   "CIP-002-6—Cyber Security—BES Cyber System Categorization." pp. 17–20 on "Impact Rating Criteria." www.nerc.com/pa/Stand/Project%20201602%20Modifications%20to%20CIP%20Standards%20DL/CIP-002-6_Standard_Clean_03162018.pdf.

44   "Synchro Phasor Domain Description." http://smartgrid.epri.com/UseCases/SynchroPhasor.pdf.

45   "Transmission and Distribution." PJM Learning Center, accessed February 10, 2020. https://learn.pjm.com/electricity-basics/transmission-distribution.aspx.

46   Sarah Freeman, in conversation, December 2019.

47   "Defense Use Case: Analysis of the Cyber Attack on the Ukrainian Power Grid." SANS Industrial Control Systems and the Electricity Information Sharing and Analysis Center, accessed March 18, 2016. https://ics.sans.org/media/E-ISAC_SANS_Ukraine_DUC_5.pdf.

48   Clifford Stoll. *The Cuckoos Egg: Tracking a Spy Through the Maze of Computer Espionage*, accessed October 23, 2001. https://en.wikipedia.org/wiki/The_Cuckoo%27s_Egg.

49   As the passage below reveals, there was no malicious intent, just one employee's desire to do something productive without realizing the ramifications of his actions. It's often difficult to distinguish between intentional attacks and accidents or configuration errors.

50   "Byres, E. J., Network Secures Process Control, InTech, Instrument Society of America, pp. 92–93, October 1998." [Requires Login Credentials]. www.tofinosecurity.com/professional/network-secures-process-control.

51   Jeffrey Carr. "The Myth of the CIA and the Trans-Siberian Pipeline Explosion." Infosec Island, accessed June 07, 2012. www.infosecisland.com/blogview/21566-The-Myth-of-the-CIA-and-the-Trans-Siberian-Pipeline-Explosion.html.

52   James Brooke. "Lima Journal; On the Front Line in Guerrilla War: Power Pylons." *New York Times*, accessed March 10, 1990. www.nytimes.com/1990/03/10/world/lima-journal-on-the-front-line-in-guerrilla-war-power-pylons.html.

53   Elinor Abreu. "Epic Cyberattack Reveals Cracks in U.S. Defense." CNN online, accessed May 10, 2001. www.cnn.com/2001/TECH/internet/05/10/3.year.cyberattack.idg/.

54   "PDD 63: Protecting America's Critical Infrastructures fact sheet." Department of Homeland Security Digital Library website. November 1998. www.hsdl.org/?abstract&did=3544.

55   "Senate Hearing 107–258: Critical Infrastructure Protection: Who's in Charge?" United States Printing Office online transcript, accessed October 4, 2001. www.govinfo.gov/content/pkg/CHRG-107shrg77434/html/CHRG-107shrg77434.htm.

56   "Proposal for Security Standards for the Electricity Sector." On NERC website, accessed July 7, 2002. www.nerc.com/comm/CIPC/Related%20Files%20DL/FERC-SMD-Conference-Presentation.pdf.

57   "Technical Analysis of the August 14, 2003, Blackout: What Happened, Why, and What Did We Learn?" pp. 32–33. NERC website, accessed July 13, 2004. www.nerc.com/docs/docs/blackout/NERC_Final_Blackout_Report_07_13_04.pdf.

58   Ron DiGiacomo. "Magmeter Basics." Accessed May 30, 2011. www.flowcontrolnetwork.com/instrumentation/flow-measurement/electromagnetic/article/15554990/magmeter-basics.

2

RESTORING TRUST

Cyber-Informed Engineering

Successful strategies must proceed from the premise that cyberspace is continuously contested territory.

—Former Secretary of the US Navy, Richard Danzig[1]

In a world of increasing connectivity and cyber threat innovation, it must be assumed that our computing environments have been compromised and that we cannot certify any system fully secure. It is reckless to presume historical analytical assumptions and approaches … can cover the unique nuances of the cyber threat.

—INL's Bob Anderson and Joseph Price[2]

Where Probabilistic Risk Assessment (PRA) or Probabilistic Safety Assessment (PSA) analysis utilizes equipment failures or human error as initiating events for a hazard, cyberattacks use the historical framework and functionality of a trusted system to perform operations outside the intended design and potentially without the operator's knowledge.[3]

—INL's Bob Anderson and Joseph Price

SIDEBAR: THE MYTH OF AIRGAPS

"We're air gapped" used to be the right thing to say to auditors. After all, if there's no network connection between the important system or data in question, there must not be a way for hackers to reach it ... right? In the earliest days of mainframes and terminals, and later local area networks with servers and PCs, the only way for computers to share data or instructions was if they were connected by a copper wire or fiber optic cable. Cut the connection, and you had complete isolation. That is, if you forgot about the other ways to move data among machines, like floppy disks, USB sticks, and other removable storage devices.

Even someone as brilliant as Maine Senator Angus King, a Rhodes Scholar and one of the most cyber savvy Senators, once recommended air gapping the grid as a strategy to thwart advanced cyber adversaries. (He doesn't anymore.)

Only problem is, the term long ago ceased to signify anything of substance, with the exception of revealing the ignorance or naiveite of the person who still believes it has value. In fact, it was never an accurate way of delivering or thinking about cybersecurity, and folks on both sides of the auditor's question were sharing a mutual delusion. Talk about a false sense of security.

Here's why there are no air gaps:

- In recent years with the rise of ubiquitous cell coverage, Wi-Fi, Bluetooth, and other wireless communication technologies, the absence of a physical communications conduit means nothing in terms of network isolation.

  Imagine a PC or other computer-based system (e.g., all "smart" devices—Figure 2.1) was entirely un-networked, with no wired connections, and all wireless connectivity not just set to off in options, but with communications physically disabled or removed. In this mode, is it useful?

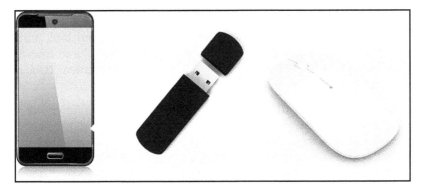

Figure 2.1 Smart Wireless and Networked Devices.

- Another system or network might be configurated to be, relatively speaking, "air gapped" by a particular administrator for
a period. Personnel turn over, as do policies, and it's often the
case that a system that was previously configured in a more
secure way becomes much less so when a new leader takes
charge or new initiative is undertaken.

The requirements of operating a plant or other engineering-heavy
organization often demand actions that further service to undermine
the concept of air gapping, including:

- Corporate networks connected through firewalls to operational
networks
- Remote access into field devices (often with little or no authentication) by engineering stations or for vendors' remote diagnostic support
- Removable media (e.g., flash drives, CDs, external hard drives,
etc.) used to perform patches, upgrades, and backups or to pull
data from a device
- Having common buses control systems and safety systems

On the positive side, if attempting to build and maintain air gaps
means there are fewer ways to reach a system or network, then that
is a good thing.

31

SIDEBAR: NUCLEAR DESIGN BASIS THREAT

INL's Bob Anderson and Joseph Price gave a long hard look and the cybersecurity threat to nuclear power plants (NPPs) and found potential blind spots via adherence to a design basis threat (DBT) that hasn't kept up with the times. They noted:

> The IAEA publication INFCIRC/225/Rev.4, also known as Nuclear Security Series #13, *"Recommendations for Physical Protection of Nuclear materials and Nuclear Facilities,"* states that a DBT is a description of the attributes and characteristics of potential insider and/or external adversaries who might attempt unauthorized removal of nuclear material or sabotage against which a physical protection system is designed and evaluated. DBT considers insiders, external adversaries, malicious acts leading to unacceptable consequences, adversary capabilities, and an evaluation of protective designs. Historically, DBT did not address cybersecurity concerns. With the cyber threat demonstrating its ability to influence physical protections systems including blended attacks, digital components and systems must now be considered as either part of the existing DBT or part of a separate cyber threat assessment. Either way, cyber-informed engineering must contribute to the analysis of credible scenarios that include the adversary compromising computer systems at nuclear facilities that lead to sabotage or the blended attack to remove nuclear material. Incorporation of the cyber threat must carefully consider new technologies, use of mobile computing, social media, and many more tactics, techniques, and procedures (TTPs) of the adversary. As these threats are considered, the engineer must design systems that reduce or remove these threats.

SOFTWARE HAS CHANGED ENGINEERING

Software arrived in our world, practically speaking, in the 1950s with the development of the Fortran programming language.[4] It took several more decades before computers and computer networks became affordable and commonplace enough to play a helpful role in the engineering-design process, as well as in the operation of computer-assisted process control functions. Previously, engineering was principally a realm of mathematics and physics, and until the arrival of the digital calculator in the 1970s, the slide rule was the engineer's constant companion.[5]

 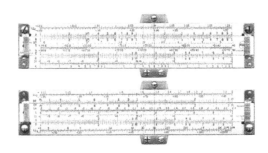

Figure 2.2   Software-driven Planning and Design Tools Develop Software-intensive Products and Systems. Calculator (left) and slide-rule (right).

"Illustrated Self-Guided Course on How to Use the Slide Rule." Web page, accessed January 4, 2020. www.sliderulemuseum.com/SR_Course.html.

"Calculator Museum." Mr. Martin's Web Site. Web page, accessed January 4, 2020. www.mrmartinweb.com/calculator.html.

While the first computer-aided design (CAD) programs emerged in the 1960s, it took until the arrival of applications on Unix workstations in the 1980s and Windows PCs in the 1990s for these capabilities to hit the mainstream and start making very large impacts in aerospace, automotive, and other industries.[6]

Imagine attempting to sabotage an engineered creation by hacking a physical slide rule (in use for centuries) or an early digital calculator (appeared circa 1970) (see Figure 2.2). To modify a single unit would require physical access to that unit and then some nifty craftwork to subtly change the devices without detection by its owner. Modifying a calculator might prove even more challenging and would require a skillset including precision soldering. To affect multiple units of either would force strategies targeting the manufacturers and/or their supply chain. While one can imagine any of these approaches employed by spy organizations, there's simply no comparison to the effects possible today at great distances and with great stealth.

INL and Engineering

Officially designated by the US Department of Energy as an applied engineering lab, INL's charter is to bring its enormous depth in engineering to solve the hardest problems of the near and mid-term future. This distinguishes it from other labs, the "science labs" that work on technical challenges of the more distant future.

There's a stereotype of inquisitive young engineers, inventors, and tinkerers who can't help themselves; they're compulsively driven to learn by taking things apart. Whether by unhurried and careful dissection, or else via sledgehammer, explosives, or other less meticulous means, there's an instinct to see how things are made by opening them up, and in so doing, determine whether they can be made better.

For the thousands of engineers and scientists at INL, better might mean a number of things, including safer, more efficient, simpler to operate, less expensive to build and/or maintain, etc. And in the twenty-first century, an increasingly essential attribute is more secure. The Idaho National Lab is an expansive government-funded test bed and playground for these types of folks. A sampling of their activities over the years would include:

- Running nuclear test reactors to the point of failure
- Calibrating battleship guns by firing Volkswagen Bug–sized projectiles at buttes dozens of miles away
- Electric grid testbed
- Water testbed
- Wireless communications range
- EMP/GMD testing
- Aurora: convincing a large electric generator to tear itself apart via a few strokes on a keyboard
- Creating extremely high-tech armor for the US Army's main battle tank
- Following the physical attack on the Metcalfe Substation serving Silicon Valley, designing and building a prototype of practical low-tech substation armor
- Operating the National SCADA Test Bed (NSTB) to take apart and find exploitable weaknesses in grid infrastructure components
- Voting machine security analysis for Department of Homeland Security (DHS)[7]
- Hosting elements of DOE's Cybersecurity Testing for Resilience of industrial control system (ICS) (CyTRICS) program today, an NSTB follow-on[8]

There's another word used to convey a constructive urge to disassemble, rearrange, or otherwise simply mess around with things: Hacking. To be called a hacker was and still is a source of pride among technical types, including but not limited to software developers, as hardware and all manner of machines can also be hacked. And biological organisms too. More recently, though, the definition of the word has skewed to include malicious intent. That's a trend that often offends the original cohort who hacked to understand and improve things, but as we all know, definitions can shift over time and no one, not even the folks in Oxford, can control them.

ENGINEERS STILL TRUST THE TRUST MODEL

Unverified Trust

In the digital world, to include almost all internetworked computing and communicating devices, the term "trust model" has signified the collective confidence derived from mutually agreed processes and protections achieved via broad conformance to standards (e.g., Secure Socket Layer [SSL], Certificates, HTTPS, password conventions, IP4, IP6, etc.). In the enterprise context, these, along with an ever-increasing arsenal of security technologies that began with antivirus tools and network firewalls, served ostensibly to protect systems and data by keeping the bad guys out. Best practices promulgated by NIST, ISA, and other standards bodies–guided organizations, but it has always been the case that targeted attacks can penetrate defenses that appear stout to their owners. With so much uncertainty, it's easy to see why the trust model has been pronounced dead by security professionals for quite a while.

Trust is more about psychology and human behavior than technology. INL's Curtis St. Michel almost always laces the opening segments of the CCE training sessions he conducts with ruminations on the dangerous position we've put ourselves in via "unverified trust." And ICS Cybersecurity educator and cyber threat analyst Sean McBride puts it this way:

> At the convergence of information technology and industrial control is a rat's nest of unseen, unknown, and unverified relationships—that for convenience and expediency we have "trusted away." Trust simplifies our decisions and puts our minds at rest: we anchor on the past to predict the future; we look for brand names; we stay in the center of the herd. But unseen, unknown, and unverified trust has immensely destructive potential. Modern societies have come to trust a convergence

of operational technologies—sensors, motors, valves, programmable controllers, and communications networks—to provide electricity, water, and manufactured goods. But the design and integration of these industrial operations are largely unverified. As a result, we have opened the door to cyberattacks intended to cause devastating physical consequences at a time of the adversary's choosing.[9]

Engineering is a different animal with a foundation built on the immutable laws of physics, more specifically in well-worn theorems from aerodynamics, fluid dynamics, thermodynamics, electrical engineering, and materials science.

In the "Old Days," the tools were physical:

- Calculations: slide rule
- Drafting medium: pencil and paper
- Storage medium: paper
- Security mechanism for sensitive intellectual property (IP): a safe protected by an analog combination lock
- Communications: via private branch exchange (PBX)/landline phone, ground, and air mail
- In Engineering (2020), the laws of physics and specific engineering disciplines are captured and reflected in software. Now the tools are:
- Calculations: software
- Drafting medium: software
- Storage medium: various digital media
- Security mechanism for sensitive IP: various software security products
- Communications: digital over fiber, wireless (and ground and air mail still)

SIDEBAR: INL'S CHUCK FORSHEE ON CYBER-INFORMED ENGINEERING (CIE)[10]

I was just talking to Bob Anderson about CIE-CCE. Bob and I go way back, designing and installing digital ICS at the Advanced Test Reactor (ATR) in the early 1990s. I believe that we are trying to make a cultural change with respect to the digital world we all live in, and the engineering challenges associated with this new reality. All new technology brings with it some new problems or faults (e.g., airbags and the warning stickers all over the inside of our cars).

In the 1990s we were just focusing on making digital ICS work. We knew components were going to fail, and there might be bugs in software, as evidenced by the ubiquitous blue screen of death. We weren't even thinking about how an adversary might use our systems against us.

We had to answer engineering design questions from a safety analysis perspective, all fault or failure based. We did not consider sabotage. When you approach a safety analyst now and tell him to design a new fault tree considering all the possible vectors a hacker might explore, you meet resistance. We try to overcome this in our CCE projects by developing sobering, sometimes shocking, but always realistic scenarios, showing the art of the possible and help them get to an epiphany.

Engineers will need to accept this new reality and develop a new culture that understands cyber vulnerabilities and employs cyber shields in all new engineering designs.

It's unfortunate that we are on our heels in a wait-and-see posture. Hoping that a new hacker doesn't exploit the holes we know exist in our systems. The hackers are getting smarter, and we are playing catchup trying to prevent their attacks. "This approach is not going well in the ransomware IT world we now live in. It's just a matter of time before the IT hackers get bored and really start to focus on OT systems. The IT stuff is most often an easy pathway to our OT systems."[11]

The C-suite knows that there are insufficient resources to patch all the holes because the OT systems were not designed with cyber vulnerabilities in mind in the first place.

TRUSTING WHAT WORKS: CIE IN DETAIL

There are a few prominent thinkers poised at the intersection of cybersecurity and physics. In the early days, circa 2003, concerned that there was too much marketing in the cybersecurity solution space, Allan Paller, the founder of the SANS Cybersecurity Training Institute, used to evaluate security tools on the basis of "What Works." Not long after he commissioned Mike Assante to build SANS ICS Security Summit and begin development of an ICS cybersecurity curricula, which now includes four different courses and certifications, from introductory level to advanced.

Richard Danzig, cited earlier, also had this to say about trimming technology down to its minimum functional requirements, so as to reduce the size of the playing field attackers have to navigate.

> Pursue a strategy that self-consciously sacrifices some cyber benefits in order to ensure greater security for key systems on which security depends. Methods for pursuing this strategy include stripping down systems so they do less but have fewer vulnerabilities; integrating humans and other out-of-band (i.e., non-cyber) factors so the nation is not solely dependent on digital systems; integrating diverse and redundant cyber alternatives; and making investments for graceful degradation. Determining the trade-offs between operational loss and security gain through abnegating choices will require and reward the development of a new breed of civilian policymakers, managers and military officers able to understand both domains.[12]

And my INL colleague, Virginia "Ginger" Wright, who played a critical role in the initial development of CIE, captures this sentiment with great concision when she says "We may not be able to engineer out all risk, but there are choices we can make during the design to simplify the cyber-security process."[13]

While INL performs research and other initiatives as tasked by multiple DOE offices (and DHS, DoD and more), the lab's primary sponsor is the Nuclear Energy (NE) office of DOE. Until recently, NE-funded efforts were primarily in materials and process research, but in 2017 it commissioned the lab to perform potentially ground-breaking research in cybersecurity challenges and opportunities facing those who own and operate nuclear plants, using CCE as its primary lens.[14]

INL researchers examined the systems engineering process across the entire lifecycle and identified 11 areas where key engineering decisions could substantially impact the cybersecurity of the operational technology:

1 **Consequence/Impact Analysis**
2 **Systems Architecture**
3 **Engineered Controls**
4 **Design Simplification**
5 **Resilience Planning**
6 **Engineering Information Control**

 7 **Procurement and Contracting**
 8 **Interdependencies**
 9 **Cybersecurity Culture**
10 **Digital Asset Inventory**
11 **Active Process Defense**

Let's take a look at each of these:

 1 **Consequence/Impact Analysis**
    The first element of CIE, consequence analysis, is concerned with
    the challenge of scarcity. Given finite money, time, and attention,
    how can limited resources be optimized to avoid the worst
    outcomes? The first task is to identify high-impact consequences
    and the actions that separately or together could bring them about.
    Mitigations that could prevent those results from occurring are
    generated. But in case mitigations are incorrect or incomplete, it's
    imperative to identify protections that diminish the consequences
    themselves. Consequence analysis can increase security simply
    through design decisions. Ideally, mitigations can be put in place
    early in the design cycle, well before the first procurement actions.
    To begin, identify
    - the bounded set of high-impact consequences.
    - the situations that must not be allowed happen.
    - systems that could contribute to or enable the negative
      consequence.
    - associated digital and communications assets.
    - protections for the system that greatly diminish negative
      consequences.

 2 **Systems Architecture**
    With the rarest of exceptions, it's not much of an overstatement to
    say that all of our systems and products were designed foremost for
    functionality, not security. However, when a team wants to under-
    take a project to build something that both fulfills its functional and
    performance requirements, and that is intrinsically secure as well,
    there are several points to keep in mind:
    - Design requires collaboration to ensure design is functional and
      secure. So the design team needs cyber expertise to ensure appro-
      priate security technology (such as data diodes, virtual local area
      networks [VLANS], network access lists, firewalls, etc.) is used
      to support the architecture. And system engineering experts

are required to fully explore and select the best approaches for meeting functional requirements.

Because any individual element cannot be trusted, the design
- avoids assumed trust.
- uses defense-in-depth principles.
- supports least privilege.
- ensures architectural boundaries are instrumented and monitored.
- documents communication flows.
- uses both horizontal & vertical network protections to enforce communication flows.

3 Engineered Controls

Engineers usually have two and sometimes several different options when making functional design decisions, and the same is true for security professionals. In a perfect and therefore unrealistic world, most security problems would be addressed through the top one or two control strategies in the list that follows. In reality, most solutions require use of some of the approaches drawn from the following list (also in Figure 2.3):

1 Elimination: Design the system to NOT have the potentially hazardous capability (often through simplification; disablement of broad "general purpose" functionality).

2 Substitution: Design the system to use a less dangerous capability (e.g., input/output information through other means).

3 Engineering Controls: If there is no way around a hazardous element in the process, then work to keep it as far away from human operators as possible. Or vice versa (e.g., use port blockers to prevent unauthorized access).

4 Administrative Controls: Develop and enforce policies and procedures that support security (e.g., structured and enforced kiosk check-in and check-out to secure mobile storage devices).

5 Personal Protective Equipment (PPE): The last line of defense. Implement cybersecurity controls. Must implement and configure correctly, patch quickly, and administer properly. (e.g., implement technical cyber controls to block unauthorized mobile devices)

In all of this, it's important to consider both IT and engineered controls as early in the design lifecycle as possible. In legacy OT systems it is often the case that patching must wait for a pre-planned maintenance activity, sometimes only on a yearly or twice-yearly basis. To take some of the pressure off of patching, investigate how vulnerabilities can be designed out or mitigated

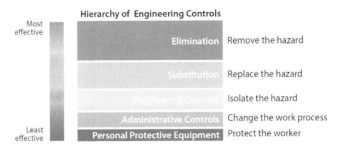

Hierarchy of Engineering Controls

Most effective

Elimination	Remove the hazard
Substitution	Replace the hazard
Engineering Controls	Isolate the hazard
Administrative Controls	Change the work process
Personal Protective Equipment	Protect the worker

Least effective

Figure 2.3   Hierarchy of Engineering Controls.

through additional engineered controls, and lastly, note that engineered controls will almost always provide more robust and dependable protection than add-on IT controls.

4 Design Simplification via ALARA

Ever-increasing system complexity is one of the trends that make defenders' lives difficult and confer advantages to attackers. ALARA—As Low as Reasonably Achievable—is a concept born from a program initially developed to reduce engineer and operator exposure to radioactivity. In the IT and OT context, it translates to reducing the functionality to only what is absolutely necessary.

A couple of cybersecurity maxims apply here. First, you can't secure what you don't even know you have. This is a comment on asset management, and the fact is that most larger critical infrastructure organizations don't achieve and maintain a comprehensive record of their assets to include the hardware, software, firmware communications, and the policy-driven and/or ad hoc processes used to operate them.

Here's another: Complexity fights security, or stated another way, you can't secure what you don't understand. An almost gratuitously high levels of complexity are what we've achieved and continue to layer on with applications and services riding on top of generous purpose operating systems undergirded by general-purpose hardware. Windows 10, while demonstrably more secure in many ways than its many generations of predecessors, includes many tools that can be turned against its users (see PowerShell, web servers, etc.). Current generation automobiles are now being recalled for patching, with multiple wired and wireless networks with processors running hundreds of millions of lines of code. All this latent functionality is a gift to attackers; it often comprises the primary playing field

41

adversaries will traverse to get where they need to go and accomplish what they seek to accomplish.

Ideally, from a cybersecurity viewpoint, a specific function is supported by a system, digital, or otherwise, customized to enable and support that function, and that function only. And if that cannot be achieved, it nevertheless can be aimed for, and the resultant reduction in complexity and therefore in attack surfaces will only serve to aid the defenders.Lastly, simplification is a specific aspect of resilience. In contrast to the massively complex and interdependent systems we have now, a better future lies in decomposing these into distributed and fundamental operations with simplified interactions, for instance, a distributed grid with primary responsibilities for local power support with microgrids and the bulk grid for supplemental needs only. Sharing or isolation can occur if the bulk grid is lost, but also, if a microgrid is compromised its effects remain localized.[15]

5 The Importance of Resilience Planning

Resilience is the ability to sustain or bounce back when stressed or compromised ... to continue operating at a minimum useful level even when impaired. There is a connection between design simplification and resilience. There is a happy medium for any system between the two.

Why is resilience necessary?

• Any digital component or system may be compromised.
• Vulnerabilities always exist, known or unknown.
• Can't always stop the process and reboot.

Current critical infrastructure and safety-critical control system designs are not able to handle multiple and coordinated malicious cyberattacks, and new failure modes from emergent properties of complex interdependencies and interactions. These systems are extremely brittle, and their operators, when faced with cascading failures and/or cyber effects, are unable to team up with the control system infrastructure engineers to achieve effective and timely resiliency responses. A more adaptive approach is needed, and this calls for new design approaches based on systems thoroughly vetted via engineering foundations.[16]

6 Engineering Information Control

Organizations and individuals should strive to make a prospective hacker's job as difficult and, therefore, as costly as possible. One way of doing this is by limiting the amount of technical information about the product or process they can find online. While documents will be created and shared as part of every engineering design and development effort, there are things one can do to reduce their accessibility and minimize the spread of this sensitive information. For example, organizations should be prepared to protect the following types of information throughout the life of a project:

- Engineering records
- Drawings
- Requirements
- Specifications
- Designs
- Analysis
- Testing
- Detailed supplier-specific technical experience listed in job postings

While every employee has a role in this, responsibility for controlling these details falls in large part to procurement offices and departments. Social media, vendor websites, press releases, conference talks, etc., any and all of these have the potential to exposure unnecessarily detailed information to the wider world. Human Resources too has a large part to play, for instance, in developing policies related to reviewing, modifying, or terminating access when authorized users or key partners leave the organization.

7 Procurement and Contracting

Approximately half of the burden of containing or limiting open source exposure can be resolved via policies followed by the organization and its employees, with the rest falling to partners, integrators and suppliers. Contracts are the first and one of the best vehicles for beginning to lock down sensitive engineering information and should begin right at the RFP/tender/requirements stage.

Procurement language must specify the exact requirements a vendor must comply with as part of the system design, build, integration, or support. Depending on the product or service being procured, some of the cybersecurity capabilities and characteristics to consider include:

- Software Security and Secure Software Development Lifecycle (Secure SDLC)
- Access Control
- Account Management
- Session Management
- Authentication/Password Policy and Management

- Logging and Auditing
- Communication Restrictions
- Malware Detection and Protection
- Heartbeat Signals
- Reliability and Adherence to Standards
  These requirements can raise procurement costs, but without them, caveat emptor. Costs related to bolting security on post procurement may be many times greater than if these functions were designed and built in the first place. Other points to consider relate to contractors and subcontractors who are allowed entry into your facilities:
- Be aware of what a subcontractor leaves behind on your network. You don't know where subcontractor devices were before today.
- Vendor tools such as calibration equipment or diagnostic equipment, which, unbeknownst to the vendor, may harbor malware (if digital).
  Here are a few vetted resources for including cybersecurity concerns in the contracting process:
- Department of Homeland Security's DHS—Cybersecurity Procurement Language for Control Systems
- Energy-Sector Control Systems Working Group (ESCSWG)—Cybersecurity Procurement Language for Energy Delivery Systems
- Electric Power Research Institute (EPRI)—Cybersecurity Procurement Methodology Rev. 1 2013 Technical Report

8 Interdependencies

Few if any modern systems are 100% free of dependencies on other systems or processes. Complex digital systems have inputs from, connections to, and protections from other systems, and it is essential that system engineers understand the people and systems on which they depend and that these interdependencies may enable cyberattacks.

While engineering design builds on experiences from multiple disciplines, (including safety, quality, maintenance, chemical, etc.), all disciplines that share information between them have to gauge how a cyberattack would affect their primary areas of concern. Questions to begin with may include:

- On what people, services, or systems do you and your product/ system rely?
- What services, systems, and people rely on your product/system?

Case in point: At the sector level, US legislators have come to realize that the reliable generation of electricity now depends upon the well-being of natural gas distribution pipelines. With a full third of US electricity now coming from natural gas, should key compressor station controls be sabotaged by either cyber or physical means, the impacts to the US grid could be substantial. Efforts are underway to tighten up cybersecurity policy and oversight for the natural gas distribution companies.

Similarly, thermal electricity generation plants (e.g., coal, natural gas, nuclear) require reliable water sources as coolant and to drive the turbines that produce electricity. And the complex modern grid completely depends upon robust communications capabilities for operator and reliability coordinators to do their jobs. And then there's financial markets, another sector without which the grid cannot function for long.

9 Cybersecurity Culture

It has become increasingly clear that damaging cyber breaches (see: NotPetya's $10 billion worldwide costs[17]) can impact the bottom line in ways similar to large safety failures.

A cyber-informed organization will ensure that while concerns with managing cybersecurity risk reduction factors will not entirely remake the way it does business (e.g., design discussions, partnering selections, M&A criteria, etc.) it will insist that a cyber professional has "a seat at the table" when any decision of consequence is being made.

But it's not just the inclusion of cybersecurity professionals in decisions they were once removed from, it's also the inculcation of a shared awareness of cyber risks in every part of the organization. All staff are part of the organization's cyber defense team and must understand, at a basic level, how damaging cyberattacks are made easier as more digital technologies (e.g., IoT, 5G, AI) are brought into everyday activities. From an engineering perspective, a cybersecurity culture must be formalized to include requirements that all interactions with digital elements receive adequate scrutiny.

As cybersecurity becomes increasingly involved into engineering process decisions, the engineering disciplines must be included in cybersecurity curricula. The Internet of Things will continue to stress organizational infrastructure while mobile technology will continue to add digital attack pathways.Bringing cybersecurity to the same level of acceptance and practice as safety would have an immense effect on the organization's defensive security posture.

And as in mature safety cultures, in cybersecurity spaces, a perpetual questioning attitude should be encouraged.

10 The Centrality of Digital Asset Inventories

For an enterprise, maintaining a comprehensive and accurate inventory of all digital assets is somewhere between a Russian nested doll, a labyrinth, and a marathon. But for an engineering firm designing a product or a system to be comprised of elements from multiple suppliers, the challenge can be similarly daunting. A digital inventory includes all hardware, software, and firmware, plus the policies and processes used to maintain it all. It drills down into the software to determine whether it's part of a packaged commercial application or platform, open source, or custom code. It needs to address whether cloud services are being used, and if so, the details of those services including how security is achieved and maintained by the cloud partners. Operating system version, patch-level, device drivers, dynamic load libraries (DLLs), and more must be annotated and tracked, for they constitute the environment adversaries will learn and leverage on the pathway toward achieving their goals.

Here's how the Atlantic Council described four types of complex software supply chain issues for suppliers and their customers alike[18]:

1 Supplier-Facilitated Risk: This refers to the cybersecurity of third-party partners who can influence energy-sector operations. For instance, systems integrators who design and implement products into energy-sector (and other industrial) operations environments, as well as other vendors who have physical or network access.

2 Counterfeit Goods: Components that come through an unauthorized channel are not authentic and would fail a sufficiently rigorous validation. Counterfeiters are typically motivated by financial gain, buying inexpensive components, and passing them off as more expensive ones. Negative impacts on operations are often an unintended consequence.

3 Malicious Taint: Components that often come through authorized channels are authentic and pass highly rigorous validation. Nonetheless, these components have some unintended functionality when placed intentionally by an adversary, which has negative implications on reliability, security, and safety. Typically,

introducing malicious taint requires very high-level capabilities and resources, such as those a nation-state may possess.

4 Unintended Taint: Components that come through authorized channels are authentic and pass highly rigorous validation. Nonetheless, these components contain quality defects in the form of software flaws or vulnerabilities, which may be known or unknown to the producer at the time of implementation.

Identification of counterfeit hardware also requires a more granular analysis that may not be readily apparent, including at the level of boards and chips. And not just for logic and memory but for I/O, interfaces, power supplies, cooling fans, and more. And as with software, the questions of provenance matter: Who made what, and when and where? And did any other third parties handle the hardware as it traversed other supply chains?

Organizations must also recognize the sensitivity of their inventories. Once collected, this information must be carefully protected, as it would be a "gold mine" for attackers. And despite the difficulties of this endeavor, this adage applies: You cannot protect what you don't know you have. And to protect it you've got to know it at least as well as your would-be adversaries.

11 Active Process Defense

Active defense is an advanced concept and requires highly skilled defenders to make it work. But as soon as resources and schedules allow, it behooves every engineering organization to begin to migrate from a purely passive cyber defense posture (e.g., network firewalls, antivirus, intrusion detection systems, etc.) to active defense. Technology researcher and writer Dan Woods describes five options available to active cyber defenders[19]:

1 Control the Scope of Damage: Quarantine the known infected systems and contain the attack in an isolated environment. This is a judgment call, often driven by the depth of expertise of the security team. The analyst may decide to watch the attacker or simply shut down the attack ....

2 Perform Forensic Analysis: Perform forensic analysis to better understand the attack. Once an attack is detected, the learning process can begin .... What does the adversary want to do next based on what they've done before? What network traffic is being generating? What payloads are they dropping? What processes are they loading? What data are they accessing?

3 Execute Standard Countermeasures: Execute playbooks for auto-mated or manual responses in the event of a cyberattack. The ability to analyze the nature of an attack can in part be automated and made into playbooks to execute at the time of an attack. This type of automation can take the form of programs that find out everything about the traffic that came from a certain IP address or that crossed boundaries that no normal traffic should ....

4 Perform Threat Detection and Hunting: Search for evidence of similar attacks. Once you understand how an attack is working and what the adversary wants to do next, you can use that insight to search methodically through your IT and OT landscape to find similar infections that may not have been detected and fully remediated.

5 Gather Threat Intelligence: Record and share the nature of the attack with others. Native integrations between vendors and actively remove internal information silos and improve productivity. As part of the cybersecurity community, companies often share intel-ligence about attacks they have detected and understood. Active defense gives an opportunity to provide deeper and richer threat intelligence so that other cybersecurity practitioners can make both their own and industrywide defenses more powerful.

SECURITY AS A CO-EQUAL VALUE TO SAFETY

Though there's no such thing as (and there never will be) a completely secure system, some degree of cybersecurity will be built into every product and featured in every service when both sellers and buyers are fully "cyber-informed." That day will come as part of a culture shift com-parable to what senior INL engineer Curtis St. Michel witnessed over the first half of his career at the lab. He recalls that when he started work in Idaho in the 1980s, safety incidents at the lab and across the country (in steel mills, in mines, in coal generation plants, on oil rigs and in refineries, in heavy manufacturing, and for telephone and electric linemen) were still somewhat common. Evidence suggests that while these types of jobs were dangerous everywhere, the United States was among the most dangerous places to work in the early-mid-twentieth century.[20]

Most accounts describe a slowly evolving safety awareness cam-paign that began with Massachusetts passing safety laws in 1887 and which gained traction with the rise of industrial manufacturing processes, and the associated deaths and injuries in the early twentieth century and reaching a peak around World War II (WWII). Even though injuries tapered after the war, robust economic expansion in the 1960s saw safety incidents rise again. The Occupational Safety and Health Act (OSHA) was signed by President Richard Nixon in 1970, following attempts by his predecessor, Lyndon Johnson, two years prior to get the bill through Congress.[21] Sentiments for OSHA became further entrenched following the worst industrial accident in history. The 1984 Union Carbide chemical plant explosion in Bhopal India was a watershed: It killed 3,800 immediately with thousands more dying within months, injured tens of thousands, and exposed hundreds of thousands to the harmful effects of methyl isocyanate.[22]

So what St. Michel initially observed was the tail end of a process that had been in motion for a century, but that had not arrived at the mature state in which we find it today. As processes became more and more governed by new safety rules, he recalls, in an echo of how many chafe against security policies in 2020, "crusty" INL engineers complaining in the 1980s that they'd never get any work done if they had to perform their tasks with so much attention to safety.[23] Skeptics notwithstanding, work got done then and is getting done today. And safety culture is now so entrenched, so thoroughly codified in organizations performing potentially dangerous functions, that St. Michel says it would be extremely difficult for him to design and build an inherently unsafe system.

Yet the arrival of connected digital technologies in the inner sanctum of safety, Safety Instrumented Systems (SISs), shows that there is a looming blind spot in safety culture. It also shows that companies are willing to trade risk for cost savings and convenience, although perhaps they have been fooled by the vendors into thinking they're not taking on any additional risk when they connect their SIS to their control systems.

SIDEBAR: THE EVOLUTION OF SAFETY SYSTEMS[24]

1960s–1970s: Mechanical Simplicity
Safety systems were called emergency shutdown devices (ESDs). They were electromechanical relay circuits with discrete inputs (e.g., pressure, temperature, vibration, etc.). When inputs went outside pre-set parameters, logic would trip pumps, motors, valves, etc., preserving them in a safe state while diagnostics were performed.

1980s: Initial Arrival of SIS Complexity

Along with the arrival of microprocessors and PCs, process engineers began switching out mechanical relays for programmable logic circuits (PLCs). As relays were prone to frequent failure, the primary drivers for this were reliability improvements and attendant cost savings. (relays were) always configured to fail in an open position, which interrupted processes and that downtime cost the asset owners money. During the transition, though, some recognized dangerous PLC failures and failure modes. Specialty vendors (e.g., August, Triconix, ICS Triplex) emerged and created "triple modular redundant (TMR)" PLC solutions with three of everything (sensors, IO's, logic cards). Two out of the three systems had to agree to cause an interrupt. Systems included firmware on PLCs and stand-alone DOS-based programming terminals, which later switched to Windows.

1990s: Open Systems and the First Moves Toward Integrating ICS and SIS

Mirroring developments in the IT world, the 1990s saw a big push for "Open" SIS solutions, including:
- Windows APIs for programming
- Ethernet
- Modbus, OPC, and others vs. proprietary protocols

Open architectures allowed asset owners and their integrators to contemplate efficiency in addition to the other benefits they might gain by connecting control and safety systems. Standards-based architectures also made it possible to move away from the vendor lock-in that came with proprietary systems. At about this time, many asset owners found themselves maintaining different providers for ICS and SIS but noticed that each company would blame the other when something went wrong, and the customer was often left in the lurch, trying to mediate the dispute and arrive at a workable solution. But one company, Exxon, placed a high value on maintaining separation for vendor independence, and of course, safety reasons.

2000–2015: ICS and SIS Integration Stampede

Asset owners now sought to avoid the finger pointing and cost, devalued independence of control & safety vendors, and didn't seem to notice that they were accepting cybersecurity trade-offs they might later come to regret. This decade and a half saw companies embrace integrated communications, HMIs, and common configurations too. Most chose to ignore the potential safety downside to the loss of independent systems, but when some asked, their vendors told them their internal development teams were independent, so not to worry.

2016–Present: TRISIS gives some Pause
As of early 2020, the roster of vendors selling integrated ICS and SIS solutions included:
- ABB
- Emerson
- Siemens
- Schneider
- Honeywell
- Rockwell
- Yokagawa

Asset owners concerned with safety are comforted by compliance to updated safety standards that are beginning to add security language to the mix, including IEC 61508 for suppliers and IEC 61511 for asset owners, the latter which added a security assessment requirement. Initially, very few did the assessments. But some, as they've become aware of the implications of 2017's TRISIS attack on an SIS in Saudi Arabia, have started to move in this direction. Still fewer than 25% do anything of substance beyond generating paper to document an assessment was performed. And everyone needs to be aware that now that safety systems are made of software and networked or integrated with other systems, like software-based control systems, safety systems themselves now have the potential to be threat vectors.[25]

Failure Mode, Near Misses, and Sabotage

Historically and still, the vast majority of working engineers, and the engineering school professors that help produce them, think of machine failure as something that happens when parts wear out. They do not consider that a machine might fail because an external actor was manipulating it or one of its supporting systems or processes.

In the software application world, in the early requirements and design stages, use cases help to establish and clarify desired functionality, look and feel, and more. Developers generate the different categories of users (e.g., administrators, customers, partners, HR professionals, etc.) and build the functionality needed for each. Access to different elements and capabilities is managed by authorization controls. One category of user rarely if ever considered by developers and their project managers (PMs) is the malicious cyber attacker. Assuming they can achieve access (and we should) the question is: What kind of experience do we want that person to have?

As every physical product is software-enabled, aka made "smart," in every engineering discipline, engineers must ask themselves what kind of experience they want criminals and other bad actors to have, then they arrive to intentionally misuse their creation. Data theft is one thing, misuse intended to cause damage or destruction, injury or death, is the province of modern cyber saboteurs.

Failure Mode and Effects Analysis

Begun in the 1940s by the US military, failure modes and effects analysis (FMEA) is a step-by-step approach for identifying all possible failures in a design, a manufacturing or assembly process, or a product or service.

- **"Failure modes"** means the ways, or modes, in which something might fail. Failures are any errors or defects, especially ones that affect the customer and can be potential or actual.
- **"Effects analysis"** refers to studying the consequences of those failures.

Failures are prioritized according to how serious their consequences are, how frequently they occur and how easily they can be detected. The purpose of the FMEA is to take actions to eliminate or reduce failures, starting with the highest-priority ones.

FMEA also documents current knowledge and actions about the risks of failures, for use in continuous improvement. FMEA is used during design to prevent failures. Later it's used for control, before and during ongoing operation of the process. Ideally, FMEA begins during the earliest conceptual stages of design and continues throughout the life of the product or service.[26]

The existing Safety Analysis and Probabilistic Risk Analysis (PRA) models were created with safety and failure mode analysis as its basis and design principles with electromechanical/analog technology in mind. With the now abundant use of digital systems for both safety and non-safety functions, this model must incorporate cybersecurity concepts and methodologies. Safety analysis should now consider previously analyzed unlikely or highly unlikely events that could potentially change those probabilities based upon an intelligent cyber aggressor. Revised analyses may yield different outcomes. Although malicious cyberattack methods may or may not change previously analyzed safety events, the potential for reactor sabotage or damage may increase.[27]

Inter-chapter Transition Thoughts and Questions

If this chapter tells you anything, it's that if we want to live in a more secure world with more secure products and services, we must have security subject matter experts (SMEs) involved in almost every decision in a product's or project's lifecycle. We're probably also going to want fewer folks in the workforce who are completely naïve about how their decisions and actions contribute or detract from the overall risk posture of their organization. So artificially marking 2020 as a starting point, here are a few things to consider:

- How do we increase the cyber IQ (if you'll pardon that term) of every member of our organization, top to bottom, without affecting adversely impacting productivity?
- Is it too early to include requirements for basic cybersecurity knowledge in every job description, with more advanced knowledge and/or skills mandatory for certain positions, and with extra consideration given to applicants who meet threshold criteria?
- Incentives for professional development in cybersecurity beyond the annual refresher training?
- How can we get more cybersecurity content into K-12 schools but especially in graduate and post-graduate engineering curricula?
- If it's going take a decade or more to include minimum cybersecurity requirements at the earliest stages of the design and acquisition processes, what can we do to better secure what we've already got? That means legacy: the industrial processes, fleets, buildings, we depend on right now and in the near-medium term.

NOTES

1   Richard Danzig. "Surviving on a Diet of Poisoned Fruit." Center for New American Security. July 21, 2014. www.cnas.org/publications/reports/surviving-on-a-diet-of-poisoned-fruit-reducing-the-national-security-risks-of-americas-cyber-dependencies.
2   Bob Anderson and Joseph Price. "Cyber-Informed Engineering: The Need for a New Risk Informed and Design Methodology." Page 1. www.osti.gov/biblio/1236850-cyber-informed-engineering-need-new-risk-informed-design-methodology.
3   Ibid., page 2.
4   Sarah Jensen. "How Did People in the Olden Days Create Software without Any Programming Software?" MIT School of Engineering, accessed April 3, 2012. https://engineering.mit.edu/engage/ask-an-engineer/how-did-people-in-the-olden-days-create-software-without-any-programming-software/.
5   "Side Rule." Wikipedia. Page accessed January 4, 2020. https://en.wikipedia.org/wiki/Slide_rule.
6   David Cohn. "Evolution of Computer-Aided Design." DE247, accessed December 1, 2000. www.digitalengineering247.com/article/evolution-of-computer-aided-design/.
7   "ES&S Sets High Standard in Elections Industry with Independent Third-Party Testing." Election Systems & Software web site, accessed April 30, 2019. www.essvote.com/blog/our-customers/idaho-national-lab-performs-independent-third-party-testing-of-voting-machines/.
8   Paul Stockton. "Securing Supply Chains." The EIS Council. Page 20. www.eiscouncil.org/App_Data/Upload/8c063c7c-e500-42c3-a804-6da58df58b1c.pdf.
9   Sean Mcbride. Written correspondence, May 2019.
10   Via email, June 2019.
11   Perspective from INL's Sarah Freeman: There's actually a ton of specialization these days in hacking …, so mostly people who learned to hack java websites are not going to become OT hackers (overnight or ever). The OT hacking space has gotten crowded not because more people are hacking OT but because there is more IT being implemented on the OT side. If you're curious about a person's background, just ask them if it's possible to hack a serial connection. The IT-focused among us will say no, that's not digital. The OT-focused hackers, however, will recognize that it's just another communication mechanism, like the rest, and capable of being manipulated like all the others.
12   Danzig, Ibid..
13   One of the lab's principal cyber and energy researchers, Virginia Wright, often kicks off her CIE talks with this statement.

14 Bob Anderson et al. "Cyber-Informed Engineering." Accessed March 1, 2017. www.osti.gov/biblio/1369373-cyber-informed-engineering.

15 INL's Dr. Craig Rieger in correspondence, January 7, 2020.

16 INL's Dr. Craig Rieger in correspondence, January 7, 2020.

17 Andy Greenberg. "The Untold Story of NotPetya, the Most Devastating Cyberattack in History." *Wired Magazine* online, accessed August 22, 2018. www.wired.com/story/notpetya-cyberattack-ukraine-russia-code-crashed-the-world/.

18 Beau Woods and Andy Bochman. "Supply Chain in the Software Era." The Atlantic Council, accessed May 30, 2018. www.atlanticcouncil.org/publications/issue-briefs/supply-chain-in-the-software-era.

19 Dan Woods. "5 Ways to Fight Back against Cybersecurity Attacks: The Power of Active Defense." *Forbes* online, accessed June 27, 2018. www.forbes.com/sites/danwoods/2018/06/27/5-ways-to-fight-back-against-cybersecurity-attacks-the-power-of-active-defense/#1cbe940646d7.

20 "History of Workplace Safety in the United States, 1880–1970." EH.net web page, accessed January 4, 2020. https://eh.net/encyclopedia/history-of-workplace-safety-in-the-united-states-1880-1970-2/.

21 Ibid.

22 "On 30th Anniversary of Fatal Chemical Release that Killed Thousands in Bhopal, India, CSB Safety Message Warns It Could Happen Again." Chemical Safety Board website online, accessed December 1, 2014. www.csb.gov/on-30th-anniversary-of-fatal-chemical-release-that-killed-thousands-in-bhopal-india-csb-safety-message-warns-it-could-happen-again-/.

23 Curtis St. Michel, in conversation, February 2019.

24 Interview with John Cusimano of aeSolutions on the evolution of safety systems, June 24, 2019.

25 Paul Stockton, in conversation, February 12, 2020.

26 "Failure Mode and Effects Analysis." American Society for Quality website, accessed January 4, 2020. https://asq.org/quality-resources/fmea.

27 Bob Andersen et al. "Cyber-Informed Engineering." Page 2. March 2017. https://inldigitallibrary.inl.gov/sites/sti/sti/7323660.pdf.

3

BEYOND HOPE AND HYGIENE

Introducing Consequence-Driven, Cyber-Informed Engineering

All of this is under our control. Cyber is not an Act of God.[1]

> —Curtis St. Michel, CTO, INL Cybercore Integration Center

We were able to work with INL directly to learn about CCE. Our CEO really wanted to connect our teams to help us build a methodology that would help protect and defend our organization.

> —Florida Power & Light (Nextera) CISO Ben Miron

Some of the most popular risk management methods are no better than astrology (with apologies to those who read their horoscope).[2]

> —Ed Gelbstein, United Nations Board of Auditors

A system that can be caused to do undesigned things by outsiders is not "reliable" in any sense of the word.

> —Marcus Ranum quoted by Dan Geer[3]

SAFETY FIRST IN IDAHO

Over the past three decades, Montana-born Curtis St Michel has worked at what's now called the Idaho National Laboratory, though he's seen the lab's name change at least four times. He's an old-school engineer who has worked on many complex engineering and industrial control challenges, including nuclear materials testing and reprocessing. During the long arc of his career, he's witnessed two profound shifts. First a reluctant, but ultimately, full-on embrace of safety culture. He remembers that during the 1980's he started to see standardized safety processes brought to hazardous operations in an attempt to decrease the number of on-the-job deaths, dismemberments, and other serious injuries.

He recalls old timers balking at the new emphasis on safety, complaining that the new and more cautious behaviors would slow them down and substantially degrade productivity. That didn't turn out to be the case; far fewer were killed or injured, balancing any reduction in speed with a reduction in training new staff and paying for medical expenses, leave, etc. Now the culture is so thoroughly entrenched with widely accepted standards and tightly enforced regulations, St. Michel says that it would be almost impossible to design, build, and field a patently unsafe system.

The second shift began in the late 1970s and then accelerated through the 1980s and 1990s. This was the arrival of digital technologies in industrial sectors, beginning with energy. General or multipurpose computing devices, made almost infinitely flexible through programmable software, started replacing single-purpose electromechanical devices. In 2020, the transformation is nearly complete, as the benefits of going digital (e.g., efficiency, cost savings, human error reduction, improved visibility into operations, and more) have vastly outweighed security concerns. In fact, except for St. Michel and a handful of like-minded others, there were no security concerns voiced in the first few decades of digitization.

Will there be a third shift, this time to security? It's funny how the crusty engineers' early laments against safety echo across the years. Similar complaints are now regularly voiced by engineers and other employees too, often labeling the cybersecurity function and those who work it as "the department of no." Perhaps because safety failures have much more visible, more tangible, more clearly consequential results, the cultural transition was a success. Your typical engineer's orientation toward working to minimize failure modes in single-purpose electromechanical systems remains an obstacle to realizing (and then working to thwart or significantly minimize) the enormous destructive potential that can be achieved via the misuse of general-purpose systems.

While a near-term transition to a full-on security culture still seems a remote possibility, security's now-irrefutable link to safety may be what ultimately helps bring it to fruition. Especially now that we're building safety systems using general-purpose digital devices and networking them with digital control systems that are too-often accessible from business networks, it's readily apparent that you can't have safety without security.[4] Imagine, if you will, a better future where security has been embraced as a design principle joining safety, functionality, and reliability.

Failure Mode Analysis, Misuse, and Mis-operation

Throughout much of the history of modern industrial engineering, machines were purpose-built with only one or two primary functions in mind (software developers, think: use cases). Complex machines, like airplanes and airplane engines, spacecraft, submarines, coal and nuclear-powered thermal electricity generation plants, and automobiles too, each an assemblage of thousands of specialized electromechanical parts, could suffer partial or complete failure if and when those parts deteriorated in ways expected or unexpected.

Understanding wear patterns and identifying the variables that influence them came to be known as failure mode analysis, which really took off during and after WWII with an initial focus on the reliability of weapons systems.[5] Robust reliability is also the objective when engineers contemplate and design for continued operation in the face of operator mistakes. Together, safety and reliability remain the twin pillars across the many industrial engineering and design disciplines.

However, when single-purpose devices, including subsystems and other components, designed to do only one thing are swapped out for general-purpose devices that can do almost anything, and they're networked in ways that make them accessible to hostile others, we've created the opportunity for intentional misuse. And while the term may sound at first to be relatively benign, the misuse of concern here is misuse with the intent of mis-operation, leading to a disruption of key services and possibly the destruction of long-lead-time-to-replace equipment. One thing Consequence-driven, Cyber-informed Engineering (CCE) personnel will ask of industrial operators is, "if someone with nearly full knowledge of your plant, your equipment and your procedures gained your credentials and authorizations, what could they do?" After the first incredulous moments, the color often drains from the operator's face once he/she fully understands the question and its implications. In this circumstance, all of the foundational assumptions on which safety and reliability have until now been predicated should be thrown out.

Origins in Idaho and Elsewhere

In the early aughts, the Idaho lab's intimate, trusted relationship with various elements of government, including particularly its parent, the Nuclear Energy office at the Department of Energy (DOE), as well as the US Department of Defense (DoD), and the newly formed Department of Homeland Security (DHS), meant it was often an important element for not just nuclear energy R&D, but in other national security roles as well. With cyber-informed engineering (CIE) still in its formative stages, its first offspring began to take form in response to what St. Michel and Assante, better informed than most via intelligence channels, were noticing going on in the world in the early-mid-2000s. Though cybersecurity products were beginning to be deployed in larger numbers, it was increasingly obvious that organizations were very, very far from being able to field adequate defenses. As St. Michel recalls, "We looked around and saw we were getting our butts kicked in the cyber arena."[6]

Previously mechanical and electromechanical infrastructure, solely governed by the laws of physics, was transforming into an ungoverned wild west of insecure software and nearly infinite connectivity via the rapidly expanding and accelerating Internet. From its inception in the last nineteenth century to approximately the late 1960s, the North American electric grid was a giant, almost entirely electromechanical machine, physics-bound, and monitored and controlled by trained engineer-operators. The advent of solid-state circuitry and not-long-after, fully digital, microprocessor-based devices running modifiable software, paired with advances in communications technologies, marked the end of days when in order to cause trouble, an attacker would have to be physically proximate to the machines he/she was targeting.

The first practical commercially available microprocessor-based digital relay appeared in the early 1980s. The mid-1990s saw digital relays replacing the solid state and electromechanical relay in new construction. And while in distribution systems digital relays took over more slowly, today, while the vast majority of relays, protective and otherwise, are digital, solid-state versions still operate where the complexities of digital are avoidable.

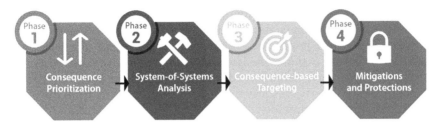

Figure 3.1   CCE Methodology Phases.

But as previously discussed, the grid is only one part of national critical infrastructure. And even if we were to protect it perfectly, successful disruption of other critical infrastructure elements could knock the grid out. As cybersecurity guru Daniel Geer simply put it: "The wellspring of risk is dependence."[7] So while the DOE is the Federal agency that serves as the Sector Specific Agency (SSA) for the grid, it must trust that DHS and the SSAs for other interdependent sectors (e.g., water, communications, natural gas, financial markets) are doing their job just as well.

For nearly two decades, INL conducted system-specific cyber assessments and performed highly specialized research, development, and deployment of technology solutions that address the significant challenges associated with securing an operational environment against high-consequence cyberattacks. Through these experiences, INL researchers came to the understanding that the cyber threat to critical infrastructure is real and that sophisticated adversaries, given time and motivation, will penetrate nearly all, if not all, operational environments. With the daunting premise that any and all vital systems can be compromised, CCE provides asset owners with an actionable means to implement an effective and efficient cyber investment strategy that is based on sound engineering principles against credible threats. The guided CCE methodology leads an organization through the steps required to protect its most essential processes from the most capable cyber adversaries (see Figure 3.1).

CCE FROM A THREAT PERSPECTIVE

There will be more on this later, particularly in Chapter 7 on Phase 3, but CCE is a methodology best performed with the fullest possible understanding of who is targeting you, what they're aiming for, where or what they need to access to create the effects they seek, and some of the most likely ways they're going to go about it.

We've seen a range of the amount and quality of threat intelligence leveraged in engagements, from extensive use of US Government sources to very little threat intel of any kind. But in every case, it's a helpful resource to leverage, and as the US Army and others have noted recently, the quality of commercial threat intelligence services has improved to the point that they are in cases the equal of, or even superior to, what the USG intel community can provide.[8]

In late 2020, CCE's infrastructure, tools, and training continue to evolve and refine its methods. There have been a handful of US Government-supported CCE engagements so far with others ongoing. Roughly in parallel, some companies who happened upon the 2018 Harvard Business Review article, "The End of Cybersecurity[9]" began to perform their own version of it on themselves, consistently reporting success, and some governments began examining some of it for potential inclusion in their national industrial infrastructure cyber policy.

The USG Is Using CCE to Better Secure National Critical Functions (NCFs)

While Assante and St. Michel deserve the lion's share of credit for developing the foundation for CCE in its earliest days, and INL's Sarah Freeman as well for laying the analytic foundation and fleshing out the four-phases, there were also a number of crucial USG support organizations along the way. Among the most important of these are several departments of the US Federal Government, most notably the DOE, DHS, and DoD. All three, as well as various intelligence organizations, had noticed the same thing the INL folks had: that established best practices in cyber defense were not nearly keeping up with the rate of improvements in nation-state offensive capabilities.

Numerous reports further corroborated this observation, including two by the Defense Science Board. One, a 2008 report on DoD Energy Strategy titled "More Fight Less Fuel"[10] included a chapter on "Managing Risks to Installations," which posited cyberattacks as a serious source of risk. Another, "Cyber Deterrence"[11] published in 2017, noted how grievously overmatched our cyber defenses were not just for weapon systems but also the energy systems that powered them as well. As the senator from Maine and member of the Senate Armed Service Committee Angus King has noted "Putin can hire 12,000 hackers for the cost of one modern jet fighter."[12]

There are also reports published by the National Infrastructure Advisory Council (NIAC), a critical infrastructure-focused assemblage of some of the best and most experienced minds in government and industry. Released in 2014, the "Critical Infrastructure and Resilience National Security Research and Development Plan" included the following passage:

> Increasing complexity is at the center of two major challenges: reliable operations and the mitigation of threat vectors. Rapid changes in technology and its use, operational dependencies on other sectors, and uncertainties in the world's natural and political environment have geometrically increased the complexity of operations. In addition, there is a sense of urgency and concern for the growing fragility of lifeline systems in the face of growing number of catastrophic natural events and growing human-originated cyber and physical threats targeting them. The expanding range of threats adds to the complexity of making informed decisions that meaningfully reduce risk within an environment where resources are subject to multiple demands and priorities.[13]

When folks in positions to know deliver cautions like this, it's difficult not to feel overwhelmed by what our critical infrastructure asset owners and operators are up against. Russia and other adversarial countries have trained thousands of skilled hackers, some within government, many in loosely affiliated commercial entities paid to do the bidding of government.

While no company, no matter how well-resourced its cybersecurity organization, can hope to hold out against a sustained national-state level campaign for long, there are some steps that can help ensure they can endure serious hits and survive. As one of the mandates of DOE national labs is to solve national challenges that others can't, wont, or shouldn't, leveraging its depth in engineering, control systems, and cybersecurity, INL has taken it upon itself to find practical approaches that go beyond cyber hygiene to demonstrably secure "things that must not fail."

For USG and INL-lead participants so far, the INL team complemented by experts in the intelligence community, the experience has been eye-opening. Over time, we'll continue to refine the methodology, train waves of expert CCE cadre, and then train the trainers. The objective is to scale up to bring many more NCF-type engagements to the organizations most in need of them.

CCE to Secure the Rest of Critical Infrastructure

Many of us have heard senior decision-makers say that while it's their responsibility to defend their companies against cyberattacks from hackers ranging from teenagers to organized crime groups, they don't have to worry about defending from Russia, China, or similar, because it's the responsibility of the DoD or other parts of the US government to defend against nation-states. While that sounds reasonable on one level, it doesn't change the fact that cyber defenders in DoD, DHS, the National Security Agency (NSA), etc. don't see and can't protect against every attack on the nation's critical infrastructure companies and assets.

Amidst this backdrop, INL sometimes shares these assumptions with audiences prepared to hear it:

1 If you are critical infrastructure, you will be targeted by nation state–level attackers.
2 If targeted, you will be compromised.
3 This means that there is a good chance that bad actors are already stealthily resident in some of your systems and networks, learning and laying the groundwork required to take you out of business or deny you the ability to perform your most vital missions.
4 There is no government or other cavalry coming to save you.

Very few organizations will be able to have an INL-led CCE engagement, at least in the near term. That leaves thousands of industrial sector companies in electric, water, ONG and other chemical production, transportation, heavy manufacturing, and more to fend for themselves. To their CEOs and board members: if you accept that your company has been or will be targeted by nation state-level attackers, what will you do differently? And to the operations personnel in these organizations: When your networks and systems are owned and operated by hostile intruders, what kinds of things could they do to you with that capability?

The case study in the sidebar shows how early on one company took the initiative and conducted a CCE engagement on itself, and several others have since done the same thing with reported success. Other companies we're tracking are engineering services delivery firms who've expressed an interest in bringing CCE to their critical infrastructure clients.

INL is seeking to help both those that seek to self-assess and those who want to add CCE to their offerings via the Getting Started Manual included in the Appendix and a two-day orientation workshop called ACCELERATE.

SIDEBAR: MINI DIY CCE CASE STUDY

After reading the mid-2018 Harvard Business Review (HBR) article on CCE called "The End of Cybersecurity[14]" and building on consequence prioritization work already in progress, a team comprised of a forward leaning and operational technology (OT)-savvy CISO and a similarly proactive senior engineer in an east coast water treatment company went into motion. As guardians of critical infrastructure looking to boost their defenses, they determined that they understood enough about how CCE is supposed to work to take matters into their own hands. This excerpt from the HBR text on how to start with CCE Phase 1 provided inspiration and guidance:

> By answering questions such as "What would you do if you wanted to disrupt our processes and ruin our company?" and "What are the first facilities you would go after the hardest?" the team can identify the targets whose disruption would be the most destructive and the most feasible and develop scenarios for discussion with the C-Suite.

The HBR brand resonated with their senior leadership, and the team was cleared to proceed. They began by asking questions along the lines of "what are the worst things that could happen to our company?" What has happened so far in INL pilot engagements happened here as well, when senior managers and engineers, when confronted, retorted with, "yeah, but that could never happen." What happened next also tracked what INL has witnessed in some of its pilots, when a little sleuthing revealed multiple pathways adversaries could take to create potentially company-ending events. Once that happens, things get interesting.

A few scenarios were drawn up in Phase 1 and investigated. The team went from facility-to-facility, process-to-process, and, as expected, encountered some real pushback. In particular, engineer-operators in charge of 24 x 7 operations who get in a ton of trouble when something goes wrong tend to resist any change from the good processes they've worked hard to establish and maintain. The idea that someone other than them could gain access to their controls hadn't entered their minds before and, to them, seemed impossible. However, once the CCE team helped them understand what was possible from an adversarial perspective, being folks whose *raison d'etre* is to solve problems, they quickly joined forces.

In all such situations, at the senior level, when it becomes clear that the worst things that could happen will probably happen, executive management has an urgent responsibility to fully understand and address those strategic risks. In keeping with some of the analog and otherwise out-of-band mitigation techniques mentioned in the HBR piece, engineers at this company devised multiple low-cost, non-digital protections to ensure that even if adversaries were to gain digital access and the ability to send destructive control signals to critical equipment, said systems would sense the imminent danger and shut down gracefully.

Please note: What felt like victory to this company and the internal CCE champions provides no guarantee of 100% protection against future attacks; of course there can be no such thing. With few resources and limited depth in OT cybersecurity to draw on, the team admitted they had to take some shortcuts from the full methodology, particularly in Phases 2 and 3, meaning:

- It is unlikely they identified all the systems, subsystems, and attack pathways adversaries might traverse to pursue destructive effects.
- Without input from the USG Intelligence Community (IC) or a top cyber threat intelligence firm or feed, there may be less insight into whether particular systems or subsystems in the company's inventory are being analyzed by hostile nations. That said, there are a wealth of open-source/publicly available indicators of nation-state interest.[15]
- Some of the mitigations they now want to deploy as a result of their CCE investigation are still being explored to insure they won't cause any unintended reliability or other problems.

Nevertheless, to the extent that security posture can be measured, they did demonstrably reduce their exposure to company-ending cyberattacks. For that, the company and its stakeholders, not to mention the hundreds of thousands of folks who depend on their critical services, should be extremely grateful. The question for this company now, and the others that will follow, is: Can it capture and communicate the lessons from this experience, and maintain and extend this new engineering-centric way of addressing its most consequential cyber risks?

METHODOLOGY HACKING AND CALCULATING RISK

Some methodologies have been a part of our professional lives so long we can't help but take them for granted. These might include Cost-Benefit Analysis, with roots in the nineteenth century but brought to full fruition by the Army Corps of Engineers in the late 1930s and more fully fleshed out in the 1950s.[16]

As previously mentioned, failure mode analysis and postmortem analysis also emerged and developed during the same approximate time frame. And if you've been in the business world long enough, you were probably exposed to one or several of these revolutionary (at the time) ways to improve operations: Total Quality Management (TQM), Lean manufacturing, Six Sigma quality control via defect management. What all of these have in common is an emphasis on measurement.

Now let's look more squarely at cybersecurity: the various National Institute of Standards and Technology (NIST) series, compliance regimes like the bulk electric sector's North American Electricity Reliability Commission (NERC) Critical Infrastructure Protection (CIP) standards, IEC and International Society of Automation (ISA) standards, and assorted top 10 and top 20 cyber hygiene best practices. All of these and more have yet to bring us to the place we've told ourselves we've been aiming for in critical infrastructure: an environment where we can proceed with business, engineering, and process control functions with near surety that only vetted personnel have access to and authorization to make changes to these systems.

CCE did not spring from the earth fully formed but rather is a unique cobbling together of a number of different previously proven analytical approaches and frameworks, albeit brought together in a way never seen before. It draws from a deep and diverse number of risk-oriented fields, including Crown Jewels Analysis (CJA), strategic risk management, red team testing, dependency analysis, process design, control theory, industrial process hazards analysis, safety instrumented systems theory and practice, cyber and physical threat analysis, including Design Basis Threat (DBT) analysis for protecting nuclear sites, nuclear reactor cyber defense, black hat cyber warfare, pure engineering first principles, and more.

All of these have a role to play, depending on the risk mitigation problem being worked. And while there are several common formulations, the field of cyber risk management is often introduced by this simple equation (or some variation of this theme):

Risk = Threat × vulnerability × consequence

On this, former NSA director Michael Hayden recommends a shift in weighting and focus that aligns almost completely with CCE's emphasis on putting consequences front and center, saying:

> Most of the history of what we call cybersecurity has been in that middle factor—vulnerability reduction… In the new paradigm, however, consequence is what matters most. Breaches are an inevitability. They're going to get in. Get over it.[17]

In fact, CCE goes against the grain of most existing cyber frameworks, methodologies, and best practices lists in how it treats vulnerabilities. Instead of recommending cybersecurity personnel, find and patch every vulnerability in their networks and systems, including the thousands of new ones announced every month,[18] CCE sees vulnerabilities as opportunities—opportunities adversaries an exploit to create high-consequence events. Thinking like an adversary shines a spotlight on consequences and in so doing helps illuminate the pathways adversaries will use to achieve them.

Many risk management formulas attempt to factor in likelihood or probability, while avoiding the reality that there is tremendous amount of uncertainly in these calculations. Significant time and money are spent acquiring data to construct the equations. But according to the non-profit information security best practices organization, ISACA:[19]

> Information security likelihood is, at best, events that can occur with uncertain frequency and magnitude. Therefore, they require an informed guess (and more often a gamble), subject to the evaluator's knowledge, experience and degree of paranoia (or optimism) when dealing with uncertainty. Stating that likelihood of the manifestation of a threat may be low, medium or high and creating a risk matrix with little boxes colored green, yellow or red is a step forward—as long as all parties involved understand the subjective nature and agree on the assumptions and ratings made.

In the cybersecurity world, CCE is uniquely focused on consequence prevention. It starts with the assumption that hackers have taken up residence in some of the networks and systems upon which your organization most depends to perform its most essential missions. That they've been with you for a while, you didn't know it, and you didn't have the means to find them. And while the methodology posits that there are sound engineering-based approaches to limiting digital access to key assets, and ways to make monitoring easier by reducing the number of pathways that must be monitored, it's perhaps most clearly differentiated from current cyber defense approaches by the types of actions it recommends to prevent the worst consequences from occurring if and when adversaries reach their targets.

As CCE draws from multiple sources, it's not unusual for certain elements to resonate with industrial process subject matter experts (SMEs) familiar with process hazards analysis (PHA), OT cybersecurity experts who've used the Industrial Control System (ICS) Cyber Kill Chain to good effect, physical security defenders who work with DBT plans, or members of the armed services and the defense industrial base (DIB) familiar with CJA. The list is not intended to be exhaustive, but here's a brief summary of a few:

1 **Design Basis Threat**[20]
Decades of nuclear energy R&D and reactor construction and defense have given INLers substantial experience with the development of DBTs, the intention of which is to imaginatively consider all the ways the buildings housing nuclear reactors and/or materials could be physically attacked by adversaries. DBT planning includes these four elements:
   - Planning to defend against both internal (insider) and external adversaries.
   - An emphasis on prioritization so as to thwart, with certainty, utterly unacceptable consequences.
   - Full consideration of the attributes and characteristics of would be attackers. In the physical realm, this includes things like weapons, explosives, tools, transportation, insiders and insider collusion, skills, tactics, and number of assailants. The cyber world analog would be tactics, techniques, and procedures (TTPs).
   - Once developed, DBT plans are used to assess the effectiveness of the policies and systems put in place to counter anticipated adversaries by evaluating the performance of the defenses vs. threat capabilities described in the DBT.

   It's important to note that DBTs are much more than an enumeration of cyber TTPs.[21] A cyber DBT[22] would also hold itself up against the best Advanced Persistent Threats (APTs), in ways akin to how nuclear power plants certify their protections as effective for certain high caliber munitions.

2 Crown Jewels Analysis[23]

Military risk assessors, whether in the Armed Forces or from commercial service providers in DIB, often find CCE Phase 1 resonates them due to their experience with CJA. According to MITRE:

Crown Jewels Analysis is a process for identifying those cyber assets that are most critical to the accomplishment of an organization's mission. CJA is also an informal name for Mission-Based Critical Information Technology (IT) Asset Identification. It is a subset of broader analyses that identify all types of mission-critical assets.... CJA is often the first step in a Mission Assurance Engineering (MAE) which provides a rigorous analytical approach to:

- Identify the cyber assets most critical to mission accomplishment—the "crown jewels" of CJA.
- Understand the threats and associated risks to those assets—via a subsequent cyber Threat Susceptibility Assessment.
- Select mitigation measures to prevent and/or fight through attacks—via Cyber Risk Remediation Analysis, which identifies recommended mitigation measures.

It's emphasis on prioritization that makes CJA and CCE compatible and gives those familiar with the former a head start in understanding the need for and approach to extreme prioritization throughout all four of the CCE phases.

3 Process Hazards Analysis

Many of the techniques that inform CCE have their roots in the early days of the industrial revolution. For many decades, industrial processes like heavy manufacturing, mechanized mining, steel making, etc. were the cause of fatalities, dismemberment, and chemical and thermal burns. Over time though, and particularly during a revolution in process safety that took place in the United States beginning in the early 1970s,[24] safety regulations and the safety culture they spawned changed everything ... for the better.

Process safety engineering firm Kenexis lays out the essentials of PHA quite well here:[25]

Facilities that process chemicals, or oil and gas, are regulated and monitored by government agencies like Occupational Safety & Health Administration (OSHA) Process Safety

Management and the UK's Health and Safety Executive to insure that they are taking the necessary steps to protect against the very real consequences of a malfunction or abnormal state where the machine, people or the environment could be damaged. This practice is well established and documented in engineering standards including ANSI/ISA-84.00.01-2004 Parts 1–3 (IEC 61511 Mod), "Functional Safety: Safety Instrumented Systems for the Process Industry Sector," as well as the IEC 61508 standard. Additionally, process industries are systematically assessed to determine what hazards scenarios might occur that could result in a significant consequence, and for each of these scenarios, the safeguards that are available to prevent the accident are assessed to determine if they are adequate. This exercise is called a "Process Hazards Analysis", and in the United States, it is required to be performed (and revalidated every five years) for all facilities that pose a significant hazard by the labor regulator—the Occupational Safety and Health Administration (OSHA 3132). Jurisdictions outside of the United States have similar requirements.

4 ICS Cyber Kill Chain

One methodology CCE leverages, but then significantly modifies and extends across all the phases, is the ICS Cyber Kill Chain, which will be covered in much greater depth in Chapter 6. Based on approaches used by DoD to take out terrorist and adversaries' weapons, this recipe for defense is a guide for offense turned upside down, and it began with a roadmap for attacking IT systems developed by defense giant Lockheed Martin. One may consider them a thought model for laying the actions or stages a cyber adversary will take as part of conducting a cyberattack.

Using IT systems to attack other IT systems is a comparatively straight-forward affair, and there is an enormous difference in the amount of work it takes, and the skillsets required, to mount a successful attack, with a particular effect in mind, in ICS environments. ICS attackers need all the knowledge and capabilities of IT attackers, plus an understanding of some or all of the following:

- Normal operating and safety procedures of target OT systems
- Regulatory and safety requirements
- Serial and routable ICS communications protocols (there are many dozens in the grid)[26]

- Safety instrumented systems (SIS)
- Supervisory Control and Data Acquisition (SCADA) systems
- Distributed Management Systems (DMS)
- Programmable Logic Circuits (PLC), Remote Terminal Units (RTU), and other embedded devices
- And most crucially, Physics

TRUE INTENT: COMPANY-WIDE CONVERSION

Initially, CCE appears as a methodology for conducting an engineering-centered cybersecurity assessment and remediation prioritized by the organization's most critical functions and values. Individuals in certain positions may start to see and understand the most potentially destructive cyber risks they've been unwittingly accepting. Longer term, CCE is intended as a vehicle to change the way employees in every function understand and manage their and the organization's cyber risks. The fact that it begins as an evaluation should not cloud its eventual, overarching purpose. Think of an initial CCE engagement as on-the-job-training. What's perhaps as important as the critical processes that are protected is the culture change lessons learned along the way that will help ensure they remain safer over time.

Additionally, whether due to retirement or by taking jobs with other companies, employees come and go. With this in mind, while changing the corporate culture at a moment in time is the intermediate goal, it's not until CCE rules and lessons are codified in durable policy that the conversion can be considered complete.

CCE has the potential to change the way the entire company understands its cyber risks, particularly the ones with the potential to cause catastrophic damage. While everyone including rank and file employees have a role to play, the conversation should start with those most senior, including the Chief Executive Officer(CEO), Chief Financial Officer (CFO), Chief Operating Officer (COO), Chief Risk Officer (CRO), and the Chief Information Officer (CIO) and Chief Information Security Officer (CISO) too. The Board of Directors should also be brought into the discussions early on. Early on, these seniors have a role to play in identifying the most consequential risks, and later, their involvement will be required in order for the Phase 4 Mitigations and Protections recommendations to be evaluated and implemented.

In industrial companies, the next group to get involved should likely the operator and engineer corps who manage and maintain the most critical processes and functions. Their hands-on experience will be invaluable to the success of the engagement.

Some might be surprised that the CIO and CISO are not considered more central in the earliest stages of CCE. Although they do have important parts to play, the fact is that their normal responsibilities typically include insuring cyber hygiene and compliance activities are in place for IT systems. In many if not most industrial companies, their role in securing OT systems is often limited. What's more, in some but not all cases, these positions rarely have access to or need to know the details and critical points of their organization's physical operations, other than their often-limited role in securing OT systems.

Nevertheless, once they come to see how it is possible for adversaries to bypass even the best IT cybersecurity defenses including good network segmentation of IT and OT networks, it will be important for them to play a large part in the development of mitigations. They will also have major roles in instilling a greater company-wide awareness of the threat vectors that, pre-remediation, were allowing access to their company's key systems.

It's important to note, here, that the fact that excellent cyber security programs can be overmatched by extremely well-resourced adversaries is in no way a mark against the CIO or CISO. Doing the absolute best possible job in implementing and maintaining a best practices cybersecurity hygiene program is an absolute must for any company these days. Absent solid cyber hygiene, harmful malware like WannaCry and NotPetya, and their descendants, not to mention the profusion of hundreds of other strains of constantly evolving forms of ransomware, can hobble profits and bring significant reputational impacts. But particularly for those in critical infrastructure sectors where they are likely to be targets of nation state–caliber adversaries at some point, CCE defines a forward-leaning defensive strategy that can help divert the worst consequences of attacks from the most capable adversaries.

TRANSITIONING TO A CLOSER LOOK AT CCE

How did this chapter work for you? If you have an engineering background, it's likely at least a portion of it made sense. If you're somewhat technical but have only known IT, some of what's been covered so far, and much of what's next may seem a little alien. The OT world has much in common with IT: While they may use different names, both environments use computers with processors and memory; both have operating systems, applications, and data; both have networks and are turning toward the cloud. But whereas the security metrics in IT most often relate to privacy and data protection, the final words in OT environments are safety and uptime, and depending on the scenario, physics is both friend and adversary. OT workplaces often include superheated steam, poisonous gases, tremendous pressures, and mechanical devices moving at high rates of speeds.

All that said, unless you're a full-time hunter-gatherer living off the grid, conditions in your work and at your home are fully dependent on industrial machines and the security of the software-based systems that monitor and control them. The developed world hasn't thought much about how to protect them from cyber attackers until recently. What follows is a somewhat detailed introduction to how it can be done.

NOTES

1   St. Michel quoted February 2019.
2   Ed Gelbstein. "Quantifying Information Risk and Security." *ISACA Journal* online. 2013. www.isaca.org/Journal/archives/2013/Volume-4/Pages/ Quantifying-Information-Risk-and-Security.aspx.
3   http://geer.tinho.net/geer.sourceboston.18iv12.txt.
4   Blake Sobczak. "The inside Story of the World's Most Dangerous Malware." E&E News, accessed March 7, 2019. www.eenews.net/stories/1060123327.
5   "Failure Mode and Effects Analysis." American Society for Quality website, accessed January 4, 2020. https://asq.org/quality-resources/fmea.
6   Personal conversation at INL, January 31, 2019.
7   David Geer. "A Rubicon." Hoover Institute. 2018. www.hoover.org/sites/ default/files/research/docs/geer_webreadypdfupdated2.pdf.
8   Mark Pomerleau. "Commercial Threat Intelligence Has Become a Key Army Tool." Fifth Domain online, accessed September 16, 2019. www.fifthdomain. com/dod/army/2019/09/16/commercial-threat-intelligence-has-become-a-key-army-tool/.
9   Andy Bochman. "The End of Cybersecurity." Harvard Business School online, accessed May 31, 2018. [Behind pay wall] https://hbr.org/product/the-end-of-cybersecurity/BG1803-PDF-ENG.

10 "Task Force Report on Energy: More Fight Less Fuel." Defense Science Board. pp. 53–62, accessed February 12, 2008. https://apps.dtic.mil/dtic/tr/fulltext/u2/a477619.pdf.

11 "Task Force on Cyber Deterrence." Defense Science Board. p. 4. February 2017. https://apps.dtic.mil/dtic/tr/fulltext/u2/1028516.pdf.

12 "King Presses Defense Department Leaders on Cyberattack Deterrence Strategies, Emphasizes Emerging Threats to U.S." Angus King press release website, accessed December 5, 2019. www.king.senate.gov/newsroom/press-releases/king-presses-defense-department-leaders-on-cyberattack-deterrence-strategies-emphasizes-emerging-threats-to-us.

13 "Critical Infrastructure Security and Resilience National Research and Development Plan." The National Infrastructure Advisory Council, accessed November 14, 2014. p. 5. www.dhs.gov/sites/default/files/publications/NIAC-CISR-RD-Plan-Report-Final-508.pdf.

14 Andy Bochman. "The End of Cybersecurity." Harvard Business School online, accessed May 31, 2018. [Behind pay wall] https://hbr.org/product/the-end-of-cybersecurity/BG1803-PDF-ENG.

15 INL's Sarah Freeman.

16 Thayer Watkins. "An Introduction to Cost-Benefit Analysis." San Jose University Department of Economics web page, accessed January 4, 2020. www.sjsu.edu/faculty/watkins/cba.htm.

17 "What Lies Beneath a Cyber Breach." *OEM Magazine* online, accessed July 9, 2018. www.oemmagazine.org/technology/machine-design-management/article/13274847/what-lies-beneath-a-cyber-breach.

18 Jai Vijayan. "More Than 22,000 Vulns Were Disclosed in 2018, 27% Without Fixes." Accessed February 27, 2019. www.darkreading.com/vulnerabilities--threats/more-than-22000-vulns-were-disclosed-in-2018–27--without-fixes/d/d-id/1333998.

19 Ed Gelbstein. "Quantifying information Risk and Security." *ISACA Journal* online. 2013. www.isaca.org/Journal/archives/2013/Volume-4/Pages/Quantifying-Information-Risk-and-Security.aspx.

20 "Design Basis Threat." The International Atomic Energy Association (IAEA) website, accessed January 4, 2020. www-ns.iaea.org/security/dbt.asp.

21 Paul Stockton, in conversation, February 16, 2020.

22 "US Views on Cyber Threat Assessment and Cyber DBT Development." United States Nuclear Regulatory Commission (USNRC), accessed August 18, 2015. www.nrc.gov/docs/ML1524/ML15240A341.pdf.

23 "Crown Jewels Analysis." MITRE Systems Engineering Guide, online, accessed January 4, 2020. www.mitre.org/publications/systems-engineering-guide/enterprise-engineering/systems-engineering-for-mission-assurance/crown-jewels-analysis.

24 M.S. Mannan et al. "The Evolution of Process Safety: Current Status and Future Direction." US National Institutes of Health, National Library of Medicine, accessed June 7, 2016. www.ncbi.nlm.nih.gov/pubmed/26979411.
25 Jim McGlone, personal correspondence, January 2018.
26 Erich Gunther. "Features and Benefits of IEC 61850." April 2012. www.enernex.com/wp-content/uploads/2012/04/Features-and-Benefits-of-IEC-61850_web.pdf.

4

PRE-ENGAGEMENT PREPARATION

We never considered sabotage. We've convinced ourselves that hygiene and compliance activities cover this ... and they don't ... at all.

Curtis St. Michel

SIDEBAR: QUESTIONS TO DRIVE ACTIONS

This isn't going to be like anything the company has gone through. Imagine a determined, well-resourced nation-state, or crime syndicate has offered to come to you and educate you on how they would destroy your company. That's incredible of course but also incredible in 2020 is that many in your company don't believe cyber adversaries could hurt you half that badly. Compliance, air gaps, and insurance are no match for what could happen to you.

Here are some questions we recommend are asked to begin this process:

- Are you aware of the capabilities of nation state–level adversaries and are you aware of the types of orgs they're targeting?

(Answer: critical infrastructure owners and operators, like electric, water, gas, transportation, etc.)

- What is the current state of our organization's cybersecurity awareness and culture, top to bottom?
- Given that even with limited resources, comprehensive and continuous adherence to cyber best practices, standards, and compliance regimes is not possible, how have you chosen to prioritize the application of limited resources?

OBJECTIVES OF PRE-ENGAGEMENT PREPARATION

Over the course of the engagements conducted to date with a variety of organizations, commercial and military, we've found that a certain amount of pre-CCE education and socialization makes it more likely all involved will hit the ground running when Phase 1 activities commence. In other words, a little more time invested up front has proven to save a great deal of time (and reduce headaches) later on. The primary objective here is to prepare the organization, particularly its seniors, for what it is about to go through, and of course, explain why. It also helps ensure the right folks are in the room, saving time and reducing the potential for miscommunication.

PRE-ENGAGEMENT PREPARATION WALKTHROUGH

Activities in this phase aren't formal or especially structured. It's really about socializing the concept to test whether the organization wants to go through a CCE engagement. And if it looks like it does, then it transitions to doing what's required ahead of time to have an excellent experience in Phase 1 (see Figure 4.1).

Establish the Need

How do you decide if your organization would benefit from CCE? The answer is simple: If your company is in any way, shape, or form associated with the production, transportation, or delivery of a service or function directly related to critical infrastructure, you are a target of cyber sabotage.

Because your company is critical, with some very important organizations, not to mention significant subsets of the population, highly

Figure 4.1   Pre-engagement Preparation Illustrated.

dependent on the reliable delivery of your service, you are a target of nation-state adversaries. Choosing to deny or ignore this well-established fact may make your life easier in the short term, but does not change the reality, and may well cost you dearly in the longer term.

Some engagements will be informed by intelligence from the USG or other government agencies and may be provided access to tangible evidence of targeting. In others, while there may be no government involvement, there are still a number of highly capable threat intelligence firms who are ready and would be able to get this fact across to sometimes skeptical seniors.

As stated in an earlier chapter, if and when the severe attack does come to your organization, it needs to be made very clear that neither the government nor the cybersecurity insurance coverage you may be carrying may be of much use—the government due to its lack of resources and the insurer because of the "act of war" clause that led to denials of coverage even in the damaging through hardly-targeted NotPetya attacks.

The value proposition, then, is that once you understand the full level of risk you're carrying, is that there are practical engineering-based ways of greatly reducing it. And they're not necessarily expensive. Also, while this engagement may seem appear at first blush to be a one-time assessment, its true objective and intent are education and culture change. Once you and your colleagues go through this process, the experience ideally will inform every significant decision going forward in ways that will demonstrably reduce risk.

Once the need for a CCE engagement has been established—and the seniors are on board—it's time to scope the activities that will ultimately lead to a radical cultural change at the organization.

Scoping and Agreements

Getting the proper paperwork in place early is an enormous time saver. Like any other prospective services engagement or product purchases, preliminary contractual discussions on expected duration, ballpark numbers of man-hours required by the entity, and likely overall costs can be discussed here. Idaho National Laboratory (INL) has enough experience with a variety of partners that we can provide good guesstimates on all of the above.

The first step is to identify the legal and information-sharing process to protect data collected and identified as part of a CCE engagement. One commonly used technique is a Memorandum of Understanding or MOU, that lays out the basis for what's soon to follow.

Another detail that can be fleshed out early has to do with roles and responsibilities. How much of this effort is INL's and how much is the entity's? And within the entity, what kinds of requirements (time and otherwise) are expected of different personnel, from the most senior to lower level operators and defenders? Organizations conducting their own CCE will need to identify the various roles and responsibilities of participants, to include which individual, department, and/or organization will be serving as lead or point.

If hosting an INL supported CCE engagement, then early scoping and agreements can also focus on logistics, as in how many on-site visits and what is the duration of the engagement? These discussions, whether conducted internally or in concert with participating organization, should be categorized by phase so that the requirements for the effort are understood by all participants.

Much depends on the type of entity and scope of the effort. For example, some CCE engagements, working with large utilities, have encompassed a wide variety of critical assets and operations spanning dozens of US states. Others have been much more focused geographically. Others still have been about looking in substantial detail about how a particular very important system is built, operated, and maintained, though even then, the logistics related to personnel access had to be worked early in order to avoid delays later on.

CCE isn't just examining one aspect of your process. It is looking at the people, processes, third-party associations, dependencies, and equipment. Since accomplishing everything at once isn't plausible (as you will see later in Chapter 5 where we take forward only a few of the most critical high-consequence events), it is important to scope your CCE engagement first. Defining these critical functions and services—those activities that absolutely cannot be lost or impaired—is the starting point for the scoping activities.

Scoping does not just include the "who" and "what"; it also considers the "how much." It is a very good practice for your organization to think thoroughly about the cost and resource lift associated with a project of this size. It's important to explore as much as you can now to prevent some pretty unpleasant surprises down the road. Once you've generated necessary buy-in from the seniors, it is the time to make sure they fully understand the level of commitment you'll need from them. This applies to the most senior decision-makers, lower level operators and defenders, and everyone in between.

Data Protection

The terms and procedures for data sharing and protection are perhaps the most important, highest risk, elements of the CCE process. Data-sharing agreements, protections, data-handling processes and connections, not to mention the wrangling over legal agreements satisfactory to both sides, should begin as soon as possible to minimize timeline risks later on. In fact, data protection and related legal agreements, in some cases, turn out to be the most time-intensive preparatory activities. One emerging practice that is proven to help with these issues is a brief from the entity on its data-handling processes. To this end, INL contracting recommends that financial, legal, and contracting points of contact be identified early on the entity side to enable agreement adoption.

The collection of your most critical functions, processes, and services requires substantial protection. After all, adversaries who achieve access to this information gain advantages we definitely don't want to give them.

With input from the scoping explorations, it's not too early to begin outlining the system that will contain the knowledgebase data and ensure it does so in conformance with the entity (and when required, USG) contracting, scoping, and data-sharing and protection requirements.

In some engagements, USG classification policies and requirements will firmly guide the protections that must be put in place before work may proceed. In others, whether an organization is performing an internal CCE engagement, or if it's hiring a services partner to lead them through the process, data protection is a must. As you go through the CCE process, remember that the information you collect provides a roadmap to target your crown-jewel, most critical business, or mission functions. So well before you begin collecting, you should create a data protection plan to protect critical information that considers and appropriately leverages the following elements from the world of classification, even if your effort will not involve officially classified information:

> Need-to-Know: Taken from the intelligence community as a fundamental security principle in safeguarding classified information, need-to-know requirements limit who can see what information. Need-to-know requires those who seek access to a piece of information have a specific need to access that information in order to perform his/her contractual duties of employment. By

limiting the audience of who can access the information to personnel who actually need that information, it helps protect key sensitive business information. This can help keep that information away from public eyes. Information doesn't need to be classified to require protection!

Aggregation: Individually insensitive or apparently unimportant items or information that in the aggregate reveal a system, objective, requirement, plan, or other aspect of your business mission, the disclosure of which would provide insight into sensitive or mission critical activities, capabilities, vulnerabilities or methods of your business. Information amassed or collected in one location should be protected.

Association: The significance of information often depends upon its context. Therefore, two unique pieces of unclassified/ unrelated information when considered together may reveal classified/sensitive information. Similarly, two unique pieces of classified information may reveal information classified at a higher level. For example, Siemens manufactures controllers, your system contains controllers, from which it can be derived that your system contains Siemens controllers.

Compilation: A document may be classified because of compilation when a large number of qualitatively similar pieces of unclassified information considered together contains some added value (such as the completeness or comprehensiveness of the information) that warrants classification.

Here are some general precepts that may help shape an organization's thinking about what information requires protection and how to protect it:

- When the information taken together may reveal vulnerabilities of systems, installations, infrastructure, or projects relating to your critical business functions.
- There are many ways that a compromise of sensitive business information could occur. If a storage medium is removed from an information system, or when the information is inadvertently stored in or transferred through an unprotected system.
- Information describing the nature or location of a system vulnerability as well as the descriptions of the procedures required to remove/mitigate the vulnerability.

- In situations where your mitigation actions only limit exploitation, the vulnerability information is still sensitive and must be protected.
- Information that could reveal, jeopardize, or compromise a device or equipment or the technology used in a system should be protected.
- Information pertaining to a system that reveals capabilities, weakness or vulnerabilities that would provide insight or motivate an adversary to develop malware or an exploit against your business should be considered sensitive and protected as such.
- Description of the design, capabilities, and functions of your information systems or software developed to process that information could reveal a method or reduce the level of effort dedicated by an adversary to achieve an objective.
- Information that reveals your organizational structure and staffing levels may provide insight to an adversary.

Lastly, one benefit of the communications that happen in these activities is that the scope of the effort begins to emerge, and that information, preliminary though it may be, can help inform the work coming up next.

Open-Source Research

While the logistics and contractual issues are being explored and potentially hammered out, for those engagements led by INL, concurrent work gets underway at the lab in the form of manual and automated open-source research. This is preliminary to the much deeper open-source and other data-gathering activities that will occur in Phase 2 once the high-consequence events (HCEs) and systems of interest have come into view. But it helps discover information that could help adversaries build out a fuller and more detailed picture of the inner workings of the entity, in particular its critical processes and dependencies, as well as key systems, personnel, and partners. Non-INL lead engagements may also benefit from access to histories of significant events or targeting activities directed against that entity from a variety of sources commercial and non-commercial sources.

The prevailing purpose of this early open-source effort is to build a threat briefing for entity seniors, providing a concise snapshot of what a determined adversary can find out—or in fact may have already learned—about the entity and its inner workings and vulnerabilities. Another product of this earliest wave research is that it will begin to help populate taxonomy that will become into greater focus in Phase 2.

Refine Initial Taxonomy and Determine Knowledge Base Requirements

Taxonomy and Knowledge Base

Regardless of the functions or functions, system or systems that will be evaluated, participants need to agree upon a common taxonomy, lexicon, or language for the engagement. This is the vocabulary that everyone can use to describe a system, its subcomponents, and functions, as well as the adversary actions and movements against these things. A number of adversary lexicons exist; for example, the SANS industrial control system (ICS) Kill Chain provides a high-level overview of adversary actions they must take to prepare for and, ultimately, execute an attack. A more recently developed taxonomy is MITRE's ATT&CK, which has been extended to address ICS, and also provides definitions for commonly observed TTPs.

Another topic that should be addressed in the early taxonomy and definition discussions is the typical elements and steps involved in a CCE engagement. Discussions centered around what is a knowledge base and what it looks like can be extremely helpful, especially if the CCE process is new to some or most of the participants.

Form and Train Execution Teams

Roles and responsibilities should be defined. Not later—when you're knee deep in the weeds of examining a seemingly foreign process or system— but before you even start, when you can clearly define requirements and expectations. Be sure to include what skills may be needed and what level of commitment you're going to need. Does anyone have any exceptionally useful or unique backgrounds, like military intelligence or OT cybersecurity experience?

Organizations conducting a CCE will need to do more than identify the various roles and responsibilities before the CCE kicks off. The specific individuals, departments, and organizations taking point on the engagement need to be identified. Do this now during pre-engagement activities to save a massive headache down the road. For example, take the time to assign someone to take notes. If you don't now, you may find you've exhausted all your human resources and end up taking your own notes. Identify who is the expert at what processes within your organization.

Once the team is formed, it is imperative each member is trained on the CCE methodology, whether it be in person or via remote means.

TRANSITIONING TO PHASE I

In the earliest days of CCE when we ran the initial pilots, there was no concept of a pre-engagement preparation. That meant that all of the tasks just described had to be worked out in an ad hoc manner in what all involved thought were the start of the CCE process. As you can imagine, confusion ensued, and target timelines were disrupted. Since preparation processes were put in place, CCE engagements have gone much more smoothly, and Phase 1 activities typically get off to a smooth start. All this to say, completion of preparation activities as described, with contractual and data issues complete or nearly so, and orientation training complete—is the best way transition to Phase 1.

5

PHASE 1: CONSEQUENCE PRIORITIZATION

"We don't know what could happen if they own it." No one has ever thought about this let alone done anything about it.

Getting people to look at risks based on trust.[1]

SIDEBAR: QUESTIONS TO DRIVE ACTIONS

The methodology begins with a series of questions designed to help the CCE team zero in on a topic many organizations have not considered in depth: How a group with ample resources, time, and skill might go about destroying the company. Generally speaking, cybersecurity need not be part of the Phase 1 discussions and scenario development activities.

Here are some questions we recommend are asked to begin this process:

- What are the absolute worst things that could happen to us?
- What functions or processes, were we to lose them for more than a day or a week, would cause a financial catastrophe?

- Are there any third-party services and/or products we use that were we to lose them for more than a few days, it would so impair out function that we'd be out of business?

Remember, the goal here is to develop a handful of worst-case scenarios that will serve as launching off points for the rest of the methodology. More than a handful, even if there are additional worst-case scenarios generated, should not be attempted until after you've gone through the complete methodology one time.

But before distilling them down to a manageable level, recommend generating potential adverse events with relative abandon. Most will drop off or collapse into groupings, the worst of which should be considered in Phases 2 and 3.

In many instances there will be a gut reaction along the lines of "that just can't happen." We have found that oftentimes the unthinkably bad outcome can happen, and once skeptical individuals are shown how their enthusiasm for the CCE process grows rapidly.

Once you've narrowed the list down to 5–10 of the worst scenarios, you are almost ready to move to Phase 2.

OBJECTIVE OF PHASE I

The primary goal of consequence prioritization is to identify high-consequence events (HCEs) that would potentially disrupt an organization's ability to provide the critical services and functions deemed fundamental to their business mission. The job is to identify the absolutely most vital processes and functions upon which your organization is completely dependent and rank disruptions of these processes and functions by severity of consequence. CCE does not seek to increase enterprise-wide security posture. Instead, the goal is to identify and develop a comparative handful of HCEs that would likely spell the demise of your company if a commercial entity, or a complete mission, fail if yours is a military or other government agency.

During the first phase, organizations are asked to generate the possible events that would significantly inhibit an organization's ability to provide the critical services and functions. Events should be physical actions that, if they occurred, would meet the threshold we defined as the boundary condition in Chapter 4. These events are evaluated to determine if they can be achieved through cyber means, and those that can be are coined cyber-events. The remaining events (those not achievable through cyber means) are discarded.

A brief narrative is generated to sketch out the actions required to achieve the cyber-event, and mission impact criteria are applied to prioritize the remaining list. The cyber-events that score above an agreed-upon threshold are designated as HCEs. By design, many of the potential cyber-events will not make it to the top of the list you construct based on impact. The level of effort required to investigate each potentially damaging HCE will often be substantial, so it's in everyone's best interest to keep the initial number limited. Nevertheless, cyber-events that don't make the HCE list the first time will likely be waiting for you when, armed with your knowledge and familiarity with the methodology, you take your second pass through it.

KILLING YOUR COMPANY— INVESTIGATING POTENTIAL HCES

Some companies go out of business because they failed to adapt to changing trends or economic conditions. Some get outcompeted. Some endure hostile takeovers. But unless you're a malicious insider, it's counter-instinctive for most employees, whether senior or junior, to spend much time thinking about how to bring about the end of the company. Or in the case of a military unit, render it 100% unable to perform its mission.

When everything you've ever thought and done has been aligned with promoting the interests of the organization, it's hard to imagine doing the opposite. You may not always have known what was the right or best course of action, but the many internal meetings, visits from consultants, teaming agreements with partners, etc. have all been to put your organization in the best position to succeed. At the onset of Phase 1, we're asking you to suspend that way of thinking for a few days and do a complete 180.

Another potentially counterintuitive aspect is that the "kill your company" question doesn't involve invoking cybersecurity … that comes later. In the beginning all we want to know is what functions or processes can your company not live without. If you were a bank, this might mean not being able to execute any transactions for an extended period of time. A commercial airline having to ground its entire fleet for several weeks or more might be more financial strain that it could bear. And a mechanized

Army brigade that loses confidence in its tanks' ability to hit their targets has lost its ability to perform its mission.

By the way, if you don't want to learn how to kill your company, that's totally your choice. But there are likely folks out there who've been doing their homework, at a minimum using freely available open-source intelligence (OSINT) about your company on the Internet. This includes:

- Press releases issued by your company as well as your suppliers and partners
- Quarterly and annual financial reports
- Information shared by your employees at conferences and workshops, presented on the stage and shared in the hallways, restaurants, and bars
- The professional and personal information broadcast on LinkedIn, Facebook, Twitter, etc.
- All systems and devices your organization has connected directly to the internet with putting them behind a firewall or a VPN, as viewed through Shodan, a free search engine for internet-connected things
- The contents of your company's webpages

Because it's their focus, they may know far more about how to put you out of business than you do. Phase 1 is the first step to turning the tables on them, and it begins with a few assumptions and boundaries.

SIDEBAR: COMPANY ENDINGS

As long as there have been such companies, electric utilities, whose mandate is to deliver electricity that's safe, reliable, and affordable, have known they have to prepare for the worst nature can throw at them. While locust plagues affect them little, hurricanes and tornadoes, blizzards and ice storms, floods and fires are all on the table. Earthquakes and volcanic eruptions too, though with less frequency. More mundane, but nevertheless challenging as they may greatly increase demand, are prolonged heat waves and cold spells.

Despite extensive planning and preparations, Hurricane Katrina's winds and the unprecedented flooding that followed forced Entergy New Orleans to File for Chapter 11 protections when it was overwhelmed by massive costs to repair the portions of its grid infrastructure decimated by the huge storm.[2]

Poor response and recovery performance in the aftermath of Superstorm Sandy essentially caused the dissolution of the Long Island Power Authority (LIPA), which lost much of its autonomy and now contracts with New-Jersey's Public Service Enterprise Group to operate LIPA's electric infrastructure.[3]

More recently is the bankruptcy declaration of California's largest investor owned utility, Pacific Gas & Electric (PG&E)[4] following tens of billions of dollars of liabilities from destructive fires demonstrably caused by faults in its equipment, though certainly exacerbated by dry conditions attributed by many to climate change.[5]

So "changing trends or economic conditions," utilities and other businesses have to have contingency plans for natural disasters. While most companies prepare for these certain categories of black swan events, CCE helps them expand that perspective to the cyber risk domain. While small and mid-sized companies have been forced out of business from ransomware and other cyberattacks, large companies like Target, Sony, Saudi Aramco, Maersk, and Merck have weathered their cyber storms with minimal long-term financial ramifications. But just because that's been the case so far, as investment broker-advisers are required to state, that's no guarantee of future performance.

PHASE I WALKTHROUGH

Getting Started with Assumptions and Boundaries

Depending on the type of engagement, before a CCE even begins, a subset of participants may be trained and know what to expect before the kickoff meeting, as well as what information to have ready to hit the ground running. They'll be introduced to a few fundamental CCE core assumptions and boundaries.

An assumption is a ground truth that is agreed upon by most or all participants as true at the start of the Phase 1: consequence prioritization process. For some, however, full acceptance of these truths comes later in the process. Here are the initial three that apply every time:

1 Access has been achieved—Adversary has logical access, including all credentials, IP addresses, firewall, and application access.

91

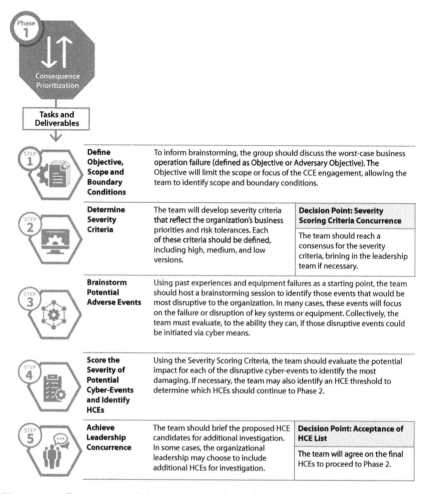

Figure 5.1   Consequence Prioritization Tasks and Deliverables.

2 Adversary is knowledgeable—They have an understanding of critical equipment and processes and all the knowledge to impact the system.

3 Adversary is well resourced—They have access to the required equipment, engineering expertise, and tools to conduct a successful attack.

To keep the scope within reason, Phase 1 requires boundaries, thresholds, or agreed-upon limits[6] for the Phase 1 working group prior to help in identifying potential HCEs.[7] While they vary by sector, a few electric sector examples might be:

1 Amount of Services Lost/Limited—amount of capacity loss necessary to impact customers
2 Level of Damage—amount in monetary terms of damage necessary to substantially impact the company
3 Duration of Outage—length of outage time necessary to cause prolonged customer impacts

The initial activity in consequence prioritization is to identify potential events that would substantially disrupt an organization's ability to provide the critical services and functions deemed fundamental to its business or military mission (specifically those that can be accomplished by cyber means). Hence, Phase 1's deliverable to Phase 2 is a small number of these company or mission-ending HCEs. It should be noted that consequence prioritization considers threats greater than those addressable by even exemplary cyber-hygiene and includes events that far exceed what's envisioned by traditional continuity of operations (COOP) perspective.

The prioritization process is most successful when organizations adopt a multidisciplinary approach, engaging operations and engineering expertise, IT, OT and physical security personnel, and more. Contributions from all of these in-depth functional perspectives are required to recognize, characterize, and eventually mitigate HCEs. For example, a utility company must identify the functions and services required to provide electricity to their customer base. In some cases, there may be multiple critical functions and services.

High-Consequence Event Scoring Criteria

One of the most prominent organizing principles of CCE is triage. By now it's obvious to even the casual observer that we can't cyber-protect everything. Some more cynical might say we can't protect anything. But CCE, as you'll see in Phase 4, allows for different and more effective protections than what the world of cyber-hygiene has produced so far. But it is triage because there is limited time and money to apply to the problem of cyber security.

This brings us to the mission impact criteria and analyses that enable the generation and selection of the most harmful cyber-events and the ones that must be examined and mitigated first to protect the processes and functions that simply must not fail.

The intent of HCE scoring is to help the organization arrive at quantified values for consequences and thereby have a means to "rack and stack" the candidate cyber-events in order of severity. While in some sectors or some situations this list might vary, for electric sector entities, Idaho National Laboratory (INL) identified six factors to use in this process:

1 **Area impacted**: One of the original severity criteria from the first CCE engagement that refers to the number of individuals or organizations or, alternatively, the geographic region, impacted by a cyber-attack. This criterion also describes whether the impact of the attack scenario is geographically localized, or it impacts the entire system.

2 **Cost for recovery**: The direct financial loss to an organization resulting from an adverse event, including restoration costs (i.e., the cost to return the system to proper operation), not including any legal or other reparations as a result of the failure (first-order effect). In the case of electric sector utilities, it also includes secondary costs such as purchasing replacement power in order to meet customer demand. (In this case, it should be noted that an organization with long-term contracts will be impacted less than one with short-term agreements.)

3 **Public safety**: Separate from the safety of those working for or in the entity in question, public safety refers to the potential harms to persons living proximate to the entity who might be subjected to the effects of explosions, fires, airborne and waterborne chemical release, etc. In addition, public safety impacts may also occur due to the ripple effects of temporary or extended loss of lifeline and other services including electricity, water and wastewater, communications, transportation, healthcare, etc.

4 **System integrity**: The degree to which a victim of a cyber-attack can validate and trust that the original risk has been mitigated. One of the severity criteria from the first CCE study, it describes whether restoration and recovery efforts can restore system integrity with confidence following an adverse event (i.e., a system not operating as expected or intended, or, alternatively, malicious operation conducted by unauthorized users). One factor to consider is whether the initial attack propagates into multiple systems and therefore complicates restoration efforts. All of these may negatively

impact an organization's confidence in their system following an adverse event.

5 **Attack breadth**: One of the severity criteria developed during Phase 1 of CCE describes the extent to which a targeted technology or system is deployed resulting in adverse operational effects. The greater the span of impacted systems, the more difficult the restoration following an adverse event.

6 **Duration**: The length of time one or more processes or functions is degraded or fully unavailable.

Consequence prioritization requires evaluating impacts resulting from potential adverse cyber-events. The CCE framework differs from vulnerability and risk assessments in that it does not attempt to evaluate the strength or effectiveness of current cyber defense. It also doesn't directly seek to factor in the likelihood of a successful attack. Instead, it is almost entirely focused on determining the consequence of a cyber-event.

To accomplish this, organizations must assume that an adversary will succeed in their attack and that some level of consequence will occur. After establishing mutually agreed assumptions and boundary conditions, the organization next identifies potential physical events, filters out those not achievable through cyber means, develops a list of adverse cyber-events with short narratives, and finally evaluates potential HCEs by using a severity scoring matrix. This resulting HCE severity score then helps inform a prioritized list of HCEs specific to an organization.

Event Development

Focusing the team's training on potential consequences, three types of targeting criteria should be considered:

- Traditional targets including choke points and extreme dependencies/interdependencies where attacker could bring operations to a standstill for a week or more.
- Widespread use of (and therefore, dependency on) a single technology for one or several critical functions. A successful attack on that one technology type might create ripple effects that could undermine or disrupt other critical functions.
- Wherever there is full reliance on automation, with no proven/test manual processes that could be depended on for a period of significant length.

95

For clarity, events are essentially the effect (e.g., "the generation plant goes down") coupled with secondary impacts (e.g., electricity cannot be produced), while cyber-events are the brainstormed events that can be achieved by cyber means. In this phase, the emphasis is on whether or not an adverse effect is possible via cyber means vs. explaining how it might be accomplished. However, sometimes the means by which a cyber-event can be achieved may be developed in tandem with the events themselves. For example, achieving a cyber-event that shuts down a utility's advanced metering infrastructure (AMI) may be possible via a variety of adversary actions or attack chains. For example, an adversary may access AMI networks via a business/IT network to manipulate all smart meter parameters or access/inject a physical AMI hub with malware that interrupts the function of meters.

To ensure helpful, high-level details are captured, each cyber-event should be concisely described, documenting these details, depending on the types of expertise present among team members, to the extent possible:

- What the adversary wants to achieve or the desired end effect of an attack (e.g., incapacitating or breaking all protective relays)
- The systems or systems that would likely be targeted
- The actions the adversary may perform on the target (at a very high level)
- And most importantly, as it has a major role in determining the HCE severity score, the most likely impacts, ripple effects, and durations

It should be noted that cyber-events in Phase 1 are developed only to the level of detail required to apply weightings from the criteria, scores, and either select or discard it from the group of HCEs moving on to Phase 2. Once in Phase 3, the process drives the team to further develop scenarios in substantial detail.

Criteria Weighting and Event Scoring

HCE severity scores are calculated using this six-variable equation:[8]

$$HCE \; Severity = \alpha(Area \; Impacted) + \beta(Duration) + \gamma(Attack \; Breadth)$$
$$+ \; \delta(System \; Integrity) + \varepsilon(Safety) + \zeta(Cost)$$

Each criterion has its own weighting coefficient or factor. During one early CCE engagement, weighting coefficient values (α, β, γ, and δ) were developed and determined by a combined team that included INL and asset owner Subject Matter Experts (SMEs), with the latter in the lead with focus on the electric sector. To expand applicability and better reflect the priorities of other utilities or organizations in other sectors, these values can and should be altered. Values can be assigned in a variety of ways, commonly the weight of "3" is used for criteria with the highest impact, while "1" is for criteria with the lowest impact, with "2" for the remaining, medium-weight items. For example, if an organization believes their primary concern is safety, then the value of ζ should be of 3.

Similarly, the severity criteria themselves can be altered to better represent the goals and risk concerns of individual organizations based on their business models, mission profile, and/or critical national or regional function they support. A weighting coefficient can be adjusted based on various factors (e.g., business risk, importance of factor to sector, etc.). For example, public safety would be weighted higher for nuclear facilities than for coal plants.

Each of the criteria is given at least three severity definitions, allowing Likert scale evaluation. Typical definitions are low, medium, and high and are given the values of 1, 3, and 5, respectively. This allows flexibility with scoring cyber-events that fall in between the written definitions (making 2 and 4 medium-low and medium-high, respectively). After all weighting coefficients and severity definitions are established, the various cyber-events can be scored. The weighting coefficients described above will be multiplied by the severity (score) that the cyber-event is given for each criterion, and then summed.

It is important that any scoring activity be consistent, so if definition changes are made, or weighting coefficients are adjusted, these needs to be applied to all the cyber-events to ensure that certain HCE severity scores are not unintentionally inflated or reduced. *Lack of care and consistency in this activity will likely invalidate the results.*

It is also vital that all original documentation be retained for future reference. It is possible that after all scoring is complete for all identified cyber-events, the resulting ranking may not "feel right." This should spark conversation among entity participants to determine if scoring or weighting changes are needed. If so, all cyber-events should be scored again (i.e., basically a wash, rinse, repeat cycle until there is consensus that the results are correct).

Ultimately and jointly, a cutoff threshold is chosen and those cyber-events that exceed it are in play for Phase 2 as established HCEs and those that fall just below, while still potentially quite serious, will have to wait until the team can circle back for them. That's the prioritization part. Figure 5.2 illustrates an example of how scoring data can be assessed and help prioritization.

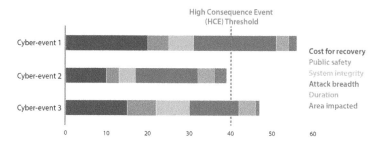

Figure 5.2   Example Events and HCE Thresholds.

HCE Validation

Before you can move onto Phase 2, your work on weighting, scoring, and selecting the HCEs to go forward must pass muster with the CEO and whichever other executives he/she includes to help make the call. The team should anticipate that decision-makers (e.g., CEO, SMEs, IC) may eliminate and/or elevate HCEs using their insight and expert judgment. In fact, we have seen entirely new events and HCEs introduced at this stage, and because the decision-makers ultimately own the risks and control funding, it's their call to make.

THE (REASONABLE) RESISTANCE

Not only does CCE call into question some of the fundamental assumptions of an entity's security program, it is a very different way of looking at risk. Therefore, resistance may be expected from several quarters. Here are a few of the positions that might be expected to quarrel with this process until they understand it more fully:

The CIO

So much depends on an organization's governance structure with this position. In some companies the CIO runs the business-side IT and doesn't touch the technologies in the industrial, operational side of the house. In others, the CIO has purview or strong influence over all significant technology decisions. In addition, as the function emerged from the IT ranks decades ago, cybersecurity is often one of the CIO's several responsibilities. This has the potential for conflict[9] when the initiatives on which the CIO is measured (e.g., improving up-time, delivering new functionality, new mobile apps, reducing costs) have the potential to weaken the organization's security posture. In most organizations, more often than not, progress on new initiatives has trumped security concerns. CIOs with only IT backgrounds may have difficulty accepting that attackers have been able to take up residence in their OT networks and systems and have been loitering there, undetected, for perhaps months or longer.

The CISO

Imagine you are the CSO or CISO of a mid-size or large critical infrastructure company. Depending on your track record, philosophy, and career risk tolerance, you may be reporting big concerns, tremendous success and confidence, or something in between. But if you've been doing your job, you've been following the accepted best practices for cyber-hygiene, which National Institute of Standards and Technology (NIST) groups into five buckets: Identify, Protect, Detect, Respond, and Recover. This was touched on in previous chapters, but for the CISO, this constitutes their entire world and easily consumes their attention across 60 or 80 work weeks.

When the target is relatively fixed, knowable, and bounded, like compliance with the NERC CIPS for bulk power system entities in North America, the challenge is difficult but doable, and reporting on status to seniors is relatively straight-forward. But for the non-compliance aspects of cyber defense, the CISO is in a much more precarious position. He or she faces the challenge of delivering the maximum amount of security for each dollar spent, to be apportioned among training, tool acquisition and maintenance, services contracts, and much more. Since there remains no way to measure security, all CISOs can do is report using the metrics at their disposal (e.g., percentage of systems patched in a specified time, percentage of employees completing a given training module, percentage of users with two-factor authentication, etc.).

The difficulty of communicating security status to CEOs—it's not just translating complex technical issues into business language—it's the uncertainty felt by both sides. Though they might choose to appear confident that the organization they're charged with protecting is fully secure against cyber threats, any well-informed CISO knows there are far too many variables—too many attack surfaces, too many unpatched vulnerabilities known and known, too many users clicking on phishing emails and inserting USB drives that haven't been through a security regime. The somewhat well-informed, tech savvy CEO will have a sense of this and yet will often proceed with an air of confidence himself/herself.

When a CCE team produces a paper, or appears in person, and says you're doing a great job but nevertheless certain adversaries will have little problem penetrating your defenses, this can be construed as a potentially threatening assertion for the CISO. It shouldn't be. Even the very best organizations can be penetrated and compromised by well-resourced, targeted attackers.

As above, the CISO's reach (or limits) depends on the governance structure. Some CISOs report to the CIO and exist solely to secure business systems. On the other hand, the most empowered CISOs report to the CEO and are charged with securing both IT and OT, cyber and physical systems. In either case, if they've shared with those senior to them their full understanding of the capabilities of well-resourced adversaries, and the uncertainties inherent in defending against them, a CCE engagement will likely be quite welcome. On the other hand, CISOs who've painted too rosy a picture about their organization's security posture (e.g., "we're solid," "there's nothing to worry about," "we're the best," etc.) will quickly find those statements undermined by evidence generated by the CCE process, and that can only cause tension. Please note: INL's intent is not to undermine confidence in the CISO or anyone else; rather it's to help everyone in the entity gain a better understanding of the cyber risks they face and arm them with the means to substantially reduce the consequences of targeted attacks by even top-tier adversaries.

Operators and Engineers

Veteran of hundreds of industrial organization security assessment Sean McBride says it is not uncommon for him to be greeted with this sentiment upon arrival on-site: "You cyber guys are here to interrupt the way my plants operate."[10] It's not difficult to understand the engineers' point of view. They are trained exhaustively to monitor processes and make changes when certain events, warnings, or alarms occur. Once processes are tuned and tested, their OT networks and workstations are configured, the last thing they want is a change not related to optimizing the process … especially one proposed by someone not intimately familiar with it.

Typically, they've had little-to-no exposure to cybersecurity concepts beyond running an antivirus program on the home computer. If they've got a work laptop or desktop, it's IT security's job to protect it, not theirs. Now imagine a CCE professional arrives on scene and begins asking them process questions. One of the letters in the acronym CCE stands for cyber, so immediately there's cause for concern.

It's only when they are shown how an adversary can reach into places that the operator thought were completely inaccessible to anyone outside the plant that the skepticism begins to fade. In CCE, it's not just a cyber professional, but a multidisciplinary team that also includes process engineers, controls engineers, and safety systems experts that have stood in the operator's shoes and understood his point of view.

The good news is that once they've seen how attackers can get in and gain control of their systems, engineers and operators who've been through this experience become among the more passionate advocates for it and also often are among the first to conceive and propose engineering-based mitigations that remove or greatly mitigate the consequences if and when attackers reach in deep.

SEQUENCING AND KEY PARTICIPANTS

As in many management endeavors, scheduling can be the most difficult part. In the case of the kickoff of Phase 1, it's essential to get as many senior stakeholders in the room as possible. The benefits of broad attendance are twofold. First, a diversity of expertise and perspectives is essential for generating a full list of candidate HCEs. Second, witnessing and participating in the scenario development process will help all in attendance attain a more visceral understanding of the methodology and, in particular, better understand what's being left to chance in the organization's current approach to cyber securing its most important processes.

The simplest sequence for involvement would look like this:

1 Initially CEO and C-Suite and Board of Directors for buy-in and top-down support
2 Then critical function/process owners and operators, safety engineers, ICS and IT cybersecurity SMEs, potentially contracting, sourcing managers as well
3 With periodic reports going back up to the Senior leadership team

Entity-Side

CEO & the Board of Directors (BoD): No one likes surprises, especially at this level, which should include the executives with access to the most accurate, up-to-date information, especially in the category of risk.

Chief Operations Officer (COO): Not a position typically noted for its expertise or interest in cyber risk, yet at the center of everything that matters, especially in industrial sector companies.

Chief Financial Officer (CFO): In conjunction with the CEO and Board and with input typically from the CIO, the Chief Risk Officer (CRO), and the CISO, the CFO gets a major say in how much money is spent on various risk reduction efforts, including cybersecurity. It may be a bitter pill for him/her to swallow to hear that their ever-increasing security expenditures do not protect them from targeted attacks.

Chief Risk Officer (CRO): In addition to ensuring the success of sector-specific and other compliance programs, CROs are charged with over-sight of insurance, financial and internal auditing, compliance, business risk, insider risk, etc. They are also often charged with implementing operational risk management and mitigation processes to avoid losses stemming from inadequate or failed procedures, systems, or policies, including business continuity and disaster recovery.

Procurement, HR/Contractor Management: These positions have enormous potential to introduce or reduce risk depending on the policies they follow, and how well your team follows them. Think: supply chain, screening integrators, vetting, and monitoring employees (including ter-mination procedures coordinated with the CIO or CISO).

The CCE Team

A major difference from other cybersecurity assessments, and perhaps the factor most contributing to the success of the engagement, is the skill and experience mix on the team leading it. Depending on the nature and pri-mary mission(s) of the entity, a CCE team could include SMEs from some or all of the following disciplines involved:

- Control
- Engineering
- Sector-specific experts (e.g., the DIB, ONG, electric, water, transportation, etc.)
- Cybersecurity
- Safety and safety systems

102

- Communications
- Threat analyst linked with the Intelligence Community

PREPARING FOR PHASE 2

After the HCEs have shaken out it's going to be time to transition to Systems-of-systems Analysis activities. Here you're going to need to assemble operators, managers, and technicians, and possibly contractors and suppliers too, to help identify and catalog, in exquisite detail, the make and model of all equipment, all software on all the hardware, the communications equipment and services, and more. Established asset management lists and inventories will be helpful, provided they are fully current and that they capture data down to the level of detail you need.

NOTES

1 Both are from Curtis St. Michel in conversation.
2 Stephanie I. Cohen. "Katrina damage prompts bankruptcy." Marketwatch.com, accessed September 23, 2005.
3 "Leadership: David Eichhorn." PSEG Long Island. Web page accessed January 11, 2020. www.marketwatch.com/story/entergy-new-orleans-seeks-chapter-11-reorganizationhttps://www.psegliny.com/aboutpseglongisland/leadershippage/danieleichhorn.
4 www.washingtonpost.com/climate-environment/inside-pgandes-choices-blackouts-and-the-threat-of-wildfires/2019/12/21/868d58e8-107c-11ea-9cd7-a1becbc82f5e_story.html.
5 In personal communications, credit ratings firm Moodys shared that some of its analysts consider PG&E to be the second climate change bankruptcy, with Entergy Louisiana as the first.
6 Sarah Freeman comment: Another category to consider is system boundaries, meaning that a CCE assessment can be limited to system or sub-system boundaries with the working group. In the electric sector, if the CCE participating organization is responsible for electricity generation, an attack against the distribution system is not relevant. Put another way, while it can be helpful to consider dependencies outside of the organization, in many cases, substantial changes to the systems cannot be made without the agreement of another party.
7 For more information on how to establish well-defined boundary conditions, see Chapter 4.

8   Six variable is accurate for this specific equation, but some entities will choose to have a larger or smaller number of criteria to evaluate, and the equation will change accordingly.

9   Andy Bochman. "The Missing Chief Security Officer." Medium online, accessed February 20, 2018. https://medium.com/cxo-magazine/the-missing-chief-security-officer-11979a54fbf9.

10 Sean McBride in conversation at INL, May 2019. Sean reports this response whenever he or his security teams enter an operational environment.

6

PHASE 2: SYSTEM-OF-SYSTEMS ANALYSIS

Successful strategies must proceed from the premise that **cyberspace is continuously contested territory.**[1]

SIDEBAR: QUESTIONS TO DRIVE ACTION

- What is your approach to company-wide asset management?
- Do you have a complete and current list of third-party product and service providers to include contractual obligations, limitations, exclusions, etc.?
- What is your policy-governing behavior of on-site contractors, integrators, and maintainers of all manner of equipment, systems, and facilities?

OBJECTIVES

- Translate high-consequence event (HCEs) into high-level block diagrams.
- Develop a functional description of the system(s) relevant to each HCE based on the preliminary block diagrams.
- Using the functional descriptions as the basis for investigation, begin collecting and organizing key details. And use these details to populate a functional data repository for each HCE (with references).
- Produce a preliminary system description, including HCE diagrams.
- Protect access and implement document control of the functional data repository.

MAPPING THE PLAYING FIELD

This phase focuses on collecting, organizing, reviewing, and summarizing the necessary information to feed into Phase 3. It is important to consider how various technologies are used, what necessary information exchanges occur, and from where.

We're trying to capture the full playing field adversaries might leverage to gain access, capture credentials, maneuver, observe, learn, and eventually put code into position, ready to carry out the attack that would create the unacceptable outcomes identified in Phase 1. Now that you've reduced the scope to a manageable set of effects, cyber events, and identified HCE's in Phase 1, Phase 2 activities include the development of high-level HCE block diagrams and data collection efforts. While this phase is labor intensive, the scope of the effort is constrained because the goal of CCE[2] is not to collect data for the entire enterprise but rather only on those elements relevant to the HCEs selected.[3] This helps to narrow the scope and thereby minimize the volume of information needed to build a deep level of knowledge of system operation and summarize the key details.

That said, this will likely require extensive effort by the team. After capturing all the necessary physical and virtual or logical data inputs into the function or process, drilling down deep and documenting in detail all the places where control and automation systems are employed, the functional diagrams can be drawn. The kinds of connections that emerge are all potential pathways for attackers, and most companies are not aware of all of them.[4]

When you start looking for internal process and configuration diagrams, you've got to remember that existing maps of these elements never fully match the reality. In fact, they may be quite outdated or just plain inaccurate in places. No organization's infrastructure is 100% static for long, and most are currently undergoing rapid change, which will likely continue as long as the twin trends of modernization and automation are with us. Assuming existing asset inventories are less-than-complete and not fully up to date (a very safe assumption), the job is straightforward to explain but laborious to execute and requires an approach that's both methodical and imaginative. Methodical in that details about all the assets that play a role in supporting each Phase 1 scenario, as outlined in the functional diagrams, must be captured.

As a start, this means rounding up information on all hardware, software, firmware, networks, communications equipment, and cloud processing and storage, and other third-party digital services associated with the systems and components highlighted in each HCE.[5] It's important that the configuration details be recorded for everything, and in detail. For example, for an operating system that supports a relevant application, info captured should include at a minimum: manufacturer, product name, version, patch version, known vulnerabilities, update process, patch process, etc.

Simultaneously, while working to collect the details of your installation, assign some individuals to conduct open-source intelligence also known as "what's findable on the Internet." Of course, many details will be missing, but it's an excellent resource most organizations have yet to tap. We look here not only to fill in blanks from the internal research, but because we know that adversaries, initially lacking easy access to companies' internal information, begin here. And as you'll see, thanks to press releases, news reports, LinkedIn and other social media, and specialized search engines like Shodan, there's an incredible amount of potentially helpful information available to adversaries in clear view.

There's also the human element to inspect—consider both full-time and part-time employees as well as full-time and occasional contractors whose access to the systems and software that support the scenario might allow them the means to contribute knowledge or actions to bolster your defenses, or aid in an attack. The vetting and monitoring processes for contractors should get substantial scrutiny here, including policies and policy enforcement practices related to the so-called transient media they bring on-site (e.g., laptops, USB sticks, and other storage devices). You'll also need to look for instances of suppliers' "secure remote access," which often isn't as secure as it sounds.

In short, the second phase of CCE is interview intensive, asking a lot of questions, looking at both internal and external sources of info, and fleshing out asset management inventories and process documents services that support the scenarios selected in Phase 1. In essence, the task is to build out the playing field the adversary will learn his way around, leverage and move through to reach targets, and create their intended destructive effects.

The key is to understand your own networks and systems at least as well if not better than adversaries you may assume have been resident and performing surveillance for years.

PHASE 2 WALKTHROUGH

These terms will also be listed in this book's glossary, but familiarizing you with a few terms here will help make what follows in this chapter easier to understand:

HCE Block Diagrams—Depict a process or system of focus in a picture format to help with visualizing the cyber manipulation required to accomplish the outcome. This exercise helps to narrow the scope of analysis, organize the physical and functional connections between the target components and the affected systems, and will minimize the volume of information collected to describe each HCE. The block diagram provides a visual starting point for identifying what information and which system accesses the adversary needs to accomplish the HCE and will be used to define and organize the data collection efforts.

Functional Data Repository—Is a taxonomical data repository that describes the origin of a device or system, how it is installed, operated, and maintained, as well as what devices and systems it feeds. Populating the data repository is an iterative process, and it is established and updated as new information is discovered. The Knowledge Base directly informs the analysis performed during Phase 3, Consequence-based Targeting.

Perfect Knowledge—Comprised of what's found via both open source research as well as information provided by the entity, this is sum total of all that is knowable about the

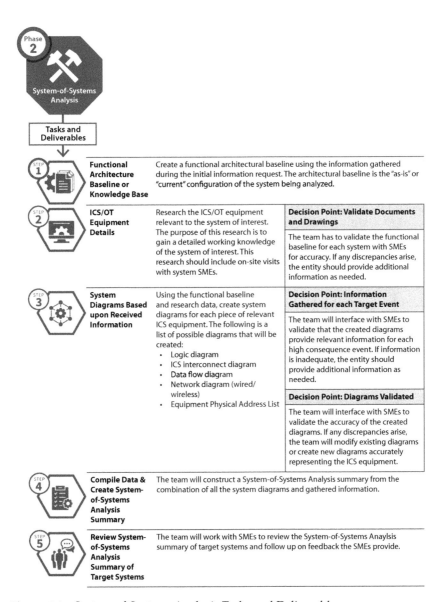

Figure 6.1   System-of-Systems Analysis Tasks and Deliverables.

operational elements that would be manipulated to bring about a particular HCE. The intent is to mirror the information collected by adversaries via their reconnaissance activities, but ideally, if done well and thoroughly, "perfect knowledge" is more complete than what the adversary can gather. Again, don't forget how important the data protection plan is in keeping this information safe.

Translating HCEs into Block Diagrams

A small number of HCEs will make the cut based on scoring and discussion by the team and the entity. For each that does, the next job is to develop a simple high-level, preliminary block diagram. This exercise helps narrow the scope of analysis, organize the physical and functional connections between the target components and the affected systems, and minimize the volume of information collected to describe each HCE. The preliminary HCE block diagram provides a starting point for identifying what information and system accesses the adversary needs to accomplish the HCE, and this information steers the data collection efforts.[6]

This process begins with sketching out the highest-level components and functions as a first step toward the development of detailed functional block diagrams to depict research results in a manner understandable by laymen, some who will be non-technical executives or middle managers.[7]

There are three main categories we want to think of when illustrating a function.[8] Systems or components of greatest interest (i.e., those whose compromise could contribute to an HCE) should be identified during this process (e.g., where digital meets analog, where the data resides, where programming changes variables, etc.). Notes from discussions between CCE team members (both internal and external) are translated into high-level diagrams with components, operations, and other relevant aspects, that interact with the targeted function. Diagrams should ideally depict the technologies, processes, and people involved in that function.

Highest impact components in systems of interest must receive very close scrutiny. It's imperative to have accurate information when assessing consequence as mistakes in estimation can lead to wasted time and/or misguided efforts in designing a system or identifying threats to a system.

110

Begin Building the Functional Data Repository

In CCE, many tasks occur in an iterative and overlapping manner. So even as you're drawing early sketches that will later mature to become highly detailed functional diagrams, you are also collecting terms to begin populating a functional data repository that over time will help you and your industry partners become more focused and efficient as you perfect the functional diagrams. As the identified key HCE Block Diagram items are collected, they'll need to be organized into functional taxonomical structures to communicate the relationship of one element to another. Functional taxonomy breaks down all of the functions that are typically necessary to provide a critical service (e.g., generation, transmission, filtration, mixing, heating, cooling, compression, protection, etc.). Included are operating procedures, logic and information flows, calibration, maintenance procedures, procurements, supply chain, vendor access, etc. Another way to think of taxonomy is as a map of the possible ecosystem of sector-specific, process-specific, system-specific, and more general things we need to know. The boundaries and HCEs help to trim the tree of the possible taxonomy.

High-level Functional Sketch Example—An Industrial Compressor

For compressor applications found in the chemical, energy, aerospace, and other industrial sectors, one of the primary safety-related functions is surge control, a critical function typically monitored and controlled via various types of networked industrial control system(s). Figure 6.2 shows, at a high level, the beginnings of knowledge base attempting to capture the sub-functions upon which the success of the anti-surge compression system depends. Drilling down further will reveal subsystems, sensors, and algorithms that could be manipulated and misused if an adversary were to gain access to topologically proximate networks and systems. You'll also want to add the people by organization and roles who support this function.

Data Collection Efforts

Once the scope of research has been narrowed to the HCEs identified in Phase 1, it's time to start drilling down to get to the level of detail attackers seek to attain and in so doing, capture the information and understanding required to begin to thwart their efforts. This will be an iterative process as the team's requests yield data, and insights prompt further requests.

111

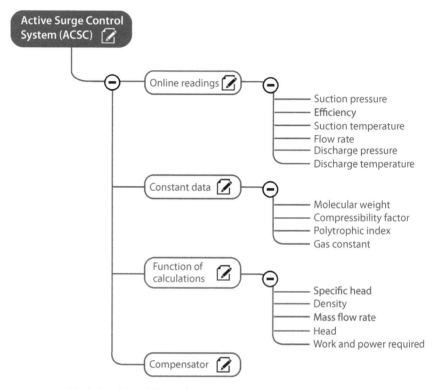

Figure 6.2 High-level Workflow Sketch of Surge Control for a Compressor Station.

Sometimes important data will be missing or outdated and must be pursued by alternate means; for example, sometimes departments may have to generate new documents or images to describe process flows internal to the company or external. Sometimes discrepancies will emerge where two documents include conflicting information, meaning there'll be more work required to get at the ground truth.

Part of this process begins with an Initial information Request (IIR), where the entity gathers information about their networks, their deployed technology, and their operational processes. Topics for collection include: Who designed it? Where is the information kept? How was it built? How was it maintained? How was it operated? Who has access to that information? How many times has it been disseminated? The IIR serves as a written record of information requests and a table of contents to direct the team to these answers.

Data Categories

In the broadest sense, the CCE team (and of course, attackers) can collect required information in two places, which are mirrored in the CCE team's collection efforts:[9]

- Open source: As in, what's available on-line and in any other publicly available forum. You should assume that whatever you find here has already been (or eventually will be) found by prospective attackers.
- Internal sources: To be found in documents internal to the organization as well as in partner services, supplier, and other organizations. Some of this information will be hard to get at but discovered as a result of interviews with subject matter experts that will be described later, and that are integral to this activity.

Depending on the entity and the composition of the team performing the engagement, this work might best be performed, at least initially, by two separate teams.

In the course of the drill-down process, systems of interest will be identified and in many cases serve as focal points for information gathering efforts as they are approached from all angles, including hardware supply chain analysis down the board and chip level. Over the course of the second part of Phase 2, with the objective of building an easy-to-navigate data repository to facilitate Phase 3 activities, we seek to answer, revisit, and update answers to questions such as:

- What information is available for systems of interest?
- Where does the information reside?
- Who has access to the information?

The remainder of this chapter will guide you through steps to help answer these questions, as well as to ensure that the answers arrived at initially are fully accurate and adequate to the task at hand.

Information from various points along the lifecycle of a system of interest can be of great value to the attacker seeking to understand the landscape and the points of easiest entry and exploit. Documents created by the asset owner, contractors, and suppliers at project initiation, through to design, construction, acceptance, and turnover will likely contain helpful data pertaining to technology products, configurations, processes, safety systems, security architectures, maintenance and spare parts, procurement, and sourcing. In particular, training materials and other artifacts can be as helpful in educating adversaries as they are to trainees.

SIDEBAR: MAINTENANCE

A particularly helpful source of current technology, people and process information can be found in the maintenance programs for systems of interest. Here is a very short list of sample questions:

- Equipment calibration and test:
  - What gets connected to the OT/ICS (e.g., meters, oscilloscopes, laptops, etc.)?
    - How does this equipment interface with the OT/ICS equipment or technology? What is typically changed? If devices are "read-only," how can you validate that nothing can be changed?
  - Does any of the OT/ICS equipment have to leave the site to be calibrated, updated, or have corrective maintenance performed?
    - Or, can the equipment be remotely calibrated, for example, by the original equipment manufacturer (OEM)?
  - Who has access to the equipment when it leaves the site? Who are your approved subcontractors and who are the approved subcontractors of OEMs, integrators, etc.?
    - What are their security requirements?
  - When equipment leaves you security sphere, what documentation, if any, accompanies it?
  - What equipment in your architecture can enable web browser integration?
- How do you protect critical information, both in use and during development?
- Where is this information/documentation stored? On secure servers?
- What does your update process look like? How are updates performed, (e.g., flash, jtag, eprom?) How do you secure the update process and the new software, firmware, configuration, etc.?
  - Where does the update code reside, is it encrypted? How is it delivered or shared with your field engineers or operators (e.g., CD, USB, network)?
- Technical specifications and safety basis concerns:
  - If you employ equipment that must operate in a certain range and accuracy to protect the plant, where is that requirement recorded? (This kind of information is invaluable as it informs adversaries what is outside the normal parameters or assumptions of the safety basis.)

There's a small universe of companies and other organizations that play a role in the successful operation of the entity in question. Informed research typically yields astoundingly rich results. Plan to research partners, collaborators, customers, service providers, government regulators, device vendors, etc. This will help your team understand how much an attacker can learn without ever accessing your networks. And then pursue answers to these questions:

- What more could an adversary find if they already have an idea of what they are looking for?
- What information could an attacker aggregate?
- What information can an attacker confirm?

Subject Matter Experts Interviews

Once you have a general idea for which systems of interest you'll be drilling down on, it's time to line up interviews with the subject matter experts (SMEs) who know the system elements, processes, and people who touch them most. Interviewing internal SMEs will help you both uncover where the most important information can be found and whether or not it's available on internal networks. They will also point you to other SMEs you might not have known about or might not have thought to interview.

Here is a list of candidate questions that might be asked of an SME knowledgeable about an automated system:

- Would you please provide a detailed description of system infrastructure components?
- How is the system (or systems) networked?
- What data exchanges occur and between what components?
- How and where is operational data stored?
- On what communications technologies does the system(s) rely?
- What ICS equipment is deployed in this system(s)?
- How are system components and functions controlled?
- What are normal operating procedures? And what are procedures for when something seems unusual?
- How is the supply chain managed?
- How is the system accessed and how is access controlled?
- How is information about the system managed? On what network is this information stored? Where specially does the information reside?

The initial answers to many of these questions will be just the tip of iceberg. For instance, to the question about ICS equipment, there may be several

115

different ICS systems from different manufacturers involved. So the follow-on guidance will be, for each please provide the manufacturer, the model, configuration details, commissioning date, and the subcontractors and services providers who performed the initial install as well as maintenance. And then you'll need to capture information about the internal hardware and software. This will likely mean calls to the vendor and to other companies once the supply chain and other sourcing details start to emerge. Remember, whereas up until a few decades ago industrial companies were relatively self-contained, in 2020 targeting a company often does not mean targeting that company directly.[10] You can visualize concentric rings of product and services providers, all who play a greater or lesser role in the successful performance of a company's core mission.

Open-source Info Resources
The following is a sample list of potentially rich open-source resources that may contain relevant information on the HCEs that have made it to Phase 2:[11]

- Federal Communication Commission (FCC)
- Federal Energy Regulatory Commission (FERC)
- North American Electric Reliability Corporation (NERC)
- US Environmental Protection Agency (EPA)
- US Securities and Exchange Commission (SEC)
- State filings, publications, etc.
- University partnerships: case studies, papers, etc.
- New articles related to proposals, partnerships, upgrades, construction, equipment for plants
- Engineering design/construction companies
- Public bids (RFPs, RFQs, tenders, etc.)
- Vendor technology websites, related publications
- Conference presentations

Other Non-internal Sources
In addition to system and process information contained in the places already mentioned, both product and services vendors may be intentionally or unintentionally storing important details about customer systems on their own. Sample questions to ask here are:

- Do any vendors have access to system-specific information?
- Do subcontractors have access to system-specific information?
- If the information resides on a network drive, who has access to the drive?

Pursuing the "Perfect Knowledge" View

In order to collect and properly reference, tag, and store information from the entity during Phase 2, the following guidance will help participants get closer to the ideal or "perfect knowledge" needed to make the most of Phases 3 and 4:

- The database must be well-organized and well-referenced to be accessible.
  - Begin to process and ingest data (tease out what matters from documents and diagrams and distill it).
  - Diligently source all documentation.
- Be prepared to return to questions and conversations multiple times. Phase 2 requires constant iteration and the collection process is a spiral, not a waterfall.
- Multiple individuals must work collaboratively to achieve success in Phase 2, including:
  - Analysts: lead effort to collect, analyze, and organize information on people, processes, and technology for each HCE/diagram, assess whether the questions have been answered.
  - Targeter and SME(s): Validate whether questions have been answered, review information, develop new questions as needed.
  - Project Manager: Validate that the requested information has been received and recorded and that project deliverables and expectations are met.
- As always, remember to protect this information: Individuals need to understand that gathering all this information in one place creates a roadmap for targeting; it needs to be protected extremely effectively.[12] Ensure that you have appropriate data protection and handling procedures firmly in place prior to beginning Phase 2.

Ultimately decision points arrive when things feel complete for a given scenario. Participants must step back, take stock, and answer this question: Has enough of the right information been collected to set the schedule for next steps?

Populating the Functional Taxonomy

Every organization, large or small, has a language to describe their work. Although it may be difficult for newcomers to translate, this language permeates the workplace, articulating an organization's mission, yearly

117

goals, and daily activities. The early CCE efforts focus on ensuring that this vocabulary is understood, not only by the CCE team but to the larger organization. For example, for years many IT and OT teams have been working to merge to a more common security language. Similarly, there has been a concerted effort to bring C-suite and top-level executives into this conversation prior to a cyber event.

There is, however, another vocabulary used to describe the work of an organization. The functional taxonomy is comprised of the ordered steps taken by an organization to meet its goals, and each step emphasizes the individuals or organizations responsible for that action.[13] Finally, the functional taxonomy notes the necessary inputs and outputs of each action. The functional taxonomy is tightly coupled with the functional diagram(s), which ultimately depicts the same or nearly the same information in a visual way.

Constructing Detailed Functional Diagrams: The Case for a Model-based Approach[14]

An object-based model is an excellent method for capturing and organizing HCE-relevant data, as it allows for classes of information that can be associated with different types of systems, components, or devices. Identifying beforehand what information is common across all types of systems within an entity or even an entire sector facilitates the construction of models that can narrow and focus the collection of information associated with systems and subsystems. It's no mere coincidence that this is the same method engineers use in designing systems. An engineer must acquire the necessary design-related information that is applicable to the specifications of which the system must be designed to in order to begin the design lifecycle. The process that engineers used to do this can be leveraged by analysts in order to study a system or subsystem and identify any related vulnerabilities or dependencies. Leveraging the object/class model approach allows for analysis of a system to obtain information within the context of the architecture that the system is based upon. Gaps are more readily spotted, and essential information elements emerge to enable a more complete understanding of even the most complex systems.

Use of an object/class approach clearly identifies classes of information that must be investigated and acquired to fully represent as much detail regarding system and its associated subsystem. Leveraging underlying databases attached to a graphical interface allows for scoping of the information within the architecture of the system design. Leveraging hierarchical graphical representations allows drilling deeper and deeper within the system of subsystems to a desired level of fidelity. This approach enables clearly identifiable gaps of information needed to understand the complexity of the system and its associated subsystems. It can also clearly identify scope and priority for acquisition of information.

SIDEBAR: RESEARCHING INTERNAL INFORMATION SOURCES[15]

Inside the entity is a vast amount of potentially helpful information for the CCE team, who seek it to ultimately inform the development of the "perfect knowledge" base. It also needs to be considered that some or a great deal of this information has been gathered by an adversary via reconnaissance. One way to order this information, using the project lifecycle as a guide, would be to collect information developed during the following phases for each potentially relevant project:

1 Project Initiation
2 Design
3 Construction
4 Startup
5 Turnover
6 Normal Operations

WHERE DOES THE INFORMATION RESIDE (EXTERNAL OPEN SOURCE)?

In both open source and as well was internal to the organization, the following is a sample list of open-source locations that may contain relevant information on the HCE being analyzed:

1 Federal Communications Commission (FCC)
    a Communications spectrum
2 Federal Energy Regulatory Commission (FERC)
    a Interconnection agreements; power flow; may identify who owns/operates parts but not system configurations
3 North American Electric Reliability Corporation (NERC)
    a Event analysis reports
4 US Environmental Protection Agency

5 US Securities and Exchange Commission (SEC)
   a All major capital investments
6 State filings, publications, etc.
   a State energy/public utility commissions or equal
   b Siting filings
   c State environmental
   d Public utility commission
7 University partnerships: case studies, papers, etc.
8 New articles related to proposals, upgrades, construction, equipment for plants
9 Engineering design/construction companies
10 Public bids
11 Vendor technology websites, related publications

WHO HAS ACCESS TO THE INFORMATION?

The entity must determine and document access levels to all system-specific information. Some questions to be asked are:

1 Do any vendors have access to system-specific information?
2 Do subcontractors have access to system-specific information?
3 If the information resides on a network drive, who has access to the drive?

PREPARING FOR PHASE 3

Phase 2 activities can be considered complete when SMEs have reviewed and validated all discovered documents and diagrams produced, and a summary is prepared that for each scenario includes:

- Access paths
- Initial assessment of attack feasibility
- Knowledge required

This process should be as exhaustive and accurate as possible because it feeds into the third phase of CCE. Note: As the team transitions into Phase 3, these diagrams should summarize the information that must be known by an attacker in order to achieve their desired effect.

NOTES

1   Richard Danzig. "Surviving on a Diet of Poisoned Fruit: Reducing the National Security Risks of America's Cyber Dependencies." Center for New American Security. June 21, 2014.

2   And the ultimate goal of CCE being to transform the way an organization understands its strategic cyber risks. Going through the four phases for each of the handful of HCE's identified is the best way we know to inculcate this knowledge in critical infrastructure owners and operators.

3   CCE Phase 2—Foundational White Paper *reference*.

4   Anecdotal. From talks with Idaho-based members of DHS critical infrastructure cyber assessment teams.

5   A secondary benefit you'll accrue from collecting all of this level of detail is you'll be much better equipped to perform incident response and system restoration when breaches occur.

6   CCE Phase 2—Foundational White Paper *reference*.

7   Ibid.

8   Ibid.

9   Ibid.

10   Curtis St. Michel, September 2019.

11   CCE Phase 2—Foundational White Paper *reference*.

12   Ibid.

13   Ibid.

14   System of Systems Analysis Methodology, R. Sadler, INL September 2014.

15   Sarah Freeman, Curtis St. Michel, and Bryce McClurg. "The Process of Consequence Driven Cyber Informed Engineering (CCE)," February 2018, INL/EXT-18-44814.

7

PHASE 3: CONSEQUENCE-BASED TARGETING

It may come across as overly clinical, but think about what this statement on the role of targeters by a senior INL engineer really means:

They "provide adversary leaders options to exploit opportunities to create specific effects."[1]

SIDEBAR: QUESTIONS TO DRIVE ACTION

Some of what you'll want to explore in Phase 3 involves examination of the following:

- Given what was learned in Phases 1 and 2, what are the highest confidence attack paths that would produce potentially catastrophic results?
- Have you considered not just direct but tangential paths (e.g., disruptive cyberattacks on a supplier of essential services to your company; prolonged physical disruption of fuels delivery, water, communications, etc.)?

- Can any of the adversarial mindset lessons be captured and codified into corporate policies, so the company does not find itself in such a vulnerable position in the future?

PHASE 3 OBJECTIVES

In simplest form, Phase 3 is where we try to find places where there is unverified trust, or in other words, trust with incomplete knowledge (e.g., a place where we think we have verified trust because we've tested to see if something performs a function but haven't tested to see all functions a component is capable of).[2]

For each HCE, fully leveraging the information just gathered from internal and external sources in Phase 2, develop and validate the high-confidence kill chains (i.e., sequenced cyber-attack instructions) to bring them to fruition. We're not going to actually execute attacks but working with process SMEs and targeters will come as close as possible to ensuring that all the technical details are correct and that the human process aspects are captured with the highest possible fidelity.

BECOMING YOUR WORST (AND BEST) ENEMY

CCE Phase 3 may seem similar in some ways but should not be confused with pen testing or "Red Team" assessments. Pen testing is often a relatively short engagement, 1–2 weeks, during which time the tester attempts to identify and exploit as many IT and OT network and system configuration vulnerabilities as they can. Results can be heavily skewed or limited based on the skills, experience, and biases of the tester. Red Team assessments are similar but typically run longer and are more targeted, and they often add additional attack vectors like social engineering. Instead of finding as many vulnerabilities as possible, the goal of Red Teaming is to stealthily test an organization's detection and response capabilities.[3]

Unlike other cybersecurity risk management methodologies, with rare exceptions, CCE participants don't spend much if any time evaluating the strength of cyber defenses or trying to close the innumerable vulnerabilities in hardware, software, and firmware. From an advanced adversary's point of view, current cyber hygiene-based defenses look at lot like France's static Maginot Line[4] strategy from WWII. It worked as long as the German's agreed to conform to France's assumption that they would approach from the Southeast ... which of course, they didn't. The best cyber adversaries are highly adaptive, and if they find defenses are easier to defeat in one place than another, they will certainly aim their attacks accordingly.

For decades, defenders have been advised to employ "defense in depth"[5] strategies, feeling more confident with each additional layer added. And while those extra defenses (e.g., more firewalls, additional authentication steps, network segmenting, etc.) mean many automated attacks as well as those by less skilled or fewer patient attackers are thwarted, they don't add up to much against the best. While they may make for extra work for professionals, there are always more than enough Achilles Heals to exploit for access and persistence and to allow for stealthy maneuvering, all while building out a better understanding of the networks and systems, the processes by which they are operated and maintained, and the highest confidence pathways to create high-consequence effects.

In Phase 3, guided by targeters and SMEs, some with hands-on experience in offensive operations from previous postings, owners, and operators (and defenders too) will be challenged to take on the role and mindset of those wishing them the most grievous harm. It's only temporary but seeing one's organization from the outside-in and coming to understand the multiple options open to attackers even when cyber defenses seem stout is something as some might say, that "cannot be unseen."

Cyber Kill Chains

Kill Chain Origins

Borrowing from a targeting term the military used to describe the steps needed to stop an enemy's mission element from achieving its goals; computer scientists and researchers at the aerospace-defense giant Lockheed Martin coined the term in 2011 "Intrusion Kill Chain for Cyber security," which was later simplified in common use as "cyber Kill Chain."[6] Here are its steps in order:

1 Reconnaissance
2 Weaponization
3 Delivery
4 Exploitation

5 Installation
6 Command and Control
7 Actions on objectives

Helpful as it was, this model or methodology was conceived for IT environments, and a number of folks, including Jason Holcomb, who had experience at both Lockheed and Industrial Control Systems (ICS) security consultancy Digital Bond started thinking about how to convert it to the less standardized world of operational technology.[7]

After all, whereas the targets of IT-based cyberattacks were primarily data and applications existing on IP networks, OT targets were often hazardous physical processes strung together via a variety of obscure communications protocols and riding on top of older and sometimes unsupported operating systems.

Whereas the amount of knowledge required to break into and move about an IT network was limited, achieving kinetic objectives in OT demands an enormous amount of research and patience on the part of the attacker, as they seek to develop a full understanding of the engineering details, configuration and design of the plant, or other industrial process provider in their sights. The number of steps the attacker must execute is much greater as well, and the ICS Kill Chain, developed by Mike Assante and Rob M. Lee and published by the SANS Institute,[8] breaks them into two stages. Nevertheless, since most ICS systems were not designed with security in mind, and most engineers and operators designed their processes without security in mind, attacks on OT are definitely doable, as some of the high-profile incidents addressed in earlier chapters demonstrate.

The CCE Cyber Kill Chain[9]

INL developed a further iteration of the Kill Chain concept to streamline the process of developing useful and realistic scenarios. Key to the CCE Kill Chain is taking the adversarial perspective, that is, stepping out of your operator or defender role and donning a "black hat" mindset to construct effective attacks.

The CCE Kill Chain is used to illustrate the adversaries' most likely actions starting with their objectives.[10] The main reason for this approach is based on CCE's focus on fully understanding (with the purpose of ultimately disrupting) the requirements for adversary actions.

Highly resourced and motivated attackers may insert corrupted component items or software several layers into the supply chain, co-opt insiders, and/or direct individuals to apply for critical positions within the target organization, its subcontractors, or its vendors. Rather than focusing only on the target network(s) and cyber hygiene obstacles for every possible cyber access, the CCE Kill Chain describes the best sources for the critical information an adversary would require while developing a capability, including where it is located and who has access.[11] Knowing this helps the CCE team focus on the most plausible paths and to identify choke points.

It is important to look at each step in the Kill Chain from an adversarial view and think about the problem from all angles and drop any biases about how the target system operates to include protections used. In fact, in some attacks the way a system operates and uses safety systems can be used against its owners. In an IT network, the access required to develop and deploy a payload is often limited to the adversary's ability to maintain persistence and elevated privileges in the target's networks. In an ICS network, the access needed to deploy a payload is often separate, more sustained, and may require physical access to the target equipment or component.[12]

Organizations may be indirectly targeted through trusted relationships and connections with vendors, subcontractors, partners, blogs, or industry associations used or visited by employees. Targeting of these outside parties by adversaries may provide critical information or vectors against their intended target.

Phase 3 Team Roles

While the targeter is the captain, Phase 3 is most decidedly a team sport. Other key roles include SMEs, analysts, and other members in a support role. Here's a little on what's expected of each.

Targeter

The targeter is trained and adept at how to identify the weakest, simplest, highest-impact points in an organization and its systems of interest and assist in devising the attack strategies to achieve the impacts. They determine where the information required to research and build the attack is held, and if not already in the knowledge base, how to access that information.

These folks have extensive experience in offensive cyber operations. Also, typically, and for obvious reasons, few critical infrastructure organizations have even one person with these skillsets on their roster.

In addition to engineering, critical thinking, problem solving, and other analytic skills, the best targeters also possess an inordinate amount creativity ... a rare combination indeed. The CIA's job description for intro-level targeting analyst positions provides some insight into the types of personalities they seek, beginning with:

> As a Targeting Analyst for the CIA, you will work on teams that bring analysis and operations together to maximize the impact of Agency and Intelligence Community resources against key figures and organizations who pose a threat to US interests.[13]

To target in a CCE context, targeters take the HCEs they're given and hold them up across Phase 2's "perfect knowledge" and get to work. They first try to identify a pathway to achieve the effect, then immediately expand to find alternative pathways that could be even easier to navigate and execute with higher confidence.

Targeters consider every angle to discover cases of unverified trust. To invoke a tree analogy, the goal is to get from the tips of the branches to the roots of the tree. Divergent branches suggest a different pathway an adversary might be able to take, and chokepoints can be found where branches converge. CCE is concerned with the chokepoints closest to the end effect (roots). Trying to cut off all the branches is like playing whack-a-mole when it's best to just cut the tree at the trunk, which is what happens with Phase 4 Protections.

Subject Matter Experts
These are the folks with the most hands-on experience and understanding of how relevant systems of interest function, are operated, how they're maintained and by whom. Their primary job in Phase 3 is to help the targeter understand specifics of how a given system works and translate relevant documentation. Examples would include an engineer's expertise in the specific boilers, flow meters, pumps, transformers, safety systems, etc. used by the entity.

Analysts
Having already analyzed and organized entity information and armed with perfect knowledge, analysts are in the best position to assist the targeter and SMEs by quickly retrieving what they need as they build and validate kill chains.

The Intelligence Community (IC)

One of the most trail-blazing aspects of CCE is the intentional involvement of the IC during selected engagements with US Department of Defense (DoD) organizations and/or commercial entities that support them or other critical national functions. In the electric sector, for example, some network traffic flows to the IC via sensors that are part of the DOE's Cyber Risk Information Security Program (CRISP)[14] initiative. The sensors are positioned just outside participating utilities' corporate internet gateways and firewalls, and the information collected is ultimately shared with the IC for analysis. The intent is that discovered tactics, threats, and procedures, (also known as TTPs or indicators) will be shared back, not just with the entity where the TTPs were observed but sector-wide via the information-sharing Electricity-Information Sharing and Analysis Center (E-ISAC). While this program has enjoyed some success and positive feedback, it's not nearly at the level of sharing most utility CEOs say they would like. And because it's IT and not OT data and intel, the IC gains little experience in assessing threats to operational energy systems and networks as part of their involvement in CRISP.

In CCE on the other hand, in some engagements, specific, high-consequence process and OT network and asset information is shared via secure channels with the IC during Phases 2 and 3. The IC investigates and analyzes potentially relevant nation-state activity and reports back to INL and entity's CCE team to inform prioritization of Phase 4 Mitigations and Protections' recommended actions. If you found out that not only was it possible for an adversary to reach deep into your networks to mis-operate key systems but also that a nation-state being tracked by the IC had recently purchased and configured multi-million dollar exact replicas of your equipment, and was apparently studying it vs. using it for its intended purpose, how might that color your risk calculus?

Of course, the IC won't have a role in engagements where an entity is putting itself through CCE, or a services company is facilitating a CCE engagement at an entity not designated as essential to the provision of a critical national function. But the capabilities of commercial cyber threat intelligence companies have greatly improved in recent years and in some the capabilities are equal or near equal to the US IC.

PHASE 3 WALKTHROUGH

Develop Scenario Concept of Operations (CONOPS) for Each HCE

Borrowing a military term, each HCE scenario requires the development of an adversarial CONOPS plan, which includes:

- The desired end effect of the ICS payload
- The precise technical element or elements being targeted
- The highest confidence access paths
- The information and access required to develop the payload

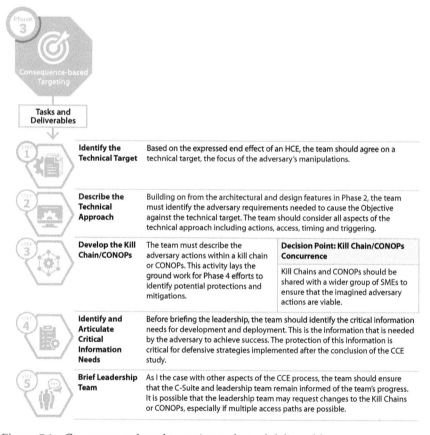

Figure 7.1   Consequence-based targeting tasks and deliverables.

- The information and access required to deploy the payload

Instead of beginning a campaign trying to see which effects might be achieved, CCE Phase 3 begins with the end in mind, identifying the objective and boundary conditions from Phase 1, and narrowing down the scenarios that could lead to those effects. As in, the targets are already selected, the requisite knowledge is already gathered during Phase 2, and it is the team's job to construct and document the most straight-forward, highest confidence attacks. By this point there's no need to recapitulate the entire CCE Kill Chain, the job is to work backward only as far as is necessary.

Note: As much of Phase 3 is circular or iterative—refinements and additions are anticipated throughout the process. The steps that follow are in approximate order, but there needs to be enough flexibility to allow for changes of direction at any point if it appears promising from the attackers' perspective.

Determining Attack Scenarios
- There may be numerous scenarios that can make the HCE occur.
- The consideration of the physics of the system is required to achieve the physical effect—SMEs have a big role here.
- Refinement of assumptions and boundaries for each HCE scenario, followed by the generation of potential approaches to meet criteria.
- As you proceed, gather more information and learn more, it becomes apparent that certain variations are not possible, and others, formerly higher in confidence, may become less likely, based on the information/steps required.

Questions to ask here:
- What is the adversary trying to achieve?
- Is the HCE physically possible?
- Where does the adversary have to be located within the organization's network to achieve the desired effect?
- What access is required to achieve the desired effect?
- What additional organization specific information would the adversary require to achieve the desired effect?

Defining a Technical Approach (i.e., the ICS Payload Requirements)
The technical approach is the detailed set of requirements the adversary needs to cause the HCE. It answers how an adversary will achieve the HCE. The steps in the technical approach define the ICS elements or targets

needed to be manipulated. Each step in the technical approach identifies a target ICS element and describes the access required to reach the target, what actions will need to occur at the target, the timing of the attack, and how it will be triggered. By describing each target ICS element in this way, it creates a possible pathway an adversary would need to follow to cause the HCE. Note: There are many different pathways an adversary could take and it's important to determine the most plausible pathway for this consequence-based targeting exercise. Consider the following when defining each step:

- **Access** are the steps, movements, and actions an adversary needs to perform to get to the target.
- **Actions** are the conditions or steps that need to be accomplished on the target to cause the HCE.
- **Timing** is the sequence of events or order of operations of the attack.
- **Triggering** is how the payload will be activated.

Things to consider:

- Establishing Command and Control (C2). If persistent, high-confidence connectivity is impossible or unlikely, then other C2 options may be explored (e.g., a time or sensor-based triggers).
- The targeter's end effect of the HCE drives the deployment. It's their job to determine where the adversary needs to be in the networks/systems/devices to achieve success.
- Thoroughly explore all potential pathways that meet the overall goals defined by each HCE.
- Remember: CCE doesn't require defining how access was achieved; this phase of CCE cares only about knocking out the critical function to bring about the HCE. And informs Phase 4, which ensures the attack won't be successful.
- Also remember: We're not trying to eliminate all access vulnerabilities; it is up to entity owners, operators, and defenders to address and secure the cyber and physical access. CCE assumes they were not at the time of the engagement—and will never be—completely successful at keeping adversaries out of their networks and systems.

Define Target Details
- The target details are identified as the result of determining precisely what specific part of the system, down to the component, needs to be sabotaged to be in position to bring about the HCE. Examples of the details collected and referenced are hardware, software, configuration files, firmware, protocols, operating system, model, vendor,

function, etc. Every piece of information should be referenced in the system targeting description.

Access Pathway
- Attack scenarios focus on the end goal of the HCE. Despite what entity defenders usually think, there are always an abundance of access paths. Focusing on access paths places the emphasis on securing network boundaries and firewalls, which even when designed, deployed, and maintained perfectly, do not block human-enabled and supply-chain-enabled attacks.
- However, all access points on the target system(s) and network(s) need to be identified. This includes the initial access point and any traversal to obtain a different access point. These should be documented in each of the following three areas for each HCE:
  - Network-based
  - Human-enabled
  - Supply chain
- Develop a summary of key system elements, by defining:
  - The information needed to develop the payload. Note: CCE does not include the development of actual payloads.
  - The information required for access allowing deployment of the payload. Note: CCE does not include the identification of the vulnerability that would be compromised to achieve access.
  - The adversarial collection plan, i.e., the full strategy for how the info above is obtained.

Other points to consider:
- If targeter or adversary only looks at how to develop and deliver payload through network operations, they miss potential real-world activities that could facilitate access (e.g., gaining physical access to components that would enable cyber access, compromising key personnel for knowledge or credentials, etc.)
- Consider attack breadth to achieve the scale of impacts needed. If the HCE being worked only requires compromising one versus ten targets, the job is that much simpler. If the effect requires ten targets be achieved, the targeter or adversary would need to find a common location for the payload versus various options for just one.
- A national-security-relevant, horizontal attack may involve compromising many or all instances of a particular device. Attackers think at this scale; defenders need to as well.

Critical Information Needs

During Phase 3, Critical Information Needs become apparent. These information needs represent key details that an adversary requires to develop the payload(s) or malicious code that initiate an HCE or deploy this code to an intended target (known as development and deployment critical information needs, respectively).

An adversary can acquire this critical information in multiple ways; however, these needs are typically dictated by the deployment of the intended target. For example, an intended payload for a system requires that an adversary first identify the deployed hardware and software versions used by a potential victim. After which, the adversary could purchase representative equipment for development.

Regardless of type of critical information needs, an organization should identify and note the location of this information, as the cybersecurity incidents that result in the theft or loss of this information serve as precursors for more damaging attacks. Similarly, organizations should also keep in mind that much of this sensitive information may reside outside of the enterprise or control network, as this data is often provided to manufacturers, service providers, or integrators.

Development of the Payload

Critical needs for development include all the information, equipment, and software needed to develop a payload. The payload is the mechanism an adversary will use to maliciously manipulate or attack a system for a sabotage effect. Often, the payload is designed to target the basic functions of a system and render these functions unavailable, or maliciously use available design features.

The goal of payload development—and its corresponding cyber-attack—is a physical effect accomplished via cyber means. In contrast to many (if not all) information technology (IT)-centric attacks, a cyber-physical attack is directed against the base functions of a system, instead of access to sensitive information. For example, adversaries targeting the wicket gate of a hydro generation station may be successful in limiting or stopping the flow of water through a dam, thereby limiting the generation output of the site.

Adversaries interested in designing payloads to sabotage physical systems need a detailed level of understanding of the target process to manipulate it for disruptive purposes. Because of the additional knowledge required, engineering design documents and other technical specifications will be a key element of the targeting process. Another exceptionally useful source of information is mechanical failure analysis or similar documentation; this information can provide valuable insight for the adversary seeking to achieve damaging or destructive attacks via cyber means.

Reid Wightman illustrated the usefulness of these design specifications when he identified a common vulnerability in a key engineering component. Wightman designed a hypothetical attack against a variable frequency drive (VFD) by rewriting the skip frequency[15] so that dangerous conditions would be obtained by the VFD during operation.[16] Wightman also noted that in many cases the skip frequency field was read/writable, allowing for potential malicious alteration by an adversary.

Deployment of the Payload
Critical needs for deployment of the payload include the pieces of critical information the adversary needs to deliver the payload to the intended location. Delivery of the payload often requires different accesses than those that were used during payload development. Other considerations include the desired scale of the attack and how many systems will need to be sabotaged to achieve the HCE.

For example, if an adversary wants to affect an entire fleet of ships—and not just one ship—the critical needs for deployment will be different. They will need to figure out how to deploy their payload to all the ships and not just one. This may be achievable through the supply chain. If the entire fleet relies on one common vendor for a target component, the adversary may only need to interrupt the supply chain in one location. However, if the ships used different suppliers for the target component, the deployment may require access to the supply chain in more than just one location.

Deliver CONOPS and Iterate with SMEs

At this point in the process it's time to critically review the HCE attack scenarios and revise them as needed. This involves the detailed descriptions of the technical approach, target details, and critical needs, and the fully referenced system targeting description that is the source of all of it. In addition to targeting information, this also includes:

- Documenting any HCEs that are eliminated because of infeasibility
- Lead by a facilitator, the team, including SMEs and analysts, going through every element to validate technical details and elicit additional information

135

Eliminating HCEs

There are times when the team gets down into trenches with the engineers and operators who know their processes inside out, and what seems like a promising attack path in every other way turns out to be 95% right and 5% wrong. And it's the 5% that eliminates the consequence, and it's usually because there's a physical process detail that didn't show up in the documentation gathered. For example, in one instance, after lengthy research, it appeared that a chemical could be added to a mix all at once that would have caused destructive corrosion and eventually, the complete destruction of an expensive, long-lead-time-to-replace machine. When the team visited the floor, however, they found that the amount of this chemical was limited to the size of the bucket that held it. And though the bucket size was chosen arbitrarily years prior, it turned out that even if it was added all at once, dilution meant the volume wouldn't be enough to cause a catastrophic effect. And there was no method, short of an on-premise employee or contractor physically added more, to create the destructive effect. That HCE was eliminated, and others have been as well for similar reasons.

Validating Details

As with the example above, there's no reason to advance the HCE through the rest of the steps if it doesn't square with reality. But assuming it holds up to scrutiny at this stage, it's imperative to ensure that the information collected is 100% reflective of the process as witnessed via direct scrutiny with the owners and operators responsible for it. Any other details that can be added at this point are welcome as the team prepares to rack and stack the HCEs ahead of presentation to senior leadership.

Attack Scenario Complexity and Confidence

Complexity and confidence play important roles in prioritizing candidate HCEs in Phase 3.[17] Generally speaking, as complexity increases, confidence decreases:

- What skills are needed to carry out the attack?
- What resources are required?
- How many number of steps would it take to carry out the attack?
- How many ways can it come about?
- What is the difficulty to compromise the target?
- What is the difficulty of getting the information needed?

While rating scenario confidence depends on the results of the complexity assessment, it then asks if the information needed to research, build, and conduct the attack is available in open source. And is there intelligence telling if this is an actual target for adversaries. The credibility of confidence ratings may be boosted substantially if there is access to known adversary capabilities, activities, and preferences.

Present CONOPS to C-Suite

This is just what it sounds like, with the full team in the room to describe the attack scenarios developed to bring about the Phase 1 HCEs that have survived the additional scrutiny received earlier in Phase 3. The team must be ready to respond to questions about how the attack scenarios were made, underlying assumptions made, internal and external information required to research and build them, etc. And even before formally launching Phase 4 activities, it's not too early to begin to start developing and describing candidate mitigation and protection strategies.

THREAT INTELLIGENCE FROM DIFFERENT SOURCES

As originally envisaged, CCE would be a tool to be used by nations—starting with the US—to defend against strategic cyberattacks on critical infrastructure conducted by hostile nation-states. And so far, the engagements guided by INL and/or INL-trained experts have involved significant interaction with the government for threat intelligence. Information about attackers and their methods and what they've been seen researching and targeting plays an important role in Phase 3.

As depicted in Figure 7.2, Phase 2-derived "perfect knowledge" is selectively shared with government experts who then report back on activities involving the same systems that they've seen around the world, and especially in countries considered unfriendly. In-depth information on adversaries' approaches and what they could achieve will be a revelation to virtually everyone at the entity involved in this process. We've found that even people who were the most skeptical in during Pre-Engagement Preparation and even Phase 1 tend to get on board by the end of Phase 3.

Interestingly, we've found that some of the methodology's central concepts can be picked up and applied to good effect without any hands-on involvement from INL or government-level threat inputs. In some instances, it's been asset owning companies that have applied the

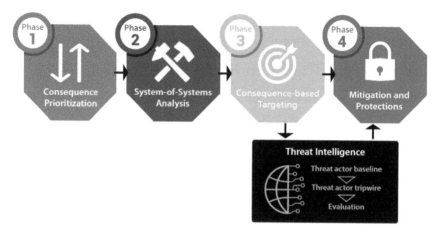

Figure 7.2   CCE process flow including threat intelligence.

methodology to themselves. Other times, security and/or engineering services firms have brought CCE to their clients and achieved significant success. As mentioned earlier, commercial cyber threat intelligence providers have in some ways caught up to their government counterparts, so there are helpful capabilities whichever way you go.

SIDEBAR: GETTING THREAT INTELLIGENCE HELP FROM THE OUTSIDE

While it's likely that your company has much of the knowledge, it needs to conduct CCE Phases 1, 2, and 4; Phase 3's call to think like an adversary—to determine the best ways to take out the systems upon which your organization most depends—will likely require talent you lack internally. Even if you have a relatively mature cybersecurity team, including one that brings a fair amount of acumen to defending OT systems and networks, it is still unlikely that anyone in the company has all the requisite experience. In other words, what is needed in Phase 3 requires professionals adept at finding pathways through corporate cyber defenders and defenses. If it seems you simply don't have the right types of folks to perform this function, you might want to turn to professionals who do this for a living. They are out there, but of course you'll want to vet them thoroughly.

Here again, prioritization is a big part of the process, as you're not interested in finding every pathway through the maze to create the effect, but rather the simplest, most high-confidence ones that require the adversary to take the fewest steps to achieve his/her nefarious goals. Those are what you'll be feeding into Phase 4. More complicated or less confident paths can and should be addressed later.

And as some have reported who've orchestrated their own internal CCE engagements, it's certainly possible to make significant and demonstrable security, safety, and resilience gains in Phase 4 without comprehensive Phase 2 or 3 efforts. For certain entities it makes sense to perform each phase in full. But for many others, the perfect may be the enemy of the good, and if a shortcut or two are required in order to get buy-in and show results that improve your defenses and begin to change minds, then that's a major win. Who should be involved? With top-down support from the CEO and Board of Directors (BoD), at a minimum: Operations and Engineering leaders with input hands-on from engineers and operations personnel, IT and OT security leads, and for Phase 3— third-party white-hat and threat intelligence firms. Also, for entities who've relied extensively on trusted integrators to design and maintain their plants and processes, there's no substitute for having integrator SMEs at the table.

PREPARING FOR PHASE 4

The transition from offense to defense happens as we prepare to move into the final phase: Protections and Mitigations. Before the new phase begins in earnest, we close off Phase 3 with a final internal assessment of whether the right types of SMEs have weighed in on the CONOPS for each HCE and whether any new or additional perspectives need to be added to the mix. It's a last-chance, pre-flight quality control effort, because what gets recommended for protections and mitigations depends entirely on the accuracy of the information that informs the development of the kill chains.

NOTES

1 Charles "Chuck" Forshee, in conversation at INL, May 2019.
2 CCE Phase 3—Foundational White Paper v2 *reference*.
3 Kirk Hayes. "Penetration Testing vs. Red Team Assessment: The Age-Old Debate of Pirates vs. Ninjas Continues." Rapid 7 Blog, accessed June 23, 2016. https://blog.rapid7.com/2016/06/23/penetration-testing-vs-red-teaming-the-age-old-debate-of-pirates-vs-ninja-continues/.
4 "Maginot Line." Wikipedia page, accessed January 4, 2020. https://en.wikipedia.org/wiki/Maginot_Line.
5 Todd McGuiness. "Defense in Depth." SANS Institute Information Security Reading Room online, accessed January 4, 2020. www.sans.org/reading-room/whitepapers/basics/defense-in-depth-525.
6 "The Cyber Kill Chain." Lockheed Martin web page, accessed January 4, 2020. www.lockheedmartin.com/en-us/capabilities/cyber/cyber-kill-chain.html.
7 Jason Holcomb. "ICS Cyber Kill Chain." Dale Peterson Blog, accessed November 29, 2011. https://dale-peterson.com/2011/11/29/1463/.
8 Michael J. Assante and Robert M. Lee. "The Industrial Control System Cyber Kill Chain." SANS Institute Information Security Reading Room. October 2015. www.sans.org/reading-room/whitepapers/ICS/industrial-control-system-$_{cyber}$-kill-chain-36297.
9 CCE Phase 3—Foundational White Paper v2 *reference*.
10 Ibid.
11 Ibid.
12 Ibid.
13 "Careers and Internships: Targeting Analyst." CIA website, accessed January 5, 2020. www.cia.gov/careers/opportunities/analytical/targeting-analyst.html#job-details-tab1.
14 "Cybersecurity Risk Information Sharing Program." US Department of Energy website, accessed January 12, 2020. www.energy.gov/sites/prod/files/2018/09/f55/CRISP%20Fact%20Sheet.pdf.
15 A skip frequency is a designated frequency for a specific piece of equipment at which unsafe vibrations and other damage can occur.
16 Kim Zetter. "An Easy Way for Hackers to Remotely Burn Industrial Motors." *Wired Magazine*, accessed January 12, 2016. www.wired.com/2016/01/an-easy-way-for-hackers-to-remotely-burn-industrial-motors/.
17 CCE Phase 3—Foundational White Paper v2 *reference*.

8

PHASE 4: MITIGATIONS AND PROTECTIONS

Physics saves the machine.

—Ed Marszal and Jim McGlone1[1, 2]

SIDEBAR: QUESTIONS TO DRIVE ACTION

This is it! The destination for which all the previous work was designed to get you to. Remember, CCE teams do not implement changes, they only describe them in a prioritized manner. Questions here include:

- What are the response times needed if/when an intrusion is detected in Kill Chains where engineered protections prove impractical or are not possible?
- In situations where Phase 3 reveals adversaries are able to reach control functions via digital means, what do the engineers and operators closest to the target processes recommend as ways to protect the most critical, long-lead-time-to-replace equipment?
- Given identified attack processes, how can you protect against the most damaging attacks? How can we alter the physics of our process to increase our immunity to digital attacks?
- In the event of a cyberattack, who do we contact?

141

PHASE 4 OBJECTIVES

The final phase of CCE methodology focuses on the identification and initial development of potential protection strategies that can be implemented within a participating organization to mitigate those attack paths and cyber Concept of Operations (CONOPs) developed during Phase 3.[3] To support this objective, the CCE team typically conducts a workshop to explore and generate potential mitigation approaches and their respective feasibility and efficacy. This resultant document becomes the basis for future discussions regarding operational, procedural, and design changes.

Phase 4 is where the entity CEOs (or their similarly senior government counterparts) earn their pay, as they will be confronted with a list of prioritized, heavily vetted recommendations for protections and mitigations to ward off company-ending scenarios. The Idaho National Laboratory (INL) CCE team and its entity CCE partners' final task is to ensure that the CEO and his or her senior staff understand, and appreciate to greatest extent possible, not only the risks described but also the types of decisions that put them in this difficult position if the first place and what their next moves are for mitigating this risk.

TAKING TARGETS OFF THE TABLE

The intent in Phase 4 is always, to the greatest extent possible, to eliminate digital exposure or dependency via engineering means, either in the technical architecture or in process, operations or all of the above.[4] Monitoring and tripwires are typically recommended in two cases: when the digital dependency cannot be eliminated or when there's disproportionate value in maintaining situational awareness via an observable chokepoint through which an adversary would have to pass to reach the target.

Relative to the five functions in National Institute of Standards and Technology's (NIST's) cybersecurity framework, CCE teams turn to the last four: Protect, Detect, Respond, and Recover for this phase and greatly prefer "Protect" actions in the form of complete, non-digital mitigations wherever possible—often phrased as "engineering-out the cyber risk."

SIDEBAR: CCE AND THE NIST SECURITY FRAMEWORK

In the fourth phase, the CCE team identifies and expands on potential mitigations that could be implemented by a participating organization to limit their exposure to catastrophic cyber sabotage. Depending on the type of entity involved, INL may articulate potential mitigations and protections within the language and terminology presented in the NIST Cybersecurity Framework, which identifies five categories of necessary cybersecurity activity. The first function, Identify, is defined as the process of developing an organizational understanding to manage cyber security risk to systems, people, assets, data, and capabilities, actions that are encompassed during the first three phases of CCE. The remaining four functions, Protect, Detect, Respond, and Recover, are defined in Figure 8.1.

Figure 8.1 The NIST Cybersecurity Framework Applying the CCE Approach.

As candidate mitigations and protections are generated, each categorized within one of the four areas. In some cases, it is possible to place a mitigation within more than one category.

In general, INL prefers actions within the protection function, as these changes are more likely to eliminate the possibility of the

143

end effect identified during Phase 3. Full Protect actions, however, are not always possible, in which case the impact of a cyber event can often be reduced by detection, response, and/or recovery actions.

INL considers four possible criteria that could be used by an organization if they require a ranking process: (1) type of mitigation or protection, (2) efficacy, (3) existing threat information, and (4) attack scenario-assessed difficulty.[5] These criteria are described in greater detail in the text box. Scores for criteria 2, 3, and 4 are indicated as low, medium, or high.

PRIORITIZATION CRITERIA

1 Type of mitigation or protection: As stated previously, INL recommends the prioritization of protect-type actions over those of the other classes (detect, respond, and recover). Therefore, in general, protection actions are prioritized over other mitigations. Only the identified primary function is recorded.

2 Efficacy: Proposed changes were reviewed in terms of their perceived efficacy (i.e., whether the proposed solution makes the attack not feasible); however, this kind of review is limited in that the end efficacy of a solution is based on the specific implementation that is adopted. Additionally, in many cases, complete mitigation of the risk is not possible, but the proposed changes may make the attack more costly or challenging for the adversary.

3 Existing threat information: Some attack scenarios may leverage techniques that have already been witnessed "in the world" (i.e., deployed against a victim) or involve the targeting of system or components that corresponds with existing adversary interest. INL assumes that the presence of existing capabilities or research directed against these systems will result in an increased likelihood that an adversary would pursue these options over other scenarios. It should be noted that INL makes these assessments with limed or imperfect knowledge.

4 Assessed Attack "Difficulty": INL assumes an increase in difficulty corresponds to a decrease in the likelihood that an

adversary would pursue that path due to an increase in relative cost and/or the increased need for specialized skills or knowledge. In this evaluation, the difficulty ranking is assessed at the level of the least challenging scenario (many of the mitigations apply to multiple scenarios identified in Phase 3).

It is possible that some of these programmatic and design changes could introduce additional risk. Entity pursuit of any of these changes should involve a thorough cost/benefit analysis and review after a specific and detailed implementation plan has been developed. This review should determine any potential unidentified consequences and/or risks that may be introduced with these changes. Additionally, additional criteria should be evaluated prior to the implementation of any changes, namely the burden for implementation and the cost of implementation and maintenance.

In order to round out the approach, when possible, INL does try to provide the entity with respond and recover mitigations options as well. When "detect" monitoring is recommended, it needs to be situated as close to the asset or process of interest as possible. That close-in monitoring can then be augmented by monitoring further away from the point of interest, which usually translates to "earlier in the kill chain." This approach may result in monitoring solutions that are IT-based, either because the full attack chain occurs within the IT domain or because an OT attack is enabled by the compromise of IT assets. Leveraging CCE principles to defend against data loss scenarios like the massive Equifax and OPM events would be examples where engineering-based "protect" mitigations are likely not possible or practical.

Protections may take several forms, including halting progress at one or more steps along the Cyber Kill Chain. Out-of-band, often non-digital protective backstops are not to be found in the RSA exhibit hall and may include selective reinsertion of trusted humans in the process decision-making loop.

Here's a succinct way to think about this phase from someone who's already been through it: "if there's a digitally controlled process or component that could be used to cause unacceptable physical consequences, then a non-digital control is required. That concept is what needs to get integrated into the engineering process."[6]

SIDEBAR: "THE ULTIMATE MAN IN THE LOOP"[7]

Figure 8.2 Former Soviet Air Defense Lt. Colonel Stanislav Yevgrafovich Petrov in 2016. (Source: Wikipedia, Used per Creative Commons 4.0. Posted by User: *Queery-54*. No Changes Made to the Image).

In the early morning hours of September 26, 1983, a Russian man you've never met saved your life. Not only your life, but your family's life and lives of at least half of the citizens of the United States and, half the citizens of, what was then, the Soviet Union, not to mention many millions more around the globe. He was Stanislav Yevgrafovich Petrov, a Lt. Colonel in the Soviet Air Defense Forces, and he defied protocol and the five computerized alarms ringing out from a command center dashboard for an early warning ICBM detection system (seen in Figure 8.2). When algorithms indicated that US missiles were headed for his homeland, Petrov remained calm. When follow-up analysis verified the alerts, Petrov remained skeptical. He did validate the findings for headquarters, which surely would have initiated massive retaliation. His knowledge, experience, skepticism, and instincts exemplify the importance of the human element in an increasingly automated world and remain, 37 years later, a cautionary tale for the future of critical infrastructure. This is what happened.

The warning system named Oko, a combination of orbiting sensing satellites and ground control computers, was intended to detect the infrared signatures of rockets launched from the continental US vectored toward Soviet territory. But on the morning in question it mistakenly interpreted sunlight reflected off high-altitude clouds as missiles.

Petrov had participated in some of the design and development work on Oko and was aware that it was rushed into service in response to a similar system deployed by the Americans. He knew it had limitations and later acknowledged he suspected it could make mistakes. When the claxons sounded, and the displays shouted 100% confidence, the sole man in the loop with the authority to confirm or question their validity made the right call.

Fortunate for the USSR, the United States, and the rest of the world that he did. Also fortunate that the Oka design allowed for a human decision-maker. One can imagine a process designer keeping humans out of the loop due to their capacity for error, inattention, or latency, in moments when speed and accuracy are of the absolutely highest import.

In the context of CCE Phase 4 candidate out-of-band mitigations, this anecdote is self-explanatory. But suffice it to say that in the nearly 40 years since this episode, we have become ever-more more trusting in the data we receive from automated systems, and as efficiency optimization drives almost all decisions involving process design, it's not hard to imagine greater numbers of critical loops running with little-to-no human involvement. After all, isn't that what we see unfolding everywhere around us in the name of modernization?

PHASE 4 WALKTHROUGH

Identifying Gaps in Expertise

Phase 4 begins with a workshop to review the now-validated CONOPs and ask whether fully sufficient expertise has been applied to the tasks at hand. The first task is to identify additional subject matter experts (SMEs) to review what's been gathered and formulated so far. SMEs, the targeter, analysts, and the PM meet to review the CONOPS for each HCE and probe for gaps in the team's expertise. If and when gaps are detected, the PM's job is to identify and bring in the right new SMEs to support mitigation and protection development.[8] Once the PM and the full team agree that all subject matter bases are covered, the PM then disseminates CONOPS information to all the SMEs to digest.

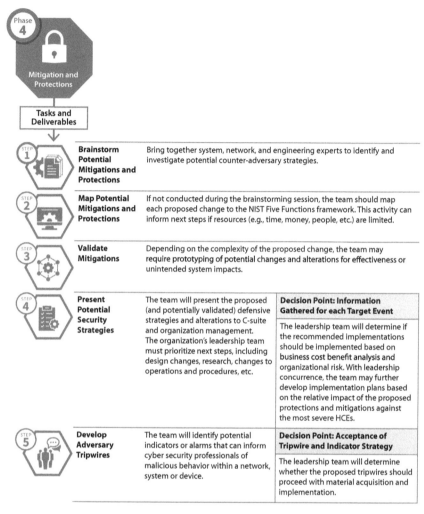

Figure 8.3   Mitigations and Protections Tasks and Deliverables.

Develop and Prioritize Mitigation Options

At this still-early stage of Phase 4 it's time to begin generating draft mitigation options[9] for each CONOPS, with the options prioritized and grouped in order of preference as follows:

- Protect: Whenever possible, this is the far and away the most desired approach. It involves conceiving of engineering change(s) that eliminate the targeter's ability to achieve the goal of the HCE scenario. If there are multiple variations of attack on one target, they can all be defeated by mitigating the target.
- Detect: Deployment of monitoring solutions to detect adversary activity—typically at a chokepoint through which the attack must pass—that enables the entity enough time to mitigate it (i.e., cut it off).
- Respond: Far less desirable than either of the two previous approaches, this one involves designing procedures to respond better/faster to a detection and/or documenting emergency procedures to limit damage of attack (i.e., limit the consequence).
- Recover: Last and least of the four approaches, here the team makes plans and procedures to return functionality after an event. Ideally this is a return to full pre-event functionality; however, if that is not possible, then the goal in the short term is to achieve an acceptable if degraded operational state.

Prioritize Mitigations

Above the prioritization was about preferring the most complete protective measures possible and falling back to less-complete measures only if/when necessary. Here it's about prioritizing recommended actions also included the likely efficacy of the proposed mitigations and protections. To keep it relatively simple we break these into two categories: completely and partially effective approaches:

- Completely effective: Solutions that eliminate the characterization of the event as high consequence (i.e., an HCE); some effect(s) may have nearly occurred, and some effect(s) will possibly continue, but the major impact is entirely eliminated.
- Partially effective: Mitigates and/or minimizes the event but does not entirely eliminate it. May include supply chain changes that are outside of operational control.

Generally speaking, "protect" options are engineered solutions that are completely effective and "detect" options are partially effective.[10] Costs do not play a role until the entity conducts its own cost-benefit analysis. The INL CCE team does not comment on or prioritize based on cost. **See Sidebar: CCE and the NIST Security Framework.**

149

Validate Mitigations

This doesn't happen for every engagement, not even the ones run by INL, but for some of the most serious ones involving one or several National Critical Functions (NCFs), the INL CCE team goes back to the lab to compare mitigations against the CONOPS and HCE criteria to more comprehensively validate the effectiveness of each mitigation. SME knowledge is crucial here, to validate mitigation options and verify that a candidate "solution" is actually effective, often through a high-level simulation. This involves integrating the proposed mitigation with the knowledge base data from Phase 2 and then subjecting that exact system to Phase 3 kill chains and CONOPS. Note: Whenever possible to ensure objectivity, it's a good idea for the validating SMEs to be separate and distinct from the SMEs who generated the options.[11]

Lead by SMEs this is the sequence:

- Run each candidate protection option back through the CONOPS to validate effectiveness
- Determine if there are ways to get circumvent or undermine the protection
- Provide additional protection and/or mitigation options (if needed)

Present and Validate Mitigations with Entity SMEs

Brainstorming Additional Mitigation Options

In this workshop the CCE team meets with entity SMEs to prepare for the presentation to entity seniors by discussing and validating all the options in detail. By now the entity team will likely have specific ideas regarding protections and mitigations and some ideas on how to message them to the CEO and the C-suite. SMEs may add their own cost-benefit analysis and recommendations, while the CCE team makes mitigation recommendations without considering cost or other risk factors. Of course, it's up to the C-suite to determine which to act on.

This sequence:

- The CCE team (Targeter, SMEs, Analysts) presents draft mitigations.
- Combined team repeats internal brainstorming and validation process with the entity SMEs, while the facilitator leads the discussion and the notetaker documents changes.

Present Recommendations to C-Suite

In this penultimate entity-facing step, the presentation is generated, led by analysts and reviewed by the targeter and SMEs. Depending on the nature of the engagement and the composition of the CCE team, the entity's CCE may be the team to revise and add to the presentation or lead development of the recommendation deck themselves.

One the presentation is locked down, it's time to brief the recommendations to the CEO and C-Suite. The CCE Project Manager leads the meeting, with other Execution Team members participating as needed, and ideally when possible, the briefing is led by entity SMEs, not INL.

When the briefing is complete, the final entity-facing step is to develop the final written output report. Prior to delivery, the report must be vetted by the SMEs and the targeter for accuracy and completeness.

Develop Adversary Tripwires (NCF Engagements Only)

With the engagement now officially concluded,[12] there's one more important task for the INL to complete: deriving essential elements of information (EEIs)[13] from each CONOPS. To do this, the INL CCE team uses the CONOPS outputs from Phase 3 to provide input to the Intelligence Community (IC) to inform the development of intelligence requirements for the IC. This does three things:

- It informs the intelligence collection process, providing invaluable input to the IC regarding what is significant adversary activity.
- As potentially helpful threat actor activity information is derived by the IC, both during the engagement as well as once it's concluded, it is communicated to the entity with assistance from INL.
- It informs the process for delivering tear lines—determination of what info can be shared outside of the IC with uncleared commercial entities—back to the entity or sector.

A LONGER LOOK AT NON-DIGITAL MITIGATIONS

Separate from tripwire sensors and other early detection approaches, non-digital mitigations are deployed to keep digital control signals from causing the damage or destruction their sender intended. This will be

151

redundant for some readers, but one thing all non-digital mitigations have in common is they neither use nor rely on anything software-based. The things they do rely on are all physics based, (e.g., gravity, known characteristics of specific alloys or other materials, electron pathways on printed circuits that can be evaluated deterministically, etc.). And one more non-digital approach will sometimes be recommended: reinserting a trusted human—removed from the process at some point via the automation of his or her function—back in the decision loop.

With the increasingly clear connection between security and safety made visible via automated vehicles including cars, drones and passenger jets, innumerable Internet of Things (IoT) devices, and our acceptance of integrated control and safety systems in dangerous industrial environments (see: **Sidebar: Safety System Evolution**), sometimes the best way to more fully secure an Industrial Control System (ICS) is to use methods proven to make a machine or process inherently safe. This excerpt from engineering process safety engineering firm provides a brief introduction to this concept:

> Several safeguards are commonly employed in the process industries that are inherently safe against cyberattack. One of these safeguards, the analog mimic of a digital safety instrumented function (SIF), can be employed to protect a process plant against virtually any conceivable cyberattack. However, the real work of protecting process industry plants lies in making the safeguard selection and installation process thorough and systematic.
>
> The common process industry safeguards that are inherently safe against cyberattack include:
>
> - Pressure relief devices
> - Mechanical overspeed trips
> - Check valves
> - Motor-monitoring devices
> - Instrument-loop current monitor relays (analog SIF mimic)
>
> Several safeguards used in the process industries are inherently safe from a hacker. These devices sense and activate electromechanically or mechanically. Consequently, these safeguards make great layers of protection against a cybersecurity attack that relies on a routable protocol.[14]

SIDEBAR: SAFETY SYSTEM EVOLUTION[15]

One example that informs the INL's team's thinking non-digital mitigations comes from the world of industrial process safety systems, also known as Safety Instrumented Systems (SIS). Up until the 1960s and 1970s, these systems, at the time called Emergency Shutdown Devices (ESDs), were comprised of simple pneumatic, hydraulic, or electromechanical relay circuits with discrete inputs calibrated a customized range of acceptable parameters (e.g., pressure, temperature, vibration, etc.). When readings indicated the system was getting close to an unsafe condition, logic would trip pumps, motors, valves, etc. There was no network, no protocols, and no software for distant bad actors to access and leverage.

But these devices weren't perfect. In fact, as they were prone to failure leading to costly production interruptions, the 1980s saw ESDs replaced by programmable logic controllers, or PLCs. As the name suggests, these were digital computers that were outfitted to support industrial process applications. However, while generally more reliable than ESDs, PLCs too suffered from unacceptably high failure rates, and when they failed, they failed open. Meaning the process(es) they were meant to protect came to a sudden halt until the problem could be diagnosed.

To counter the issue of PLC failures, specialty process safety vendors emerged like August, Triconix, and ICS Triplex created "triple modular redundant" (TMR) configurations with three of everything, including sensors, IO buses, and logic cards. In order to pull this off, these solutions became more complex, with firmware included on the three PLCs and a stand-alone DOS-based programming terminal, which later switched to early versions of the Windows operating system.

The 1990s saw big push for "Open" solutions, with Windows APIs for programming and communications via Ethernet, and Modbus and OPC competing against proprietary protocols. These trends meant that safety systems could now be integrated with other networked systems, including industrial control systems. While some large industrial process users like Exxon valued separation of control & safety for safety reasons, many companies who initially sought to keep these systems independent eventually gave in to the economic and efficiency benefits of fully integrated process and safety systems.

From 2000 onward the trend toward integration and convenience went into overdrive, with fully integrated communications,

HMIs, configuration tools, and more. The market didn't seem to notice or care about the loss of separation and independence, and customers concerns were mollified by vendors who told them their internal development teams operated independently. Today, Exxon still has policy supporting independence, but the company is a rare exception, and even with the TRISIS attack's clear shot across the bow, the following is a list of vendors who make and market integrated control and safety systems:

- ABB
- Emerson
- Siemens
- Schneider
- Honeywell
- Rockwell
- Yokagawa

That said, TRISIS is having some effect. Since 2017 asset owners are paying more attention to standards including IEC 61508, "Functional Safety of Electrical/Electronic/Programmable Electronic Safety-related Systems"[16] for suppliers and IEC 61511 "Functional safety— Safety instrumented systems for the process industry sector"[17] for asset owners. IEC 61511 was updated in 2018 to add a requirement for recurring security assessments.

In the bygone pre-digital, software-less era, safety systems were easy to understand and had failure modes that were well defined. That is good safety design could be verified by deterministic methods. The logic of hardwired circuits and their *and*, *nand*, and *or* gates could be verified with maximal confidence via truth tables that mapped known inputs to known outputs. Then this on the introduction of complexity and what it means to risk:

> Electronic and programmable electronic systems came into use in safety functions during the 1970s. Electronic and programmable electronic systems have indeterminate failure modes. They do not inherently fail into a safe state. They are subject to hidden or latent faults that can be difficult to eliminate. Failure modes and behaviors cannot be completely determined and predicted. Programmable systems, in particular, have hidden complexity, and the complexity has been increasing exponentially for several decades. Complex systems are subject to the risk of systematic

failures, failures caused by errors and failures in the design and implementation of the systems.[18]

Seems unwise to introduce so much uncertainty into domains so inherently dangerous. Wouldn't you want to do just the opposite, especially when there is now the distinct possibility, if not the likelihood in some circumstances, that external actors are in the systems, plotting failure modes of their own. Given that, IEC 61511 provides some insights into the origins and goals of CCE Phase 4:

> There are many hazards in process industries that can lead to loss of containment, resulting in an impact on health, safety, environment and plant assets. Process safety is best achieved by using inherently safe processes. However, when this is not practical or possible, protective systems are required to mitigate the risk of hazards to an acceptable level.[19]

In CCE, for national critical assets, there is no "acceptable level" level of risk beyond. Now that SIS is fully digital and accessible to certain adversaries via their integration with other systems, an "inherently safe" process is one that is also inherently secure.

One old-world example that demonstrably reduces but doesn't eliminate risk to a target or the second-order effects to transportation infrastructure and public health is the steel barrier, augmented with hydraulics, such as the buffer stop shown in Figure 8.4. It's relatively low cost; it relies neither on software nor networks; measuring its effectiveness is a straight-forward process; and it's not an easy thing to sabotage. Or at least, if sabotaged, it would be difficult for any inspector not to notice it.

Figure 8.5 shows an "attack surface disruptor,"[20] a software-free circuit board, custom-printed to allow the safe operation of a large, expensive, and hard-to-replace piece of energy equipment. In fact, you could think of it as a machine safety system in contrast with SISs intended to protect human operators as well as processes. Custom-made and yet comparatively inexpensive, it allows operation only within safe working parameters. The instant the equipment begins to move toward an unsafe boundary, a trip signal is generated putting it into a safe condition.

Of course that trip event is a problem, a costly, unplanned, and unwanted interruption to process-business as usual. And it's going to require a significant amount of incident analysis and forensics to uncover what caused the trip. But considering the alternative: destruction of a

155

Figure 8.4   Train Station Buffer Stop—A Physical Backstop.

Figure 8.5   An Attack Surface Disruptor—An Electromechanical Failsafe. Photo by permission of Ralph Langner and Tim Roxey.

156

long-lead-time-to-replace piece of capital equipment, or perhaps several at once if the attack is horizontal and successful and against a number of the same make and model equipment, guarded by the same protections with the same weaknesses. In that case, defeat once = kill many.

In the realm of processes involving high volume and/or pressure fluids, there are upper bounds to what pipes, pumps, and other related equipment can tolerate. When a fault, human-induced or otherwise, causes a jump in pressure beyond established safety parameters, a rupture disk (see Figure 8.6a) can bring the processes to a quick but safe halt. A more gradual means for avoiding damage or destruction, and one that, depending on design and configuration allows processes to continue, is a pressure relief value (see Figure 8.6b).

Large motors and drives have important roles in many industrial processes and can be damaged or destroyed by excess heat caused by current flow in overload conditions. The most common cooling methods are air or liquid, and if these are disrupted, that too could kill a motor even one operating in otherwise normal parameters. The largest industrial electric motors can be found providing ship propulsion, pipeline compression, and pumped-storage applications with ratings reaching as high as 100 megawatts.[21] While fuses and circuit breakers can provide protection short circuits, ground faults, or overloads, they are not the proper

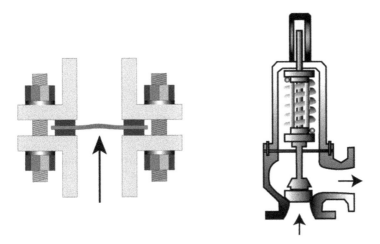

Figure 8.6   (a) A Rupture Disc and (b) Pressure Relief Valve.

157

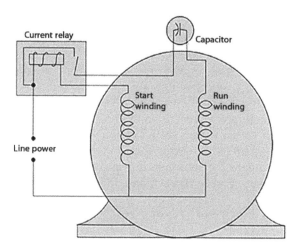

Figure 8.7   Motor Overload Relay.

protection device for motors, as motors pull significantly more amps at startup than their full-load current rating. Any fuse used with a motor would need to be rated to handle this higher startup amp draw; therefore, it would fail to protect the motor from overload conditions beyond normal startup. Circuit-based, non-digital overload relays are designed to allow temporary overloads for a specific period during startup; however, if the overload persists longer than defined by process safety engineers, the overload relay will trip and break the circuit to protect the motor (Figure 8.7).[22]

Humans Back in the Loop

In a 2012 keynote titled "Criticality, Rejectionists, Risk Tolerance," security futurist Dan Geer opined:

> Should we preserve manual means? I say "yes" and I say so because the preservation of manual means is a guarantee of a fall back that does not have a common mode failure with the rest of the interconnected, mutually vulnerable Internet world. That this is not an easy choice is the understatement of the day if not year. I cannot claim to have a fully working model here, but neither do our physicist friends yet have a unified field theory.[23]

In the long-ago days before the arrival of software and cell phones, trusted humans engineers and operators were the essential link between the sensors on a distant machine and other humans back at headquarters or a control center. In the electric sector, substations were often manned by an engineer living in or near the substation. When a voltage reading from six large transformers housed there was needed, a control center operator using a dial-up phone would call the substation engineer to read the voltage meters and report back the findings. At the point, depending on other indicators about the state of the local or regional grid, Fred[24] (Figure 8.8) might get a call back prompting him to increase voltage by 2.5% using the manual tap changer. Once he made the change, he'd then call the control center one more to confirm the update.

Figure 8.8   "Fred's" Truck.
Note: "Early Power Substations and Switching Stations." Water and Power Associates website, accessed January 5, 2020. https://waterandpower.org/ museum/Early_Power_Substations.html.

While it was expensive to maintain such a large cadre of personnel across dozens or hundreds of substations, there simply was no other way to get the job done. Fast forward to now, and the vast majority of substations in the world are remotely monitored and controlled, using a combination of SCADA and inter-substation communication protocols. Their performance with other substations, as well as their adjustments to the continuously changing weather conditions and demand for electricity, is coordinated by complex automation software packages (e.g., energy management systems and distribution management systems).

Only thing is we saw something in Ukraine in 2015 that is impossible to forget. When a Russian cyberattack on multiple distribution companies, including dozens of substations, made it clear that the Ukrainian engineers were no longer operating their own equipment, the utilities were able to dispatch trained and trusted personnel to substations to run important elements of grid equipment without full reliance on automation. In the face on ongoing attacks since then, Ukrainian operators now value the ability to run in less efficient, but more secure and reliable manual mode.

The lesson for CCE Phase 4 here is clear: Social engineering notwithstanding, and until neural link interfaces become more common, humans are non-digital and cannot be hacked. Where they have been completely removed from the industrial process monitoring and control loop, we are 100% dependent on digital systems. For modernized critical infrastructure entities with substantial reliance on automation, this gives them an option they might not have remembered they have. For modernizing entities, it means maybe thinking twice before becoming fully automated and letting your last cadre of trusted engineers retire.

REVISITING PHASE 1'S NEXT-WORST HCES

A decision was made at the end of Phase 1 to select the handful of most catastrophic potential HCEs, those capable of producing the highest consequence events, and the team proceeding on from there. If you recall, this triaging action is performed because CCE is best executed by focusing on a comparatively small number of scenarios, as each requires an intensive focus and a fair amount of effort to produce high-quality Phase 4 Mitigation and Protection recommendations.[25]

What was left on the table, however, were the one or several scenarios that were fleshed out but fell just short of the cut-off threshold. In all likelihood, these scenarios would also produce effects that the entity would find damaging, if not completely unacceptable. So what's needed, after the recommendations have been made to seniors, cost-benefit analysis has been performed to leadership's satisfaction, and mitigations and protections have been put in place, is a return to Phase 1 and a visitation of the next-worst HCEs.[26] Armed with the knowledge and experience the team acquired by conducting a full CCE engagement, the second pass (and all subsequent passes) through the methodology will serve two purposes.

First, it will ensure that the second batch of HCEs gets the examination they deserve. And the experience will reinforce lessons learned the first time through and may help as the entity seeks to make permanent the structural, process, and policy changes needed to achieve and maintain a markedly higher level of confidence in its cybersecurity posture.

CODIFYING CCE'S LEARNINGS IN POLICY

When people hear about CCE for the first time, it's hard for them not to think of it as a new approach for performing cyber assessments, albeit one that begins with the assumption that adversaries have already achieved access, and one that puts great emphasis on the engineering disciplines as sources of risk reduction. And in the pre-engagement preparation activities, as well as in the four phases that follow, it's clear that a principal objective of all this activity is to identify and eliminate the greatest sources of strategic business or US Department of Defense (DoD) mission risk. And that's not wrong.

Over the course of every engagement some entity participants, at first skeptical, begin to understand the nature of the forces allayed against their organization and its most vital functions. CIOs and CISOs who've been doing their level best to keep the entity as cyber secure as possible come to see how even the best cybersecurity programs still leave gaping holes for well-resourced adversaries to climb through. Engineers who previously believed there was no cyber risk to their most important systems and processes learned there was not one but several ways a cyber adversary might reach and establish control. Though most lack the contemporary hands-on engineering or cyber experience of their rank-and-file employees, CFOs and other seniors who've felt that cyber defenses were a necessary precaution to nuisance level risks often come to see that they've been living with a risk far more dangerous than they'd imagined.

These conversion experiences are often so thorough that the best Phase 4 out-briefings to CEOS are conducted by entity personnel themselves. It's then up to the seniors to act on recommendations as they see fit. However, INL doesn't consider the mission fully complete until the lessons of this experience are codified in company policy. It's a cliché to say that cybersecurity needs to be embedded in the culture of organizations, but that's exactly what's intended.[27] When the lessons of the CCE experience are captured in corporate policy and promulgated by leadership to all corners of the company, from operations to procurement, to partners and suppliers, to human resources, etc. so that all significant business decisions are "cyber-informed," then that organization will be far more ready to survive and even thrive in our now "continuously contested"[28] world.

NOTES

1   Please note, however, that while it's tempting to call processes protected these ways "unhackable" it's best not to go there. When persuadable humans inside the entity and throughout the supply chain are targeted by saboteurs wielding immense amounts of money and other forms of compulsion, almost anything can be achieved. Hence, while CCE represents a dramatic improvement over current approaches, it should not be thought of as silver bullet, or the single answer to all critical infrastructure security challenges.

2   Ed Marszal and Jim McGlone, *Security PHA Review for Consequence-based Cybersecurity*. Accessed June 26, 2019.

3   CCE Phase 4—Foundational White Paper *reference*.

4   Ibid.

5   Ibid.

6   Anonymous by request, 2018.

7   Sewell Chan. "Stanislav Petrov, Soviet Officer Who Helped Avert Nuclear War, Is Dead at 77." *New York Times*. Accessed September 18, 2017. www.nytimes.com/2017/09/18/world/europe/stanislav-petrov-nuclear-war-dead.html?smid=nytcore-ios-share.

8   CCE Phase 4—Foundational White Paper *reference*.

9   Note: CCE teams make recommendations only; they do not construct or deploy the non-digital engineered solutions nor do they write code, select sensors or sensor locations. Those decisions are ultimately in the hands of senior decision-makers in conjunction with their hands-on operators, engineers and defenders, etc.

10   CCE Phase 4—Foundational White Paper *reference*.

11   Ibid.

12   Clarification: Though the initial engagement is over, the CCE process should continue at the entity with the next worst HCEs (the one's that didn't reach the Phase 1 cutoff threshold the first time) getting attention.

13   From https://fas.org/irp/doddir/dod/jp2_0.pdf: A description of EEIs in larger context:

> Priority intelligence requirements (PIRs) receive increased levels of intelligence support and priority in the allocation of intelligence resources …. Based on identified intelligence requirements (to include PIRs), the staff develops a series of more specific questions known as information requirements—those items of information that must be collected and processed to develop the intelligence required by the commander. A subset of information requirements that are related to and would answer a PIR are known as essential elements of information (EEIs)—the most critical information requirements regarding the adversary and the Operational Environment (OE) needed by the commander to assist in reaching a decision. The development of information requirements (to include EEIs) leads to the generation of requests for information (RFIs).

14   Edward Marszal and James McGlone. Chapter 6 "Non-Hackable Safeguards" in *Security PHA Review for Consequence-Based Cybersecurity*, accessed June 26, 2019.

15   Phone interview with John Cusimano on Safety Systems evolution, accessed June 14, 2019.

16   "Functional Safety." International Electrotechnical Commission website, accessed January 5, 2020. www.iec.ch/functionalsafety/explained/.

17   International Standard IEC 61511-1. 2003. Web page accessed January 5, 2020. www.sis.se/api/document/preview/562724/.

18   Mitek Generowicz. "Functional Safety: the next edition if IEC 61511." CGErisk.com website, accessed January 5, 2020. www.cgerisk.com/2017/06/functional-safety-the-next-edition-of-iec-61511/.

19   "Functional safety—Safety instrumented systems for the process industry sector—Part 0: Functional safety for the process industry and IEC 61511." IEC Webstore. Web page accessed January 5, 2020. https://webstore.iec.ch/publication/60766.

20   This one designed specifically to thwart "Aurora" style attacks of the kind demonstrated at the Idaho National Lab and discussed earlier. https://spectrum.ieee.org/energywise/energy/the-smarter-grid/unplugging-digital-networks-to-safeguard-power-grids.

21   "Electric Motor." Wikipedia, accessed January 5, 2020. https://en.wikipedia.org/wiki/Electric_motor.

22   Lynn Dreisilker. "Electric Motor Protection: Basics of Overload Relays." Dreisilker Electric Motors, Inc. website, accessed March 14, 2018. https://dreisilker.com/blog/electric-motor-protection-basics-overload-relays/.

23   Daniel E. Geer, Jr. Talk titled "Criticality, Rejectionists, Risk Tolerance." SOURCE Boston, accessed April 18, 2012. http://geer.tinho.net/geer.sourceboston.18iv12.txt.

24   Tim Roxey has referred to Fred and his dog in similar scenarios for many years when discussing their removal from the substation monitoring and control function with the advent of SCADA and automation.

25   INL-EXT-16-40341_Consequence   Prioritization—Updated   4.7.2020   NHJ *reference*.

26   CCE Phase 4—Foundational White Paper *reference*.

27   Ibid.

28   Danzig, Ibid.

9

CCE FUTURES

Training, Tools, and What Comes Next

CCE TRAINING OPTIONS

There may be a little irony here, since Consequence-driven, Cyber-informed Engineering (CCE) itself is less about gaining momentary benefits from going through an assessment, and more about changing the way everyone in an organization understands strategic cyber risks and how they might eliminate or reduce them. So with that established, CCE orientation training in the case of ACCELERATE helps one get prepared to initiate an entity-led, "do it yourself" CCE engagement. And for those who seek to become CCE "black belts" if you will, capable of playing leading roles in NCF-level engagements, CCE Team Training has substantial pre-requisite requirements, is longer, extremely rigorous, and includes extended follow-on supervised on the job training (OJT). In short, it's not for everyone, but those who can complete it successfully will play a major role in helping scale the methodology to reach many more critical infrastructure organizations.

ACCELERATE Workshops

For the first year or two of CCE's existence, all that anyone could find to learn about it were a couple of older and none-too-detailed whitepapers[1] and an article intended primarily for senior decision-makers published by the Harvard Business Review[2] in mid-2018. But starting in early 2019 the core CCE group teamed with the training experts at INL who, among other things, created and still run the renowned, hands-on Industrial Control System (ICS) Cybersecurity 301 training[3] better known at INL's DHS-funded Red Team/Blue Team training.

ACCELERATE is a two-day class, with the following learning objectives:

- Describe the CCE methodology
- Identify roles and responsibilities for a CCE team
- Prioritize consequences (Phase 1)
- Conduct system-of-systems analyses (Phase 2)
- Develop consequence-based targeting (Phase 3)
- Identify mitigations and protections (Phase 4)

ACCELERATE sessions are delivered by INL in three primary scenarios:

- As part of pre-engagement preparation activities for NCF-level organizations about to go through a government-sponsored engagement
- For other entities seeking to put themselves through an internal CCE engagement
- For services firms planning to help entities with their CCE engagements

CCE Team Training

Where ACCELERATE is intended as a lightweight introduction to CCE for anyone about to go through an engagement, CCE Team Training takes place over one full week and is much more intensive. It has significant pre-requites in terms of skills and experience, and the subject matter is difficult enough that it's likely not every student will pass. To test out, using information presented and the CCE Tool Suite, trainees will be able to complete a simulated CCE engagement fulfilling identified roles and responsibilities.

Attendees will need to have substantial experience in one or preferably more of the following categories:

- Engineering and engineering design (e.g., mechanical, electric, fluid, chemical, etc.)
- Electric grid operations
- Weapons systems
- Plant operations
- Safety systems
- Cybersecurity, particularly ICS/OT/embedded systems cybersecurity

The training itself includes an introduction to and training on the CCE application suite and prepares successful students to train future CCE engagement entity participants to perform as CCE team members (train-the-trainer). The intention is to create CCE practitioners and CCE process experts who can facilitate an engagement on site. They will also be expected to train entities on the CCE process.

Learning objectives include:

1 Define CCE
2 Identify roles and responsibilities of the CCE team members
3 Describe CCE methodology
4 Describe pre-engagement activities required to perform a full CCE
5 Complete Phase One: Prioritize consequences
6 Complete Phase Two: Conduct system-of-systems analyses
7 Complete Phase Three: Conduct consequence-based targeting
8 Complete Phase Four: Develop and prioritize mitigation and protection options

The initial evaluation consists of gauging the trainees' ability to demonstrate a baseline understanding of the methodology and demonstrating their skills by fulfilling identified roles and responsibilities in a simulated CCE engagement using case studies. Successful completion of the course and trainee qualification for college education units (CEUs) is dependent upon their performance in a simulated CCE engagement, as well as scoring 80% or better on the final exam. Trainees may also receive additional OJT during an on-site engagement under the direction of a senior team member.

CCE TOOL SUITES AND CHECKLISTS
Tools

NCF-level engagements are supported by access to a suite of custom software tools developed by the lab to standardize and speed up the process, as well as capture and store sector-specific information that may aid future engagements. It's possible if not likely that a version of these tools will eventually be made available to others via commercialization, but at the time of publication they remain proprietary and are reserved only for USG CCE use.

Here's a brief overview of the main modules and what they do for those who use them:

Initial Research—Allows team members to add, organize, view, and edit information relevant to the subject entity during Pre-CCE and Phase 1 activities. This includes both the external and internal collection activities which eventually inform the perfect knowledge database the targeter and others will use to inform their Phase 3 kill chain development.

Event Development—Helps the Phase 1 team develop severity criteria and adjust weighting, generate Events, and Scenarios, and to identify the HCEs that will move on the Phase 2 as a result of scoring higher than the agreed threshold score.

Taxonomy Population—Assists in the construction of taxonomical representations ("tree" structures) of the system or systems related to each HCE. A Taxonomy allows users to visually organize the information, or Artifacts, required in conducting Phase 2: System of Systems Analysis activities. The Taxonomy Population module helps users understand the parts and functions of systems associated with HCEs, and in identifying gaps in collected and available information.

Diagram—Stores and facilitates viewing of diagrams created for HCEs. While the CCE Tool stores documents and files but relies on external programs to create, edit, and view them. Use local system programs (e.g., Visio, Adobe, MindManager, Excel, etc.) to create, edit, and view files stored in the CCE Tool.

Kill Chain Builder—Used to construct Kill Chains, the primary output of Phase 3 activities. The Kill Chain module leverages information added to the Taxonomy Population module to allow

168

users to create diagrams that depict plausible attack paths an adversary might use to achieve an HCE. The ultimate deliverable for those using this module, is the Targeter and others can rank Kill Chains using various indicators, including: special knowledge requirements, degree of difficulty, number of steps, confidence, etc.

Mitigation Collection—This module is used to create, store, and prioritize mitigations, the primary output of Phase 4 activities. For each HCE, users have the ability to tag applicable NIST Framework categories: Protect, Defend, Respond, and Recover. Special knowledge requirements, degree of difficulty, number of steps, confidence—all feed into prioritization calculus for Phase 4 Mitigations and Protections. Phase 3 Kill Chains are only prioritized by impact. Ones found to be not possible are removed or de-prioritized.

An example would be a Kill Chain in which compromise of the safety system is necessary and the safety system is fully air-gapped from the primary controllers. As this would require physical access to compromise these devices, the Kill Chain would likely be eliminated because the perceived risk (e.g., likelihood of occurrence is substantially reduced). Another example might be when, in the course of Kill Chain development, the team determines that the required exploitation is not possible due to a physical or segmented stopgap. In this case, the scenario would be deprioritized or dropped altogether.

Checklists

You can get a good high-level feel for what it's like to prepare for and conduct a CCE engagement by reviewing the questions and attempting to follow the sequential instructions in the checklists included in Appendix B. These same materials are used in the group breakout exercise portions of ACCELERATE training sessions, but even on their own, and especially if you've made it through most of this book, putting oneself in the shoes of people actually conducting an engagement can be quite instructive.

A MORE INHERENTLY SECURE
CRITICAL INFRASTRUCTURE

Certification and Scaling via Partners

In the first year or two, CCE engagements occurred in several ways. First, the US government supported pilot engagements with a handful of energy companies and DoD organizations. Separately, a number of US water utilities took it upon themselves to go through the four phases. And similarly, while other nations were inquiring, a Japanese energy company performed its own internal CCE, and the federal agency charged with securing critical infrastructure in Japan is now teaching CCE principles to early and mid-career engineering and cyber defense professionals.

You could say the United States, from the federal perspective, is doing CCE deep but narrow. The engagements to date with DoD and critical infrastructure organizations have been 6–12 months each, and in order to achieve maximally secure connectivity and share info back and forth with the US Intelligence Community, required laying substantial contractual groundwork, not to mention technical infrastructure.

Outside the United States, we're seeing countries go shallow but wide, meaning whether through policy and/or training, and without the burden (or the benefits) of involvement with their ICS, they are spreading the methodology's emphasis on prioritization, adversarial approaches, and engineered mitigations comparatively quickly.

And back in the United States, the water sector, which falls under the sector-specific agency (SSA) oversight of the US Environmental Protection Agency (EPA), is having to demonstrate the adequacy of its cyber preparations for the first time in 2020, and the sector is introducing CCE's engineering emphasis into its cyber assessment activities. Some utilities have performed their own internal CCE assessments, though not necessarily performing all four phases in full. Others have teamed with engineering services firms who've picked up the methodology and run with it.

But CCE will not go broad and deep until a large cadre of trained, certified, and experienced professionals is created to bring engagements. This begins with CCE team training as described above but will greatly expand when engineering firms and consequence-focused cyber defense consultancies get trained and grow trainers of their own, en masse.

Ensuring Cybersecurity for Safety

In 1974 a chemical plant in the village of Flixborough in northeastern England exploded killing several dozen plant workers and wounding many dozens more. This tragedy prompted chemical safety engineer Trevor Kletz to inquire about the assumptions that led engineers to allow a huge amount of highly explosive chemicals to be processed at temperatures and pressures where one or several engineering design decisions produced catastrophic results. Perhaps the most memorable and impactful result of the proceedings that followed was the definition of an IST—inherently safer technology (or sometimes design or process)—the short version of which reads:

> IST permanently eliminates or reduces hazards to avoid or reduce the consequences of incidents.[4]

This now-fundamental concept in the safety world is very much aligned with how CCE considers cyber risk, with often substantial safety implications, during the design and operational phases of complex industrial processes.

In industrial sectors, though many plant and process designers remain unaware of the inseparable union, cybersecurity and safety are now fully wed. We have the TRISIS/Triconix attack in Saudi Arabia for elevating public awareness, but as discussed in Chapter 8, process safety engineers have been aware of the risk of connecting digital safety systems to digital control systems for a long time. Today, even with good network segmentation and other well-implemented cyber hygiene controls, pathways exist for certain attackers to achieve access, pivot to the ICS network and control systems, and from there reach some safety systems. More than ever it's clear you can't ensure safety if you don't have very sound cybersecurity in place, and this holds true in the consumer realm (e.g., vehicles, home automation) just as much as in industrial plants.

Sometimes working back from logical extremes can help one plot a better course. On the opposite end of the spectrum from an insecure, cyber-dependent ICS is a hypothetical fully secure system: Its digital elements are unplugged and unpowered, their memory is wiped, every communication port is closed, and input–output devices are destroyed or removed. Lastly, it's buried at least six feet but preferably more feet underground. Not much utility in that approach, right?

So we're tasked with identifying and then moving toward a middle ground (skewed more than a little closer to security than we are at present) that maximizes operational benefits while minimizing security risks and therefore safety risks—which by the way are also operational risks. Industry is going to continue to innovate (see next section) and claim to be doing so in a safe and secure fashion, but with a focus on unacceptable consequences, and given the track record, we cannot afford to take infrastructure companies at their word. We're intent on finding ways of constraining cyber risk particularly for things that are too important, or too dangerous, to fail, and of driving that risk as close to absolute zero probability as possible.

Policy Prognostications

Whether it's to standards, frameworks, best practices, or mandatory policies, just exactly how much security is achieved by compliance is unclear. There's no end of commentary online and at conferences about the detrimental effects of compliance cultures. Money spent achieving and demonstrating compliance to others arguably might have made a greater impact on improving security posture had it been left to the entity's discretion.

In addition to the early engagements and training sessions, some non-US governments and one US critical infrastructure sector have moved to incorporate elements of CCE into policy. In particular, its emphasis on leveraging engineering skills and knowledge to achieve demonstrable improvements in security and thereby, safety. Credit agencies and cyber insurers are motivated to ascertain financially quantifiable cyber risk exposure, and there appears to be an appetite, if not a hunger for something more tangible, a return on security investment more measurable.

Tim Roxey's Aurora Attack Surface Disruptor (ASD) is designed to disallow destructive consequences to important elements of the electric grid and other equipment essential in large industrial operations. It's about as big as a hockey puck and contains a custom board with the logic captured in circuitry. Powered by a long-life battery, there's no software, no digital connectivity, and it can be tested for effectiveness via deterministic methods. That's also the case for some of the protective measures recommended by CCE, and why in some cases it "takes the target off the table" by removing the adversary's ability to create the effect they're seeking. These protections can be proven/demonstrated to be effective, whereas one never knows how much protection they're getting with a 1,000-user antivirus subscription, a managed security provider (MSP) contract, email security, two-factor authentication, recurring user training, pen testing, 100 firewalls, 10 intrusion detections systems, and more feeding a security incident and event management system (SIEM) in their Security Operations Center (SOC).

In 2018, INL fielded an inquiry from international researchers looking at how to best secure the ITER—the International Thermonuclear Experimental Reactor—the largest fusion energy experiment to date. CCE concepts formed the core of our recommendations for how to cyber protect what is sure to be a tempting target to cyber bad actors. The researchers reported they were looking at astronomical costs to deploy and maintain traditional cyber hygiene defenses at ITER, and it seemed, at least at first blush, that there might be ways to "engineer out" some of the cyber risk and help keep the program's cybersecurity expenses more down to Earth.[5]

Outside advertising,[6] few business domains spend more money on a capability with benefits so difficult to measure. In most sectors, the way we've chosen to measure security so far is the path of compliance. This is security by inference, as in, if your company is seen to be performing generally accepted good security behaviors, then we will infer that you are more secure than if you were not. The bulk electric sector in North America remains the only industrial sector to have mandatory security controls promoted with few carrots but enforced with North American Electricity Reliability Commission's (NERC's) sizable-fine sticks.

One might think nuclear power plants would get at least as much cyber oversight and perhaps they do, but if a recent audit of the Nuclear Regulatory Commission's (NRC's) approach to regulating cyber controls[7] is any indicator, it sounds like a strategy that depends on a fair amount of hope and hygiene as well:

> NRC's cyber security inspections generally provide reasonable assurance that nuclear power plant licensees adequately protect digital computers, communication systems, and networks associated with safety, important-to-safety, security, and emergency preparedness…. Additionally, the current cyber security inspection program is risk-informed but not yet fully performance based. The cyber security inspection program has not identified performance measures because of technical and regulatory challenges in program implementation, and there are challenges in predicting the level of effort required to conduct inspections.

The "challenges" cited arise from the indeterminate nature of the efficacy of cyber defenses against adaptive and ever evolving cyber threat actors. For indeterminate, we might easily substitute "unknown" or "variable,"[8] both words that accurately describe how much confidence we can

173

ascribe current hygiene-based approaches to cybersecurity. As IT controls replaced earlier physical engineered controls, risk analytics thought (or maybe hoped is the right word), they'd be good enough to be a full replacement. But while printed circuits that can be evaluated deterministically are still in use as final line of safety at US nuke plants, they are steadily being replaced by software.

Every critical infrastructure sector, including the ones slowest to modernize, allows the unknown into their operations as they embrace automation, tolerate convenient connectivity to safety systems that shouldn't be tolerated, and allow their employees' skills to atrophy. Referenced in Chapter 1, automation systems are "competitive cognitive artifacts,"[9] meaning as we become dependent on them, our own knowledge and competencies decline, and later we lack the skills and knowledge to recreate the engineered systems we once knew enough to build and run.

The words below, crafted by former NERC CISO and nuclear power plant risk analyst Tim Roxey, are an attempt to help codify the necessary shift back to engineering *terra firma* for critical infrastructure. Roxey first introduced these words at the National Academy of Science in late 2019:

> Those systems, structures, or components deemed necessary to protect the health and safety of the public (nuclear energy context) or deemed critical via relevant regulations for non-nuclear CIKR[10] SHALL be protected by systems that can be shown effective via deterministic methods. This means formal methods for SQA— Software Quality Analysis and other appropriate testing for physical systems such as structures or components.[11]

This was briefed at the US National Academy of Science in late 2019, and the intent is to inform new procurement language that would drive suppliers to certain classes of entities to deliver systems and products that are demonstrably secure and therefore can give owners and operators more confidence in their safety systems and processes. But whether by policy or by market forces that—propelled in part by cyber insurers and credit ratings firms—eventually reward suppliers who build and market inherently more secure offerings, it's clear the current approach to cybersecurity, especially of critical infrastructure entities, is not sustainable.

Other potentially helpful language intended to inform legislation was developed by the bi-partisan Cybersecurity Solarium Commission co-chaired by Senator Angus King and Representative Michael Gallagher. Among other recommendations, the Commission's report calls for a "Critical Technology Security Center" including:

A Center for Connected Industrial Control Systems Security to test the security of connected programmable logic controllers, supervisory control and data acquisition servers and systems, and other connected industrial equipment.[12]

The center described might be just the place to put Roxey's language into practice.

Emerging Technology Only Elevate CCE's Importance

Most of these technologies are already with us, but their eventual fully realized impact remains years in the distance.

- IoT = connectivity that's even more pervasive and ubiquitous in every aspect of our work and personal lives.
- 5G = much more data in motion at much higher speeds, enabling new, previously unimaginable applications.
- AI = as the algorithms begin to improve themselves, automation is transitioning from human decision logic encoded in software to alien decision logic encoded in inscrutable black boxes.
- Quantum Computing = appears to have the potential to increase processing power enormously and its ability to break RSA encryption will definitely have a profound impact and will force us to update the ways in which some aspects of cybersecurity are accomplished.

Each of these adds immense new complexities and uncertainties. Blended they will produce a multitude of unknown unknowns. Taken together, all four only serve to make the cybersecurity professional's job vastly more difficult, and it's going to be difficult to resist the temptation to throw more buzzword-bearing digital cybersecurity technologies at the problem. The cybersecurity professional is going to need a huge helping hand from outside her domain of expertise. Perhaps we are at a tipping point where those responsible for managing risk will see a return to first principles engineering design concepts as the best and perhaps only means to keep these challenges within bounds we can all live with.

Injecting Cyber into Engineering Curricula

Not only does it remain unusual for courses on cybersecurity to be required in undergraduate computer science curricula, unless the college or university is struck by a cybersecurity attack, it is similarly unlikely for the word to be even uttered during any of the four years a student is earning a degree in mechanical, chemical, civil, electrical, aviation, or any of the other classic engineering degrees.

And yet, everything—literally everything—uses or is dependent upon computer-based technology now. They are part of the design process, parts sourcing, fabrication, testing and certification, logistics and delivery, and support. And that list doesn't include the fact that related technologies are an essential part of many products and services themselves. How is it possible, then, that we expect workers to "bolt-on" security knowledge to their college experience with any more efficacy than companies and government agencies attempt to address security matters only after acquiring the systems upon which they depend?

Let us consider moving from legacy mitigation to future designs via CIE and CCE—both fundamentally about culture change—on our existing critical infrastructures and engineered functions and with a focus of consequence prioritization while recognizing the cyber realities of our present near-term future technologies. CCE's Phase 2 Systems-of-Systems Analysis and Phase 3 consequence-based targeting are applied to already designed and operating facilities and systems—legacy infrastructure. Equally important is the need to fundamentally change how we design new systems and the to-be-created technologies of the future. Instead of applying the security technology at the end of the design process (integration of market-driven technology), we should consciously and holistically design cyber-physical system with security in mind throughout all stages—just as we do for safety.

Wayne Austad, Technical Director of INL's Cybercore OT security organization, riffs on Marty Edwards' "Think like a hacker, act like an engineer," like this:

> Looking at CIE's V-Model of a systems design lifecycle, there is a series of steps that start with concept and requirements through formal testing and operations. To embrace security as culture like we've done with safety, there are principles to apply well before "systems integration" and engineering/risk fixes applied to existing operations. A framework of "1st Principles" should guide what a good design process looks like. These first principles drive the creation of methods and measures as well as the models and tools that assist designers as they create and validate their work. First versions of these principles were developed and published

as part of an International Atomic Energy Agency effort.[13] Now, in cooperation with university partners, the methods and trial cases studies are being developed with goal to impact the curriculum and textbooks for the engineers of the future. This is important and diverse effort—the risks and designs for a chemical engineer is very different than a power engineer, even if they use similar or same digital controllers.

Last Word

I came in contact with all kinds of folks as I was assembling material for this book. This piece—a caution and a hint from an anonymous observer[14]—struck me for both its ominous tone as well as its upward-inflected ending:

> Please remember a tiny thing if you will. The adversary has someone like me working for them. In a manner of speaking—if I were with your adversary, I would **deny you** the use of Detection or Mitigation and then **shove you** into a design basis accident. Your day would be difficult. You could prevent me or temper my efforts through CCE.

From a US national security perspective, the strategic concerns for the nation expressed in a 2017 Defense Science Board report likely are shared by all nations:

> The unfortunate reality is that for at least the coming five to ten years, the offensive cyber capabilities of our most capable potential adversaries are likely to far exceed the United States' ability to defend and adequately strengthen the resilience of its critical infrastructures.[15]

One desirable outcome of a broad adoption of CCE principles will be to sap the confidence of top-tier attackers that their efforts will create the damaging or disruptive effects they intend. This would be a boost to what some in national leadership positions call deterrence by denial, as in "deterrence by denial operates by reducing the expected benefits of attack."[16] Thanks to the early vision and gigantic efforts of Mike Assante, Curtis St. Michel, Sarah Freeman, and numerous others at INL and elsewhere building up and fleshing out the methodology, we now have the ability to begin deterring the most damaging attacks and save the day.

NOTES

1 Sarah Freeman et al. "Consequence-Driven Cyber-Informed Engineering (CCE)." Accessed October 18, 2016. www.osti.gov/biblio/1341416-consequence-driven-cyber-informed-engineering-cce and Joseph D. Price and Robert S. Anderson. "Cyber-Informed Engineering: The Need for a New Risk Informed and Design Methodology." Accessed June 1, 2015. www.osti.gov/biblio/1236850-cyber-informed-engineering-need-new-risk-informed-design-methodology.

2 Andy Bochman. "The End of Cybersecurity." Harvard Business Review, accessed May 31, 2018. https://store.hbr.org/product/the-end-of-cybersecurity/BG1803.

3 "Training Available through ICS-CERT." DHS Cybersecurity and Infrastructure Security website, accessed January 5, 2020. www.us-cert.gov/ics/Training-Available-Through-ICS-CERT#workshop.

4 "Final Report: Definition for Inherently Safer Technology in Production, Transportation, Storage, and Use." The Chemical Security Analysis Center, US Department of Homeland Security. June 2010. www.aiche.org/sites/default/files/docs/embedded-pdf/ist_final_definition_report.pdf.

5 From interviews with Andy Bochman conducted with consultants from Thales UK Limited in late 2018 and early 2019.

6 And advertising has gotten much more measurable on mobile devices and the web.

7 "Audit of NRC's Cyber Security Inspections at Nuclear Power Plants, OIG-19-A-13." Office of the Inspector General, US Nuclear Regulatory Commission, accessed June 4 2019. www.oversight.gov/sites/default/files/oig-reports/OIG-19-A-13-Audit%20of%20NRC%27s%20Cyber%20Security%20Inspections%20at%20Nuclear%20Power%20Plants%20Final%20Report%28BXK%29.pdf.

8 Thomas Becker and Volker Weispfenning. *Gröbner Bases: A Computational Approach to Commutative Algebra*. Springer, New York, NY. 1993. Cited by Wolfram MathWorld on page named "Indeterminate." Accessed January 5, 2020. http://mathworld.wolfram.com/Indeterminate.html.

9 David Krakauer, President, and William H. Miller, Professor of Complex Systems at the Santa Fe Institute, calls technologies that obviate the need for human mastery of once-common skills: competitive cognitive artifacts. On Sam Harris podcast (transcript), accessed November 13, 2016. https://samharris.org/complexity-stupidity/.

10 CIKR = Critical Infrastructure and Key Resources.

11 Included in brief by Tim Roxey to the Committee on Computing, Communications, Cyber Resilience, and the Future of the US Electric Power System, at the National Academy of Sciences, Washington DC, accessed November 1, 2019.

12 Cybersecurity Solarium Commission Report, section 4.1.1, accessed March 11, 2020. www.solarium.gov.
13 R. Anderson et al. "Cyber-informed Engineering." INL/EXT-16-40099 Rev 0. March 2017.
14 Received via email November 6, 2019.
15 Defense Task Force report on Cyber Deterrence, February 2017. p. 4.
16 Ibid.

ACKNOWLEDGMENTS

Three individuals played an outsized role in bringing Consequence-driven, Cyber-informed Engineering (CCE) and this book about it to life. Mike Assante and Curtis St. Michel created the spark, nursed it to a blaze, laid down the conceptual framework, briefed and re-briefed US government seniors until the messages stuck. They were joined by Idaho National Laboratory (INL) super analyst and cowriter Sarah Freeman in describing the four-phase approach and executing the first-ever CCE engagement. This could not have happened without the advocacy of INL Cybercore director Scott Cramer and the staunch support of Florida Power & Light CEO Eric Silagy. Thanks also to Florida Power & Light's (FP&L's) Ben Miron, CCE's first encounter with the real world proved to be a tremendous success, and since then Miss Freeman's contributions have proved essential, helping the INL team build a solid structure atop the well-laid foundation. Mike is gone now, and Sarah is continuing to move mountains. But all that said, though: no Curtis, no CCE. No Sarah, no CCE or CCE book.

It's impossible to adequately convey enough appreciation to Mike's wife Christina. During two intensive bouts of cancer treatments separated by approximately 10 years of remission in between, Chris was the rock that miraculously held everything together, ensuring their children Alex, Anabel, and Asher were immersed in love no matter the gathering dark clouds.

An essential partner in the larger Industrial Control Systems (ICS) security story, particularly in the field of training and workforce development, is Tim Conway. Tim was Mike's close friend and right-hand man in the construction of ICS curriculum at SANS and continues to this day, developing and delivering new courses. In all, he's trained and educated thousands of early- and mid-career professionals, in the United States and around the world in this increasingly crucial domain and shows no signs of stopping.

To be sure, senior executives at the lab own a share of the credit. That's INL director Mark Peters who approved CCE as one of only a highest priority lab initiatives, Zach Tudor, who runs the National and Homeland Security (N&HS) Directorate and who insisted this book be written, and Zach's predecessor in that position, Brent Stacey, who provided valuable insight and encouragement during the early stages. Finally, thanks to Dan Elmore, who half a dozen years or so recruited me into the Critical Infrastructure Protection division of N&HS.

Support and guidance from the Department of Energy (DOE's) recently established Cybersecurity, Energy Security, and Emergency Response (CESER) office proved essential to the development of CCE. The most significant contributions came from notably principal deputy assistant secretary Sean Plankey, senior technical advisor Ed Rhyne, and CESER's first director Karen Evans. Also instrumental over the long run has been principal deputy assistant secretary in DOE's Office of Electricity Delivery and Energy Reliability, Pat Hoffman.

The first time any concept is put into practice is simultaneously full of potential and fraught with peril. Yeoman's work from these three Florida Power & Light professionals: Tom Beck, Tom Atkins, and Rob Adams, helped ensure the initial pilot was an unqualified success.

Crucial for getting the manuscript across the finish line was senior internal editor Michelle Farrell. As providence would have it, she joined the lab and dove into the book project at just the right time to drive high-quality text, graphics, and formatting. This thing would have been a mess without her sage guidance over the final several months.

Analyst Kara Turner provided outstanding editorial support, as did her Cybercore colleagues Jeff Gellner, David Kuipers, Nathan Johnson, Stacey Cook, Cory Baker, Steve, Rawson, Matthew Reif, Theo Miller, Brandon Odum, Matthew Kress-Weitenhagen, and Douglas Buddenbohm.

The list of other INL professionals who played pivotal roles includes: CCE PM Rob "Too Tall" Smith, Rob Helton, Tom Andersen, Joseph Price, Ginger Wright, Wayne Austad, Rita Foster, Chris Spirito, Rob Hoffman, Bob Anderson, Craig Rieger, Vergle Gipson, Rob Pate, and the core CCE team: Jeff Klingler, Amanda Belloff, Chuck Forshee, Megan Kommers, Jeff Gellner, Colleen Glenn, Stacey Cook, Greg Jentzsch, Nathan Johnson, and Matthew Reif. Also, INL's Steve Hartenstein, Eric Barzee, and Jon Cook deserve a shout-out as their guidance in the run-up to signing with the publisher was supremely helpful, not to mention the commercialization discussions and bearing the brunt of the patent process. Appreciation to Ethan Huffman for essential marketing and messaging leadership. And I really wouldn't be able to do much on time or under budget without often daily assistance from INL's Debbie Payne, Rhee Lusk, and Dori Nelson.

INL alum and former ICS-CERT director Marty "Think Like a Hacker, Act Like an Engineer" Edwards has been banging the CCE drum at RSA and other high visibility venues almost since its inception. To say he got early, and helped many others get it, would be an absurd understatement.

We owe a heaping helping of respect and appreciation to four intellectual giants, all who played an enormous part in OT security education and in certain elements of this book. They are: former Secretary of the Navy Richard Danzig, former NERC CISO and E-ISAC Director Tim Roxey, former Assistant Secretary of Defense Paul Stockton, and cyber luminary Dan Geer. Rarely can I get through a conference presentation or a conversation with senators, representatives, or their staffers without leaning on the wisdom of at least one of them.

Reviewers of early drafts steered the text in ways that produced profound improvements. Among them we count Paul Stockton, Mark Weatherford, Sean Plankey, Eireann Leverett, Jason Larsen, and Sean Mcbride.

Mark Listewnik, Katie Horsfall, and the rest of the team at CRC Press, Taylor & Francis have made our job getting this book across the finish line so much easier than we anticipated. And thanks to INL's Ron Fisher and Mike Fagel of Argonne National Lab who connected us. And while on the subject of publishers, I am indebted to the two-man team at Harvard Business Review who built a "Big Idea" on Cyber around CCE, Steve Prokesh and Scott Berinato, as well as to Michael Sulmeyer, of Harvard's Kennedy School who introduced us. Some say national labs aren't particularly focused on marketing, and the HBR article and cheesy case studio it contained carried much of the messaging and awareness burden for nearly three years.

For their contributions to OT and critical infrastructure security knowledge and education large and small, and in many cases, friendship, the following have all played a role we want to acknowledge here: Dale Peterson, Eric Byers, Art Conklin, Bruce Schneier, Ralph Langner, Rob M. Lee, Chris Sistrunk, Monta Elkins, Mark Bristow, Steve Dougherty, Jack Danahy, Joe Weiss, Stuart Brimley, Patrick Miller, Steve Parker, Jacob Kitchel, Slade Griffin, Erich Gunther, Jason Dely, Cherrie Black, Ralph Ley, Bob Timpany, Chris Peters, Stacy Bresler, Justin Searle, Joe Slowak, Josh Corman, Arthur House, Miles Keogh, Joel Gordes, Billy Rios, Jack Whitsitt, Bobby Brown, Kai Thomsen, Daniel Thanos, Beau Woods, Juliette Okafor, Lynn Costantini, Sam Chinoski, Jennifer Silk, Bryson Bort, Isiah Jones, Liza Malashenko, Jim McGlone, Bryan Owen, Tobias Whitney, John Cusimano, Jacob Kitchel, Daniel Groves, Andrew Ohrt, Tyson Meadors, Darren Highfill, Stuart Brindley, Steen Fjalstad, Russ Johnson, Andre Ristaino, Massoud Amin, Matthew Carpenter, Ross Johnson,

Andrew Hildick-Smith, Kevin Morley, Ernie Hayden, Andrew Ginter, Keith Flaherty, Chris Villarreal, Gus Serino, Mark Fabro, Mike Toecker, Joel Langill, Bryan Singer, Bob Radvanosky, Ron Brash, Ben Miller, Jamie Sample, Sam Chanoski, Samara Moore, Bill Lawrence, Peter Singer, August Cole, Scott Aaronson, David Batz, Cynthia Hsu, Jason Christopher, Monta Elkins, Michele Guido, Jens Wiesner, Sarah Fluchs, Tomomi Aoyama, Koichi Tsuneda, Koji Ina, Hiroshi Sasaki, Javier Diéguez Barriocanal, and Samuel Linares.

Lastly, thanks to my sig other Tracy Staedter for not merely tolerating the prolonged disruption to our work-life balance, but as a professional science writer, offering up some excellent suggestions on structure and tone.

Apologies to anyone we've neglected to mention. A quality beer or whiskey will be your reward when you make the grievous omission known to us.

GLOSSARY

Actionable intelligence Information shared by the intelligence community or private cyber intelligence field that allows for meaningful changes to be made by the private sector in order to improve their security posture.

Actions One of four elements required to fully understand an adversary's technical approach. Actions refer to the conditions or steps the adversary must accomplish to initiate the payload. Actions may also describe what the payload will do once it's initiated.

Advanced persistent threat (APT) Often used to describe nation-state cyber intrusions and long-term unauthorized access into a network. APT activity can be used to track growth or capability within the field of cyber intelligence (e.g., APT 1, APT 28, Energetic Bear etc.).

Adversary Synonymous with attacker, adversaries discussed in CCE are the individuals or organizations that seek to cause damage and destruction to victim organizations via cyber-enabled sabotage.

Adversary intent This refers to desired outcome (or outcomes) of cyber-enabled sabotage, similar to an adversary's objective. Common examples include financial loss, damage to public reputation, and physical damage, within the area of critical infrastructure.

Aggregation Individually insensitive or apparently unimportant items or information that in an aggregate reveal a system, objective, requirement, plan, or other aspect of your business mission, the disclosure of which would provide insight into sensitive or mission critical activities, capabilities, vulnerabilities, or methods of your business. Information amassed or collected in one location should be protected.

Analyst The analyst role includes collecting, compiling, and analyzing information to find relevant data. Using structured analytical techniques, the analyst will identify gaps and conduct further research to fill those gaps. Understand how to document, organize, and access data stored in a database. Use critical thinking skills to come to conclusions based on research done.

Association The significance of information often depends upon its context. Therefore, when two unique and innocuous pieces of information are considered together, they may reveal sensitive information.

Assumptions Within the context of CCE, assumptions represent the core foundation of the CCE philosophy, namely that a well-resourced, determined, and sophisticated adversary can bypass the security controls of an organization. Typically defined as: (1) if targeted by an advanced cyber-adversary, organizations will be compromised, (2) traditional IT security is focused on cyber hygiene and insufficient to repel non-targeted attacks, (3) critical infrastructure, and the complex systems created to control it, was designed to meet engineering requirements, not security requirements. Other common assumptions include that the adversary is knowledgeable, well-resourced, and has achieved access. Assumptions are set prior to or during the first phase of CCE.

Attack breadth One of the severity criteria developed during Phase 1 of CCE describes the extent to which a targeted technology or system is deployed resulting in adverse operational effects. The greater the span of impacted systems, the more difficult the restoration following an adverse event.

Attack node Synonymous with technical target, the attack node is the location where the primary payload must be deployed.

Attack path The steps an adversary takes to navigate a target, typically in reference to network operations.

Attack step This is the final step of cyber-enabled sabotage. This step is within the deployment stage of the CCE Kill Chain.

Attack tree A model in cybersecurity that depicts all the motions of an adversary (sequence of events) that can lead to control of a particular resource.

BIOS Basic input/output system. Non-volatile firmware that initializes hardware at computer system startup.

Black box research Open-source research conducted with no inside knowledge from the entity.

Blended attacks Cyber-enabled sabotage combined with traditional, kinetic effects in order to increase the impact or severity of the attack (e.g., initiating physical damage to multiple transformers while simultaneously damaging energy management system [EMS] servers).

Boundary conditions The combination of the objective and the scope. Boundary conditions establish the thresholds for which impacts would be too devastating or substantial to critical functions or services. This is an understanding of how an adversary's intent is able to become a high-consequence event that can be examined using the CCE methodology.

CCE engagement The process of reviewing one's architecture through the CCE methodology.

CCE Kill Chain   Used to visualize the process and steps an adversary would take during a cyber-enabled sabotage attack. The CCE Kill Chain is used to illustrate an adversary's actions and objectives, starting with the end effect and working backward. The main reason for this method is based on CCE's focus on understanding (and ultimately disrupting) the requirements (critical information needs) an adversary needs to achieve the end effect.

CCE team   The group of people at the organization (including third-party participants from government and industry) working on CCE activities.

CCE tool belt   A proprietary software program developed to document CCE engagement information.

Choke point   A node within the environment of a critical function (such as a person, piece of information and/or equipment) that the adversary needs to know/manipulate/engage to facilitate sabotage.

CIE   Cyber-informed engineering. The concept that modern cybersecurity of industrial control systems should consider the cyber implications of an engineering design in all stages of a system's lifecycle, just as with reliability and safety.

Command and control (C2)   The C2 phase involves the adversary establishing remote access to the organization's system of interest using either in-band communications over the corporate network or remote out-of-band communications via cellular networks or other means.

Concept of operations (CONOPS)   A description of the actions necessary to achieve an end goal. In relation to Phase 3, it refers to the ends, ways, and means by which an adversary achieves a desired outcome. See also: Attack scenario.

Conditional trigger   A mechanism that an adversary employs to remotely initialize a payload after some pre-programmed conditions are met. Although a basic timer does represent one type of conditional trigger, the phrase typically refers to code that initializes after a more complex situation is reached (e.g., disabling lubrication oil system of a turbine generator at system startup).

Consequence   Within CCE, the impact an adverse event resulting from cyber-enabled sabotage.

Consequence Prioritization   The first step or Phase 1 in CCE, during which a participating organization identifies potential adverse events that could, potentially, result from cyber-enabled sabotage. The most severe of these events are defined as high-consequence events or HCEs.

187

Consequence-based targeting The third phase of CCE. The information gathered throughout Phase 2 is applied to a targeting exercise with the end goal of identifying potential attack scenarios and choke points.

Consequence-driven, cyber-informed engineering (CCE) An INL-developed methodology that provides an alternative and surgical approach to traditional cyber security risk mitigation approaches. The CCE methodology addresses existing exploits, current and future vulnerabilities, and potential process and organizational weaknesses in an organized fashion based on the potential impact of cyber-enabled sabotage. The CCE methodology represents one approach under the umbrella of the CIE philosophy.

Cooperative research and development agreement (CRADA) An agreement between a government agency and private company to work together on research and development.

Critical functions and services Those actions or activities that comprise a business organization's primary purpose (e.g., the generation, transmission, and delivery of electricity to a utility customer; a military organization's primary mission). In many cases, an organization will meet these critical functions and services by relying on specific technologies or processes (e.g., a municipal utility's reliance on a Distribution Management System [DMS]). Participating organizations identify critical functions and services during Phase 1, Consequence Prioritization, as a precursor to HCE development.

Critical need Key data that an adversary must acquire in order to successfully sabotage a system. By identifying this data, a participating organization determines information that can serve as indicators or tripwires of adversary activity.

Cyber-event An event, as defined for CCE, that specifically requires cyber-related efforts by an adversary. Written down, they include a description of the end effect as well as a brief, high-level explanation of the cyber means that could be employed. This term precludes events that are caused solely by natural disaster, face-to-face interaction from an adversary, or methods that do not include (even partially) the use of cyber means. In Phase 1, after events are brainstormed, those determined to be achievable by cyber means are considered to be potential high-consequence events (HCEs) that should be evaluated and are termed cyber-events.

Cyber hygiene Practices when using computer technologies that are aimed at improving the cybersecurity of a given user or organization. These practices may include the use of firewalls, antivirus software, prompt software updating/patching, strong password rules, multi-factor authentication, encrypted communications protocols, etc.

Cyber intrusion   Cyber intrusion is an attempt by the adversary to gain access to the system of interest. Access may be achieved via a variety of methods, such as targeted internet-based drive-by attacks, social engineering, vulnerable services exposed to the Internet, affecting the supply chain, or insertion by trusted insiders.

Cyber-enabled sabotage   A focused attack upon an organization, which causes disruption, degradation, or destruction of critical functions or services through the use of cyber means. This is not limited to network attacks, as supply chain, third-party dependencies, and insider threats are all possible avenues for cyber-enabled sabotage.

Cyber-physical attack   Cyber-enabled sabotage that results in physical damage (e.g., Stuxnet).

Cyber-physical effect   Cyber-enabled sabotage that results in changes to the physical environment (e.g., 2015 Ukrainian cyber-attack).

Data collection plan   While conducting a System-of-Systems Analysis, the ability to track down key details about documents, information, devices, protocols, software, vendors, and other items of interest is imperative. Key question words to consider when attempting to gather all relevant information include who, where, what, why, when, and how.

Data protection   This is completed before data collection activities begin and refers to the manner in which the entity, INL, government partners, and any other CCE participants agree to handle and secure the information and materials gathered, as well as the outputs generated, the analysis performed, and any other details deemed necessary to protect while performing a CCE engagement. It provides details about all regulations, classifications (if applicable), locations, accesses, disclosures, information sharing, transmission methods, etc. that are to be observed, applied, or allowed for a specific CCE engagement.

Deployment   The steps, movements, and actions that an adversary performs to reach a target. This stage of the CCE Kill Chain includes the Payload Delivery and Attack steps while incorporating Targeting and Information Gathering for each of these steps.

Design vulnerability   A weakness within a digital device or component based on the foundational design.

Detect   Refers to the timely discovery of adversarial activities. Within Phase 4, recommended mitigations and protections are classified by

Protect, Detect, Respond, and/or Recover, with preference placed on Protect.

Development stage   The technical requirements for the payload(s) that will be delivered to cause the HCE.

Duration of outage   The length of time of interruption to key services (e.g., electricity delivery, production interruption, etc.)

End effect   Within CCE, the final result of cyber-enabled sabotage, similar to a technical effect, but distinct in that it speaks to the organizational or system impact of an event rather than the impact to a digital device. For example, cyber-enabled sabotage may require the replacement of millions of smart meters (end effect) after a malicious payload pushes firmware overwrites to the communications module (technical effect).

Essential element of information (EEI)   An intelligence requirement, EEIs are those central questions and pieces of information being requested by an intelligence consumer/customer (e.g., information collection related to ACME brand of equipment by a malicious actor). Often presented in question form.

Event   A negative, physical end result. Within the CCE context, an event does not necessarily refer to an adverse impact originating from cyber-enabled sabotage. Instead, adverse events may be the result of human error, engineering failures, or resultant from natural causes.

Exploit   The means by which an adversary takes advantage of a vulnerability or weakness. Distinct from, although commonly and incorrectly referred to as malware.

Facilitator   Process expert that facilitates the CCE engagement but does not provide technical input for its content (it may even be helpful for a facilitator to lack technical expertise in order to remain objective and maintain a broader view of meeting progress); elicits information from the entity; present at all workshops with entity and for internal INL workshops.

Functional diagram   Similar to a logical or physical diagram, a functional diagram describes the procedures and steps for the use of a specific technology or system. Although it is not imperative that this model be developed by the CCE participants during Phase 2, it can be a useful tool for describing the full lifecycle of a technology.

HCE severity score   The final score of a scenario using the scoring matrix. A weighting coefficient values in the equation are determined by engineering and sector SMEs to reflect the priorities of the criteria.

HCE threshold   The HCE point value threshold that determines which HCEs represent a high enough impact to warrant further analysis during a CCE engagement. This level is selected by the CCE Team prior to or immediately after the scoring of HCEs.

High-consequence event (HCE)   HCE refers to the adverse events deemed most significant in terms of the severity of impact. HCEs are cyber-events that received the highest severity scores identified based on the severity criteria, which should be aligned to best represent the organization's mission and business values. Initially only some of the identified events in Phase 1 may become HCEs to carry through the CCE methodology; however, other events may later be deemed HCEs as the CCE process is repeated.

Horizontal application of technology   This is one of three areas of focus for potential targets. They address the effects of impacts on a technology that is widely deployed, either within a system or across a geographic region. This may include technology that supports a function performed by multiple organizations.

ICE payload   Also known as primary payload, the main malicious code that results in an adverse condition that causes an end effect.

Impact   Synonymous with consequence. Within CCE, the result(s) of cyber-enabled sabotage.

Implementation vulnerability   A weakness not inherent to the design of a technology but the result of how a specific organization or individual employs a technology.

Indicators   The warning signs of adversary activity. An entity will identify indicators of adversary activity as a result of the analysis completed during Phase 3. Although some of these indicators may be visible by the victim organization, some are only visible as a result of cyber intelligence collection from the intelligence community or private cyber intelligence firms.

Industrial control system (ICS)   A collective term used to describe different types of control systems and associated instrumentation, which include the digital devices, systems, networks, and controls used to operate and/or automate industrial processes.

Information gathering   Activities performed throughout a CCE engagement to collect all the system information specific to an HCE. From the adversarial view, the activities include information gathering techniques such as open-source collection, social engineering, remote access, etc.

191

Information sharing analysis center (ISAC) An organization that provides cyber security and threat information, typically by critical infrastructure sector.

Initial information request (IIR) Developed at the start of Phase 2, the IIR serves as a record of the specific questions or pieces of information that the CCE team requests of the participating entity. These requests and their answers are typically stored in a table with the date requested, date received, and a reference to where the original source information is located.

Initiation Within the CCE methodology, the process of steps an adversary takes to trigger the payload.

Intelligence community The collection of 16 individual government entities that work collectively to meet the government's intelligence and national security needs.

Kill Chain A military and terrorism studies concept used to describe the process of kinetic attack development from target identification, attack preparation, and execution. See also, CCE Kill Chain.

Knowledge base The output of Phase 2, System-of-Systems Analysis, a taxonomical data repository that describes the origin of a device or system, how it is installed, operated and maintained, as well as what devices and systems it feeds. The knowledge base directly informs the analysis performed during Phase 3, consequence-based targeting.

Likert scale Type of rating scale used to measure opinions. There are usually three to five responses to choose from, and each is assigned a number on a scale basis. The sum of these responses designates a final score for a scenario.

Logical diagram A logical diagram (or logical data flow diagram) is a depiction of how data is shared between systems or organizations. One of the outputs of Phase 2 is the development of logical diagrams for each of the systems of interest identified in the HCEs.

Malware Code intended to adversely manipulate a digital device, system, or process, in the case of critical infrastructure, to achieve unauthorized access, disruption, or damage.

Mitigations and Protections The fourth phase of CCE. The goal of this phase is to either remove the possibility of the end effect via the implementation of often-engineered "protections" (preferred) or to develop "mitigations" strategies to detect, respond to, and/or recover from adversary activity.

Need-to-know This is the fundamental security principle in safeguarding classified information. Requiring a need-to-know for data access ensures that such information is available only to those persons with appropriate managerial approval and clearly identified requirement to use the information.

NIST five functions National Institute of Standards and Technology (NIST) has identified five functions that are key to a successful cybersecurity approach. The five functions are Identify, Protect, Detect, Respond, and Recover. The first three phases of a CCE engagement are used to identify, and Phase 4 addresses the other four functions.

Notetaker A CCE role that's more important than it may seem at first blush. Captures real-time discussions during CCE collaboration meetings in an organized manner.

Objective Identified in Phase 1, the objective is the adversary's intended effect from cyber-sabotage. The objective is often linked to an organization's worst-case operational failure.

Open-source intelligence (OSINT) Data collected from publicly available sources that is used in an intelligence context.

Operational technology Operational technology (OT) refers to any technology used to manage industrial operations. ICS is a subset of OT. The term cyber-physical system is also roughly synonymous.

Payload delivery This is a step in the CCE Kill Chain. The adversary delivers a payload that causes the desired end effect to a technical target. The adversary also establishes command and control to trigger at intended times. This step includes targeting and information gathering tasks to gain the critical information needs of the system, accesses needed, and the physical affect the payload has on the targeted process. This step is also linked to payload development and testing.

Payload development and testing During this step of the CCE Kill Chain, the adversary is developing and testing a payload that would cause the desired end effect. This step includes Targeting and Information Gathering tasks to gain the critical information needs of the system, accesses needed, and how the payload will physically affect the targeted process. The adversary must also establish command and control to be able to trigger at the intended time and have access to develop the payload. This step is linked to Payload Deployment in that the development of the payload must be completed before delivery can occur, but if a barrier or new information appears during the Payload Deployment step, Payload Development and Testing will also need to change.

Perfect knowledge The gathering of data, documents, and people with full inside access to fully understand the processes and implementations specific to the entity.

Phase 1 The first phase of CCE, Consequence Prioritization.

Phase 2 The second phase of CCE, System-of-Systems Analysis.

Phase 3 The third phase of CCE, consequence-based targeting.

Phase 4 The fourth phase of CCE, Protections and Mitigations.

Physical damage As an escalation of cyber-physical effects, the most impactful of cyber-physical attacks that results in destruction or damage to equipment, property, and loss of lives.

Physical infrastructure and interdependency This is one of three areas of focus for potential targets. It includes sabotage on a single piece of the system (like one line on a transmission system) with the primary goal of having compounding effects on the greater system (transmission network and underlying distribution system, for example).

Physics payload Also known as primary or ICS payload, the main malicious code that results in an adverse condition that causes an end effect.

Preliminary HCE diagram A relatively simplistic functional and physical block diagram used to describe each scenario. This helps to narrow the scope and thereby minimize the volume of information needed to examine and convey HCEs.

Protect Refers to the ability to remove the objective of cyber-enabled sabotage. Within Phase 4, recommended mitigations and protections are classified by Protect, Detect, Respond, and/or Recover, with preference placed on Protect.

Reconnaissance Adversary actions, both on and off the target networks, to collect information about a victim and target. Reconnaissance is identified as a necessary preparatory action of cyber-enabled sabotage and included in Stage I of the SANS ICS Cyber Kill Chain.

Recover Refers to the timely restoration of critical functions and/or services. The Recover function supports timely recovery to normal operations to reduce the impact from a cybersecurity incident. Within Phase 4, recommended mitigations and protections are classified by Protect, Detect, Respond, and/or Recover, with preference placed on Protect.

Reliance on automation This is one of three areas of focus for potential targets. This describes cyber-events that may inhibit an organization's ability to automate, monitor, or control critical functions and services.

Remote access trojan (RAT)   Malware that tricks user into opening or allowing it to run, then provides a backdoor for an adversary to communicate with the compromised machine.

Respond   Refers to the ability to contain or disrupt adversarial activities. The Respond Function supports the ability to contain the impact of a potential cybersecurity incident. Within Phase 4, recommended mitigations and protections are classified by Protect, Detect, Respond, and/or Recover, with preference placed on Protect.

Restoration   In the context of cybersecurity, the processes and procedures employed by an organization to recover from cyber-enabled sabotage. Proactive development of restoration plans could also refer to contingency plans.

SANS ICS Cyber Kill Chain   A variant of the Lockheed Martin Cyber Kill Chain, the SANS ICS Cyber Kill Chain describes an adversary's actions for preparation to execution of cyber-enabled sabotage.

Scope   This describes the extent that an adversary's objective (disruption, degradation, or destruction) which meets the level of concern for an organization or industry. This is an understanding of how an adversary's intent is able to become a high-consequence event that can be examined using the CCE methodology.

Scoring matrix   The scoring table used to quantifiably evaluate the impact of conceptualized scenarios. Criteria and thresholds in the table are tailored to the organization's priorities. The finalized scoring matrix is a key output of Phase 1.

Scoring threshold   When developing the impact scoring matrix, each criterion needs to have the details for each threshold defined. For example, a scoring matrix developed for an electric grid customer with one of the criteria being "Duration," and the scoring elements of this category would be defined as: Low = Return all service in less than 1 day, Medium = Return all service in between 1 and 5 days, and High = Return to service in greater than 5 days.

Severity criteria   A collection of criteria that are used by CCE participants to measure the impact of potential cyber-enabled sabotage. Each criterion has a definition, including by high, medium, and low versions of that definition, and a weighting factor, which indicates the criterion's relative importance (according to the participating organization).

Smart trigger   A pre-positioned initiator that allows for remote and future action by an adversary.

Subject matter expert (SME)   Person with deep specialized expertise in an area or topic of need. In CCE context, often a specific technology, process, or function.

Supply chain   The origin, including development, design, and production of a commodity; this includes the entire ecosystem—software, hardware, and production.

Supply chain co-option   An adversary takes advantage of the normal installation, maintenance, or end-of-life activity to deploy their payload (or payloads) to a target environment (e.g., Havex).

Supply chain interdiction   An adversary accesses materials, software, hardware, or other components in transit with the goal of delaying, disrupting, or destroying this equipment before it can be received by the procurer/purchaser.

Supply chain substitution   The deliberate insertion of malicious "substitutes" into the supply chain for future manipulation by an adversary.

System description   This activity is completed at the end of Phase 2. The system description is a summary of all the pertinent information that must be gathered during Phase 2. It consists of all the system information related to each HCE to include personnel, safety documents, engineering documents, equipment descriptions, etc. In other words, the system description is a digestible summary of the HCE relevant data used to develop the CCE Kill Chain.

System integrity confidence   The degree to which a victim of cyber-enabled sabotage can validate and trust that the original risk has been mitigated. One of the Severity Criteria from the first CCE engagement, it describes whether or not restoration and recovery efforts can restore system integrity with confidence following an adverse event (i.e., a system not operating as expected or intended, or, alternatively, malicious operation conducted by unauthorized users). One factor to consider is whether or not the initial attack propagates into multiple systems and therefore complicates restoration efforts. All of these may negatively impact an organization's confidence in their system following an adverse event.

System targeting description   The system description from Phase 2 will be the groundwork that becomes the system targeting description in Phase 3. The system targeting description includes additional key details that are identified during targeting analysis and complete the summary of information required for the attack scenarios to cause the HCE.

System-of-systems analysis   The second phase of CCE, during which CCE participants collect the information necessary to identify a viable cyber-enabled sabotage process for Phase 3. Typically, this information is collected from interviews and documentation and stored within the knowledge base, the critical output of Phase 2.

Target   This might be a device component, system process, memory module, programmable chip, or logic circuit. The target can also be non-cyber or human components of the process, like personnel with direct access to the system.

Target details   The target details describe the operating position(s) for a cyber-attacker; it is the "where" in the question. Where does an adversary need to be to control and execute the attack?

Targeter   An individual who specializes in the development of tools and techniques to target a system.

Targeting   The process of selecting the appropriate tools and techniques to apply against a target.

Taxonomy   A classification structure that indicates relationships and hierarchy among devices and systems. In relation to Phase 2, data compromising the knowledge base is organized taxonomically.

Technical approach   Detailed requirements used by the adversary for the development and delivery of a payload, developed in Phase 3. This identifies "how" the desired effect will be achieved by defining the steps required to place the payload in the desired location and maintain command and control. This requires taking advantage of how existing systems and components communicate and interact while highlighting both the existing and potential flow of information. The technical approach includes four components: access, actions, timing, and triggering.

Technical target   A specific element (e.g., device component, system process, memory module, programmable chip, logic circuit), the compromise of which is achieved via a technical approach and deployment and enables an adversary's terminal goals. Knowing the technical target provides the "what" needed to understand how an HCE can be achieved.

Timing   One of four pieces required to fully understand an adversary's technical approach. Timing refers to the sequence of the adversary's steps.

Trigger   A pre-positioned mechanism used by an adversary to remotely initiate a payload.

Triggering   One of four pieces required to fully understand an adversary's technical approach. Triggering refers to the system conditions or timing required for the adversary to activate the payload.

Tripwires   Pre-positioned indicators or alarms that can inform cyber security professionals of malicious behavior within a network, system, or device.

Uninterruptible power supply (UPS)   A backup battery through which power is wired, so power failures will not immediately affect device connected.

Unverified risk   By trusting people, services, processes, and systems without performing thorough evaluation, risk is assumed. CCE's methodology suggests that all such risk should be acknowledged and documented. Closely linked to unverified trust.

Unverified trust   The blind reliance we place in people, services, processes, and systems. By giving this trust without deliberate and thorough verification, an organization assumes unverified risk.

Vulnerability   Refers to a flaw in hardware, software, processes, or systems that can leave it vulnerable to an attack. For the CCE methodology, it is crucial to understand that vulnerabilities do not merely exist in an IT context. Rather vulnerabilities may be present in any aspect of an organization's operations.

Weighting coefficient   A value placed on each scoring criteria to reflect the priorities of an organization. A higher weighting coefficient signals a higher priority of that criteria to the entity. For example, an electric sector company may place a higher priority on the area impacted by an event and the duration of the outage as compared to the cost of an event.

Appendix A: CCE Case Study

Baltavia Substation Power Outage

Cybercore Integration Center
Idaho National Laboratory
Cybercore Integration Center
Idaho Falls, Idaho 83415

www.inl.gov

Prepared for the U.S. Department of Energy, Office of National & Homeland Security, Under DOE Idaho Operations Office
Contract DE-AC07-05ID14517
INL-EXT-20-58092

DISCLAIMER

US Government or any agency thereof. The views and opinions of authors expressed herein do not necessarily state or reflect those of the US government or any agency thereof.

INTRODUCTION

In this case study, we will examine a fictional event broadly inspired by the real power outages in Ukraine that took place in December 2015 and December 2016—both the result of cyber-enabled sabotage. The adversaries in these well-documented attacks gained access to a few power companies' corporate networks, pivoted to industrial control system (ICS) networks, and created widespread physical effects in the form of power outages.

2015 Ukraine Attack

Figure A.1 is an infographic that helps summarize the 2015 Ukraine power system cyber-attack.

The December 2015 power outages in Ukraine were the result of a coordinated cyber-attack on three power distribution companies involving roughly 53 substations within their associated service areas. The attack focused on supervisory control and data acquisition (SCADA) and distribution management system (DMS) platforms and leveraged the unverified trust of established remote access capabilities.

2015 Ukraine Event Summary

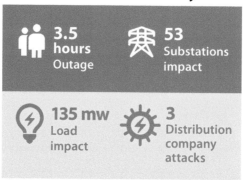

3.5 hours Outage

53 Substations impact

135 mw Load impact

3 Distribution company attacks

Figure A.1   Graphical Representation of the 2015 Attack on Ukraine's Electrical Grid.

The attackers caused outages by using the engineered functionality of the controls platforms to manipulate circuit breakers within the substations. Attackers also prevented an immediate restoration of normal power delivery by targeting core supporting functions of centralized control: field communications (altered firmware uploaded to station Serial-to-Ethernet gateway devices) and operator visibility ("wiping" hard drives of operator workstations and servers). Malicious modifications to uninterruptable power supply (UPS) configurations were also discovered. Attack preparation involved first gaining access to the companies' business networks (via spear phishing), harvesting credentials and escalating privileges, and using the stolen, trusted ICS accounts for remote VPN access to the power system networks.

Although many customers were affected by the outage, the utilities' field personnel were able to perform manual system operations; consequently, they restored power to customers in a relatively short amount of time—less than 4 hours.

2016 Ukraine Attack

Now we will look at the 2016 Ukraine power system cyber-attack. Fewer details related to this event have been made public. Figure A.2 is an infographic that summarizes what we do know about the Ukraine power system cyber-attack.

2016 Ukraine Event Summary

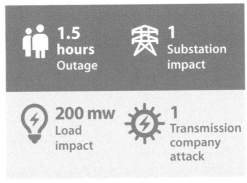

Figure A.2 Graphical Representation of the 2016 Attack on Ukraine's Electrical Grid.

The December 2016 events in Ukraine were quite different from those in the previous year. For example, the 2016 attack impacted a single transmission-level substation and 200 MW of customer load.

A switch to manual operations again aided the quick recovery of power delivery functions at the affected substation. While the total customer demand loss was greater than it was in the 2015 incident, the 2016 event was of shorter duration (just 1.25 hours), and fewer individual customers experienced a power outage.

Investigation by private cybersecurity firms following this outage uncovered malware capable of mapping networks and executing commands within an ICS environment. While the 2015 attack relied on direct interaction with a SCADA/DMS platform via a remote operator, the malware discovered following the 2016 attack was designed to automatically enumerate on-network ICS devices using specific ICS communications protocols. The malware also contained capabilities to issue commands to those devices.

Note the increased risk presented to asset owners/operators—instead of having to maintain covert access, the adversary is only required to get the malware to the right network "by hook or by crook" and provide a trigger for execution. In addition, this approach also potentially shortens the amount of time needed for an adversary to position itself for an attack. The approach is also modular (configurable and transferable) to other organizations leveraging similar communications protocols.

The Fictional Attack on Baltavia

With the 2015 and 2016 attacks in mind, we will now explore how to apply the CCE methodology to identify worst-case functional impacts and determine high-consequence events (HCEs) in a fictional case study.

DISCLAIMER #1

This case study is a work of fiction. It is the product of the authors' imaginations, written to reinforce the understanding of the CCE methodology. Names, locations, events, corporations, regions, countries, and incidents are fictitious. Any resemblance to actual countries or events is purely coincidental.

DISCLAIMER #2

Any references to specific equipment, vendors, or technologies in this study does not imply increased susceptibility to cyber-attack over other brands or devices. The equipment in this study is "typical" equipment often found in the industry. As a work of fiction, some features were modified to support the narrative.

It is January 2017, and Baltavia's transmission[1] utilities seek to better prepare themselves in the face of threats posed by adversaries. Despite the operational risks presented by a rapidly aging coal-fired generation fleet, Baltavia is working to establish itself as a net power provider (see Figure A.3) to European markets.

Capital projects are approved for transmission substation upgrades with a focus on reliability and modernization. A portion of the preparation involves upgrading transmission substations with new direct current (dc) power management systems that will automate battery health monitoring and emergency ac/dc power[2] transfer. Additionally, this will improve remote control and monitoring capabilities.

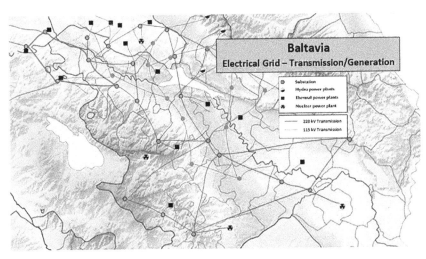

Figure A.3   Asset Systems in the Baltavian Electrical Power Grid.

1   See Appendix A for a glossary of key electric sector terminology.

2   "alternating current." See Appendix A for a glossary of key electric sector terminology.

Foreign adversaries are concerned with Baltavia's ambitions to be viewed as a reliable net power provider. They wish to deny any opportunity for the country to discuss potential sales of electricity to European markets. Utilities and the Baltavian government fear that a cyber-enabled outage would be a roadblock to their business goal of selling electricity to western Europe, if not ruin the prospect altogether.

Baltavia's ability to deliver energy to Western markets relies on infrastructure connectivity (transmission and distribution) and power generation capabilities. Figure A.4 provides a snapshot of Baltavian power system assets, their geographic dispersion internally, and their proximity or interface with neighboring countries.

Electrical power generation and local demand are met via the generation and distribution systems, respectively. The critical function of power delivery to the Eurozone market relies on the Baltavian transmission system.

The five substations that comprise the western portion of the transmission system are arranged roughly in a ring structure to provide redundant pathways for power delivery (see Figure A.5). The ring structure ensures that if a single substation is taken completely out of service by a disruption, the remaining substations on the loop will still be able to provide connectivity.

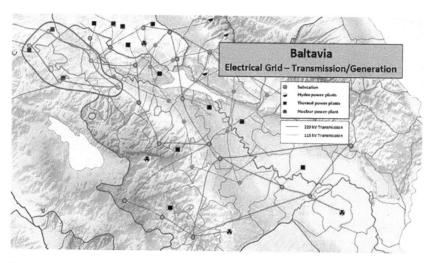

Figure A.4   Asset Systems in the Western Baltavian Electrical Transmission Grid.

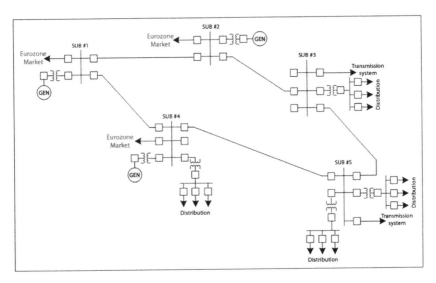

Figure A.5   Bus One-line Diagram of Asset Systems in the Western Baltavian Electrical Transmission Grid.

While power delivery to the Eurozone market is still possible with an outage at a single key delivery point, both throughput and system resilience capabilities would be negatively impacted if the outage lasted more than 6 hours. More importantly, such an event (especially a malicious cyber-enabled event) would erode European Union (EU) confidence in Baltavia's ability to reliably supply power. This would damage the EU's perception of energy security in Baltavia. Compromise of a critical control or operational component in the transmission system would also lead the utility to question their own ability to restore and maintain system integrity.

Each critical substation shares similar general topology. Dual transmission feeds provide the connectivity to the greater loop, and a third line provides connectivity to the target European market systems. Transmission voltage at each is established at 220kV. The bus structure of each substation is shown in Figure A.6. As mentioned earlier, each of the substations also provides some generation capacity to offset internal (Baltavian) and external power demands.

The three critical transmission substations with connectivity to the EU Market have been equipped with a new auxiliary dc power system (see Figure A.7). The dc system is comprised of a battery management system

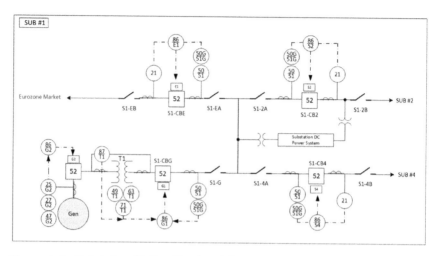

Figure A.6 Substation #1 Bus/Breaker Schematic, Illustrating the Bus Structure of Each Substation.

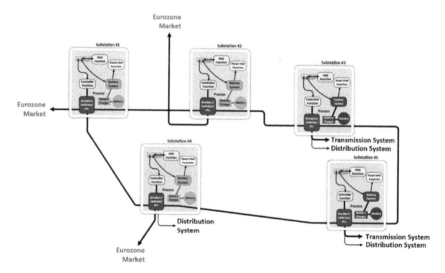

Figure A.7 Critical Substations with the New Auxiliary dc Power System and/ or SCADA Upgrades.

(controller, ac/dc rectifier electronics, on-board maintenance bypass, and transfer capabilities), dc power distribution infrastructure (breakers, panels, wiring, etc.), a battery bank, and a resistive load bank. The dc system is a redundant system with multiple taps used to provide power to all substation control and protective devices, communications infrastructure, breakers, and switch actuators. If the dc power system is incapacitated (battery failure, controller failure, loss of ac power supply and charging, etc.), the ability to automatically and remotely control and monitor the substation is lost. The battery management system provides control and monitoring of the dc system, a configuration interface, communications capabilities, and battery bank charging functions. Battery health/charge is critical—from a degraded charge state, it can take up to 24 hours to restore batteries to a usable voltage level.

Centralized transmission system operations, as well as generation dispatch, are performed remotely from a control center at the utility headquarters. Transmission operations (control/monitoring of the transmission system infrastructure) are implemented via a commercial-off-the-shelf (COTS) SCADA platform, while generation dispatch uses an automatic generation control (AGC) module within the utility Energy Management System (EMS). Each of the five transmission substations in the western ring have been recently commissioned with full SCADA capabilities via new front-end servers located at the HQ control center. The other transmission substations have active telemetry and metering; however, because necessary upgrades have not been made, they do not have supervisory control capability from the control center.

Communications and control engineering staff have access to the SCADA system network for station device configuration and troubleshooting activities. Although individual substation control and protection devices function independently from the SCADA system, without SCADA operability, automated remote management of stations and the greater transmission system is reduced to manual operations via radio. Because of staffing "cost optimization" measures, there are only enough linemen available to handle manual local response duties at a limited number of substations at any given time. Travel and staging time for a site visit averages 3 hours or more.

Operating procedures are such that if a station's SCADA system values are suspected of being erroneous, field personnel will be deployed for validation of the subject substation device/system telemetry points. Loss of communications similarly requires dispatch of field crews to verify system integrity. Because of the travel time involved to and from substations and the limited availability of field personnel, the absolute minimum estimate for issue resolution time is 3 hours per site.

Due to present elevated political and economic pressures, an extended outage (6+ hours) at a critical substation would be intolerable. Although a somewhat shorter outage (2 hours or less) could put Eurozone power delivery hopes at risk, such an event may be recoverable through transactions by government officials and utility management.

CCE STEPS—SUBSTATION CASE STUDY

Phase 1: Consequence Prioritization

Objective

Functional disruption of Baltavia's full-power delivery capabilities to Eurozone markets for 6 hours or more.

Scope

This transmission system loop was designed for high reliability, but it can only operate at full capacity using all three critical substation "Eurozone market" delivery points. While it is conceivable that three separate transmission substations could be taken down as a result of a simultaneous attack on the utility, an outage at even a single critical substation would negatively impact the power system delivery capability and raise doubts around Baltavian transmission operation reliability.

Boundary Condition

Functional disruption at a single critical transmission substation, resulting in a reduction of Baltavian full-power delivery capabilities to Eurozone markets for 6+ hours.

Events

1 Transmission-level interconnect breakers are opened at a critical power delivery substation.
2 Transmission-level interconnect breakers at a critical power delivery substation are opened, and the SCADA system at the control center is made inoperable.
3 Loss of local and remote communications capability at a critical power delivery substation.

4 The dc power system capabilities in a critical power delivery substation are degraded, and transmission-level interconnect breakers are opened.

Cyber-Events

1 Open all transmission-level interconnect breakers at a critical delivery substation.
   a Adversary gains access to the substation network and triggers station isolation and de-energization by opening breakers on the three transmission-level interconnects.
2 Open all transmission-level interconnect breakers at a critical delivery substation, and then disable the HQ control center SCADA capabilities.
   a Adversary gains access to the substation network and triggers station isolation and de-energization by opening breakers on the three transmission-level interconnects. Adversary then delivers and executes a "KillDisk"-type program on the primary and backup front-end field communications servers at the control center, rendering SCADA functions inoperable.
3 Disrupt local and remote communications (including SCADA) at a critical substation, prompting the dispatcher to deploy field crews to investigate.
   a Adversary gains access to the substation network and disrupts communications and SCADA functionality by installing malicious firmware on the substation communications gateway device. Dispatcher follows protocol to "roll" a field crew and manually isolate communications at the critical substation pending on-site inspection and resolution.
4 Degrade substation station dc power system capabilities in a critical power delivery substation and open all transmission-level interconnect breakers.
   a Adversary gains access to the substation network and manipulates the configuration of the battery management system. Modifications reduce battery bank recharging capability and dc power availability. The dc system capacity is degraded to a level insufficient for sustained support of substation SCADA, protection, and operations infrastructure. Attack ensures that no indications are presented to system operators, while the charging system is at reduced capacity. Adversary triggers station isolation

and de-energization by opening breakers on the three transmission-level interconnects.

Scoring

Here is a list of potential criteria:

- Area Impacted (Not Applicable): Severity determined by the number of substations that are impacted by the event. All four cyber-events occur at a single critical delivery substation (so not a differentiator) and power delivery at present demand levels can be maintained (1st paragraph, p. 6).
- Attack Breadth: Severity determined by the extent to which a targeted technology or system is deployed. The greater the span of impacted systems, the more difficult it will be to restore following an adverse event. Of note, attack breadth moves beyond the number of devices impacted, since this value also considers the additional resources needed for restoration, such as additional personnel or financial expenditures
- Cost (Not Applicable): Severity determined by direct financial loss to the utility as a result of the failure scenario including restoration costs, which is the cost to return the system to proper operation, not including any legal or other reparations as a result of the failure. Mostly labor costs are associated with these cyber-events, no major equipment damage, or long-term outages to critical customers. Hence, cost is not a significant differentiator.
- Duration: Severity determined by length of power outage resulting from event.
- System Integrity Confidence: Severity determined by the degree to which restoration and recovery efforts can restore system integrity with confidence following the event (i.e., a system not operating as expected or intended, or, alternatively, malicious operation conducted by unauthorized users). One factor to consider is whether the initial attack propagates in multiple systems and therefore complicates restoration efforts. All of these may negatively impact an organization's confidence in their system following an adverse event.
- Safety (Not Applicable): Severity determined by the potential impact on safety, including injuries requiring first aid or loss of life. For example, the power system outage results in health hazards or mortalities directly tied to the lack of available electric power. No large-scale or long-term power outages (public safety) and no major

equipment damage that could cause an explosion/other. These cyber-events essentially focus on unauthorized use of engineered functions and/or loss of visibility.

Scoring Cyber-Events

	Severity Scoring			
	None (0)	Low (1)	Medium (3)	High (5)
Attack Breadth $\beta = 1$		Elements of the system are vulnerable to an exploit that is active and causing operational effects, but recovery is possible using immediately available resources. These events are covered within the utility's recovery plan.	Multiple system elements have the potential to be or have been successfully attacked causing operational effects. Recovery is possible but requires additional resources (i.e., time, personnel) not immediately available.	Many system elements have been successfully attacked causing operational effects. Restoration is complicated by the dispersed deployment of devices or scale. Timeline for recovery is unknown.
Duration $\delta = 3$		Return of all service in less than 2 hours.	Return to service in between 2 and 6 hours.	Return to service in greater than or equal to 6 hours.
System Integrity Confidence $\epsilon = 2$		Asset owner has an ability to restore and is confident in restoration integrity.	Asset owner has knowledge to restore but does not have the resources (financial, time, personnel, etc.) to restore confidence in the system.	Asset owner has ability to restore but is not confident of restoration integrity.

211

Scoring Cyber-Event 1

Adversary gains access to the substation network and triggers station isolation and de-energization by opening breakers on the three transmission-level interconnects.

	Severity Scoring			
	None (0)	Low (1)	Medium (3)	High (5)
Attack Breadth $\beta = 1$		Elements of the system are vulnerable to an exploit that is active and causing operational effects, but recovery is possible using immediately available resources. These events are covered within the utility's recovery plan.	Multiple system elements have the potential to be or have been successfully attacked causing operational effects. Recovery is possible but requires additional resources (i.e., time, personnel) not immediately available.	Many system elements have been successfully attacked causing operational effects. Restoration is complicated by the dispersed deployment of devices or scale. Timeline for recovery is unknown.
Duration $\delta = 3$		Return of all service in less than 2 hours.	Return to service in between 2 and 6 hours.	Return to service in greater than or equal to 6 hours.
System Integrity Confidence $\varepsilon = 2$		Asset owner has ability to restore and is confident in restoration integrity.	Asset owner has knowledge to restore but does not have the resources (financial, time, personnel, etc.) to restore confidence in the system.	Asset owner has ability to restore but is not confident of restoration integrity.

Score for cyber-event 1: $\beta 1 + \delta 1 + \varepsilon 1 = 1 + 3 + 2 = \mathbf{6}$.

Scoring Cyber-Event 2

Adversary gains access to the substation network and triggers station isolation and de-energization by opening breakers on the three transmission-level interconnects. Adversary then delivers and executes a "KillDisk"-type program on the primary and backup front-end field communications servers at the control center, rendering SCADA functions inoperable.

	Severity Scoring			
	None (0)	Low (1)	Medium (3)	High (5)
Attack Breadth $\beta = 1$		Elements of the system are vulnerable to an exploit that is active and causing operational effects, but recovery is possible using immediately available resources. These events are covered within the utility's recovery plan.	Multiple system elements have the potential to be or have been successfully attacked causing operational effects. Recovery is possible but requires additional resources (i.e., time, personnel) not immediately available.	Many system elements have been successfully attacked causing operational effects. Restoration is complicated by the dispersed deployment of devices or scale. Timeline for recovery is unknown.
Duration $\delta = 3$		Return of all service in less than 2 hours.	Return to service in between 2 and 6 hours.	Return to service in greater than or equal to 6 hours.
System Integrity Confidence $\varepsilon = 2$		Asset owner has ability to restore and is confident in restoration integrity.	Asset owner has knowledge to restore but does not have the resources (financial, time, personnel, etc.) to restore confidence in the system.	Asset owner has ability to restore but is not confident of restoration integrity.

Score for cyber-event 2: $\beta 3 + \delta 3 + \varepsilon 5 = 3 + 9 + 10 = \mathbf{22}$

Scoring Cyber-Event 3

Adversary gains access to the substation network and disrupts communications and SCADA functionality by installing malicious firmware on the substation communications gateway device. Dispatcher follows protocol to "roll" a field crew and manually isolate communications at the critical substation pending on-site inspection and resolution.

	Severity Scoring			
	None (0)	Low (1)	Medium (3)	High (5)
Attack Breadth $\beta = 1$		Elements of the system are vulnerable to an exploit that is active and causing operational effects, but recovery is possible using immediately available resources. These events are covered within the utility's recovery plan.	Multiple system elements have the potential to be or have been successfully attacked causing operational effects. Recovery is possible but requires additional resources (i.e., time, personnel) not immediately available.	Many system elements have been successfully attacked causing operational effects. Restoration is complicated by the dispersed deployment of devices or scale. Timeline for recovery is unknown.
Duration $\delta = 3$		Return of all service in less than 2 hours.	Return to service in between 2 and 6 hours.	Return to service in greater than or equal to 6 hours.
System Integrity Confidence $\varepsilon = 2$		Asset owner has ability to restore and is confident in restoration integrity.	Asset owner has knowledge to restore but does not have the resources (financial, time, personnel, etc.) to restore confidence in the system.	Asset owner has ability to restore but is not confident of restoration integrity.

Score for cyber-event 3: $\beta 1 + \delta 3 + \varepsilon 1 = 1 + 9 + 2 = \mathbf{12}$

Scoring Cyber-Event 4

Adversary gains access to the substation network and manipulates configuration of the battery management system. Modifications reduce battery bank recharging capability as well as dc power availability. The dc system capacity is degraded to a level insufficient for sustained support of substation SCADA, protection, and operations infrastructure. Attack ensures that no indications are presented to system operators while the charging system is at reduced capacity. Adversary triggers station isolation and de-energization by opening breakers on the three transmission-level interconnects.

	Severity Scoring			
	None (0)	**Low (1)**	**Medium (3)**	**High (5)**
Attack Breadth $\beta = 1$		Elements of the system are vulnerable to an exploit that is active and causing operational effects, but recovery is possible using immediately available resources. These events are covered within the utility's recovery plan.	Multiple system elements have the potential to be or have been successfully attacked causing operational effects. Recovery is possible but requires additional resources (i.e., time, personnel, etc.) not immediately available.	Many system elements have been successfully attacked causing operational effects. Restoration is complicated by the dispersed deployment of devices or scale. Timeline for recovery is unknown.
Duration $\delta = 3$		Return of all service in less than 2 hours.	Return to service in between 2 and 6 hours.	Return to service in greater than or equal to 6 hours.
System Integrity Confidence $\varepsilon = 2$		Asset owner has ability to restore and is confident in restoration integrity.	Asset owner has knowledge to restore but does not have the resources (financial, time, personnel, etc.) to restore confidence in the system.	Asset owner has ability to restore but is not confident of restoration integrity.

Score for cyber-event 4: $\beta 3 + \delta 5 + \varepsilon 5 = 3 + 15 + 10 = \mathbf{28}$

215

HCE Identification

Using these criteria, *cyber-event four scores the highest and will serve as the HCE.*

HIGH-CONSEQUENCE EVENT

Adversary gains access to the substation network and manipulates the configuration of the battery management system. Modifications reduce battery bank recharging capability, as well as dc power availability. The dc system capacity is degraded to a level insufficient for sustained support of substation SCADA, protection, and operations infrastructure. Attacker ensures that no indications are presented to system operators while the charging system is at reduced capacity. Adversary triggers station isolation and de-energization by opening breakers on the three transmission-level interconnects.

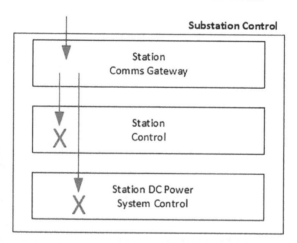

Figure A.8 Block Diagram of the HCE

PHASE 2: SYSTEM-OF-SYSTEMS ANALYSIS

Creating a Preliminary Block Diagram

The starting point for Phase 2, System-of-Systems Analysis (SoS Analysis), is the creation of a relatively simple, high-level block diagram for each

HCE to help with visualizing the cyber manipulation required to accomplish the outcome. This exercise helps narrow the scope of analysis, organizes the physical and functional connections between the target components and the affected systems, and minimizes the volume of information collected to describe each HCE. The block diagram provides a starting point for identifying what information and system accesses the adversary needs to accomplish the HCE and will be used to define and organize the data collection efforts. See Figure A.8 for an example HCE block diagram.

"Perfect Knowledge" Benefits

Most of the activity in Phase 2 will involve identifying, collecting, and organizing documentation relevant to an HCE to build a comprehensive knowledge base of key details for the SoS Analysis. The goal is to obtain "perfect knowledge" of the system(s) relevant to the HCE. To help organize the collection and analysis activities, a functional description can be developed based on the HCE block diagram. This is often best done by starting with the target components that must be affected to cause the HCE and working backward. Consider the following:

- What systems and equipment are involved in the HCE?
- What documentation is needed to describe interconnected systems and dependencies?
- What relationships with other entities are involved?

The functional description can be represented as a hierarchical data structure or taxonomy. Using this functional taxonomy as the basis for investigation, the CCE Team will begin collecting and organizing key details. Relevant information to support this work includes details of interconnected systems and dependencies, controllers, technical manuals, diagrams, protocols, access lists, associated manufacturers, trusted relationships, contractors, suppliers, emergency procedures, and personnel.

The SoS Analysis proceeds in parallel during information collection by building an understanding of the critical systems and processes. The process is iterative, and as the CCE Team identifies specific information gaps from the SoS Analysis, time is taken to adjust the detailed information collection to close these gaps. While not all inclusive, the resulting information will build upon the initial HCE block diagram and will ideally result in perfect knowledge.

217

This will benefit the organization by both identifying critical information and determining where it resides. For example, is the critical information on internal servers or a public-facing server? To help ensure continued data collection efforts remain focused on the HCE, it may help to build out the original diagram throughout Phase 2. This helps produce diagrams with greater detail as more data is collected and aggregated. The point of Phase 2 is to be aware of all the information that an adversary would need to execute a successful attack. A typical taxonomy for this use case is shown in Table A.1.

System Description

In order to analyze the system to develop Attack Scenarios in Phase 3, the CCE Team must collect as much relevant information as possible. The information helps summarize the key details to support a deeper level of knowledge of the system operations, personnel support activities, system configuration, and other aspects of the operation. To accomplish this, a System Description is developed that details the key information that an adversary may need to obtain access and accomplish the HCE through cyber means. This description should summarize the functional block diagram and provide traceability to all the information collected in Phase 2 by describing where the information resides and who has access to it. This will be the output of Phase 2 and the input to Phase 3. A System Description for this use case is shown and detailed below.

Transmission System

Power delivery to the European market is delivered via the western Baltavian transmission grid. The five substations[3] that comprise the western portion of the transmission system are arranged roughly in a ring structure to provide redundant pathways for power delivery (see Figure A.9). The ring structure ensures that if a single substation is taken completely out of service by a disruption, the remainder of the substations on the loop will still be able to provide connectivity. Power delivery to the European markets is provided via substations #1, #2, and #4 specifically. All three substations need to be online for maximum stability and power delivery capacity.

---

3   See Appendix A for a glossary of key electric sector terminology.

Table A.1 Substation HCE Taxonomy Example

HCE Taxonomy: Substation Case Study

What: By Company Business Function/Equipment/Entity

Function
  Group
    Role
      Info Object
Engineering
  Physical System Design
    Hardware (Electrical/Mechanical/Process/Civil Engr)
      Physical System (Main) Layout Drawings
        Single-line diagram(s)
        Sub#1 one-line diagram
        Sub#1 Switchgear Layout
        Sub#1 Battery system one-line diagram
      Physical System (Ancillary) Layout Drawings
        Station Battery and Battery Monitoring and Control System
      Physical System Equipment User Manuals
        Station Battery and Battery Monitoring and Control System
  Control System Design (Digital & Analog)
  Personnel
      Power System Design Engineer
        Contact Information
      Substation Engineer
        Contact Information
      ICS/SCADA Design Engineer
        Contact Information
      Relay/Protection Engineer
        Contact Information
  Software / Firmware
      Software (Main) Specs
        ABB MultiProg PRO RTU560 Software
        ABB RTUtil560 Configuration Application
        BMT Battery Management System application (DGK Enterprise)
  Automation/Control—Control Center System
      System-wide Network Communications Diagram
        SCADA comms diagram(s)
      SCADA Vendor/Make/Components
        SCADA ICS
      SCADA I/O Tagname Configuration and List
        HMI I/O associated with Sub#1 Device Status and Control

(continued)

219

Table A.1 (Cont.)

HCE Taxonomy: Substation Case Study

Function
  Group
    Role
      Info Object

Platform Components—App Server: I/O Server
  Make/Model of Computer
    Dell Precision 3630 Tower - MSWin
Platform Components—App Server: HMI
  Make/Model of Computer
    Dell Precision 3630 Tower - MSWin
  Program/Config Files
    SCADA HMI Sub#1 HMI Layout
Platform Components—App Server: Engineering WorkStation
  Make/Model of Computer
    Dell Precision 3630 Tower - MSWin
Platform Components - File Server: Utility Engineering File Server
  Make/Model of Computer
    Dell Precision 3630 Tower - MSWin
  Program/Config Applications
    BMCS Configuration Software
    ABB MultiProg PRO RTU560 Software
    ABB RTUtil560 Configuration Application
  Utility Documentation
    Remote Access Policy and Procedure
    Remote Access Security Configuration and Approval
  Control System Component Logic Flow Diagrams
    Sub#1 SCADA Circuit Breaker Logic Flow Diagram
Platform Components - Substation Engineer Laptop
  Make/Model of Computer
    Dell Precision 7540 Laptop
Automation/Control - Remote System
  Control System Layout Drawings
    Sub#1 SCADA system block diagram
  Control System Wiring Diagrams (Components)
    Sub#1 Bus, Device & Relaying wiring diagrams
    Circuit Breaker S1CB-E, S1CB-2 and S1CB-4
      Sub#1 CB-E/-1/-2 wiring diagrams
    Disconnect Switches: S1-EB, S1-EA, S1-2A, S1-2B, S1-4A, S1-4B, and S1-G
      Sub#1 wiring diagrams—each switch component unit
  Control System Wiring Diagrams (I/O)
    Sub#1 RTU560 wiring diagram
    Sub#1 Bus, Device & Relaying schematic diagrams

220

Table A.1 (Cont.)

HCE Taxonomy: Substation Case Study

Function
  Group
    Role
      Info Object

Sub#1 RTU Rack Module Configuration
Sub#1 RTU I/O wiring diagram
Control System Wiring Diagrams (Comms)
Sub#1 ICS Communications Diagram
Control System Wiring Diagrams (Pwr)
Sub#1 RTU560 Power Wiring Diagram
Control Platform Components (RTU)
  Make/Model of RTU
    ABB RTU560
  Program/Config Applications
    ABB MultiProg PRO RTU560 Configuration Application
  Program/Config Files
    ABB RTU560 and I/O Module System Components
    ABB MultiProg PRO RTU560 Configuration Application Sub#1
    Config File(s)
    ABB MultiProg PRO RTU560 Configuration Application
    Configuration Software Screenshot
  Component User Manuals (including auto / manual capabilities)
    ABB RTU560
    ABB MultiProg PRO RTU560 Configuration Application
  Component Subsystem Specs
    ABB RTU560 tech specs
    Sub#1 Relay/RTU Platform Config Applications specs
Control Platform Components (BMCS)
  Make/Model of BMCS
    BMT Battery Monitoring and Control System Product Specs
  Program/Config Applications
    BMT Battery Monitoring and Control System BMCS
    Configuration File
  Program/Config Files
    BMT Battery Monitoring and Control System BMCS Panel
    Screenshot
  Component User Manuals (including auto/manual capabilities)
    BMT Battery Monitoring and Control System BMCS Operation
    and Service Manual
  Battery System Equipment Sizing Calcs
    Operation and Failure Mode Study

(continued)

221

Table A.1 (Cont.)

HCE Taxonomy: Substation Case Study

Function
  Group
    Role
      Info Object

Communications
  Design/Operations
    Network Architect/Engr
      Architecture Directory Services/Authentication Design
        Certificate-based authentication
      Logical network diagrams - Internal ICS Zones
        Logical network diagrams - Internal OT infrastructure
      Comms Components - Fiber Optic Network
        System Fiber Optic Layout
          Area Fiber Optic Infrastructure
      Remote Comms Components
        Gateway Configuration Backup and Documentation
          Sub#1 ICS Communications Diagram
        Switch User Manual
          Ethernet switch (24-Port Ethernet Switch)
  Operations
    Personnel
      Contact Information
        Contact Information
    Operations Documentation
      System Operations Procedures
        ICS HMI Operating Procedures (including HCE Critical Components)
          ICS HMI Operating Procedures (including Bkrs/Switches)
        ICS Abnormal Operating Procedures (including HMI/Panel Alarms)
          ICS Abnormal Operating Procedures (including HMI/Panel Alarms)
        Other Systems Monitor and Control Operating Procedure
          Battery Monitor and Control System Operating Procedure
      System User Manual Documentation
        System SCADA User Manual Documentation
      Control/Automation Component User Manuals
        ABB RTU560 tech manuals
        BMT ADV1 Battery Monitoring and Control System
  Maintenance
    Personnel
      Contact Information
        Contact Information

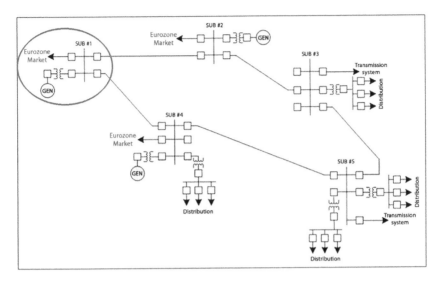

Figure A.9   Transmission System Western Ring Bus/one-line.

Critical Substations

Each critical substation shares similar general topology. Dual transmission feeds provide the connectivity to the greater loop, and a third line provides connectivity to the target European market systems. Transmission voltage at each is established at 220kV. The bus structure of each substation is shown in Figure A.10. As mentioned earlier, each of the substations also provides some generation capacity to offset internal (Baltavian) and external power demands.

System Operations

Centralized transmission system operations, as well as generation dispatch, are performed remotely from a control center at the utility headquarters. Transmission operations (control/monitoring of the transmission system infrastructure) are implemented via a COTS SCADA platform, while generation dispatch uses an AGC module within the utility EMS. Each of the five transmission substations in the western ring have been recently commissioned with full SCADA capabilities via new front-end servers located at the HQ control center. The other transmission substations have active telemetry and metering; however, they do not have supervisory control capability from the control center since the necessary upgrades have not been made.

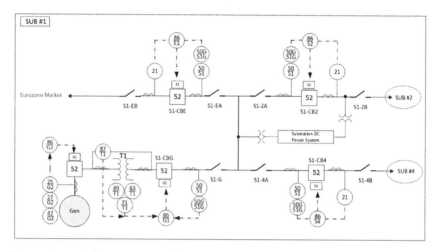

Figure A.10   Substation #1 Bus/Protection Schematic.

Communications and control engineering staff have access to the SCADA system network for station device configuration and trouble-shooting activities. Although individual substation control and protection devices function independently from the SCADA system, without SCADA operability, automated remote management of stations and the greater transmission system is reduced to manual operations via radio. Because of staffing "cost optimization" measures, there are only enough linemen available to handle manual local response duties at a limited number of substations at any given time. Travel and staging time for a site visit averages 3 hours or more.

System Communications

SCADA and individual substation operational environments reside on separate dedicated subnets within the corporate private network address space, see Figure A.11. SCADA functionality is communicated to each substation controller (ABB RTU560) over Ethernet on the SCADA subnet. The ABB RTU560 provides communications to local devices on the substation control subnet via separate on-board Ethernet interface.

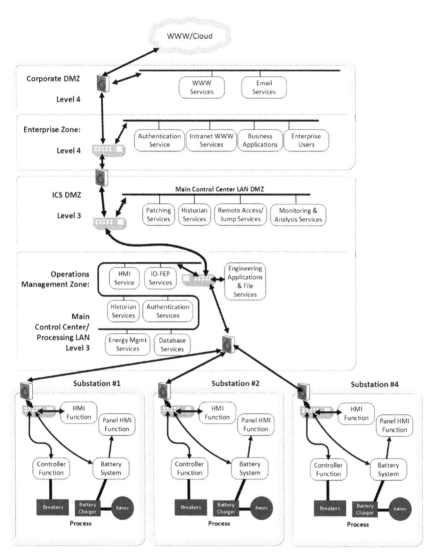

Figure A.11   Utility Power System SCADA Communications.

Substation Control

Local monitoring and control capabilities are provided via a dedicated station controller platform. At the western grid critical substations, this critical device is an ABB RTU560. The station controller provides capabilities for SCADA communications, field device (e.g., breaker and switch actuator) operations, power system protection task/sequence logic processing, physical and logical I/O tagging, dc power system communications, station events analysis, alarming, and protocol concentration. See Figure A.12 for substation major functional grouping and group relationship to station control.

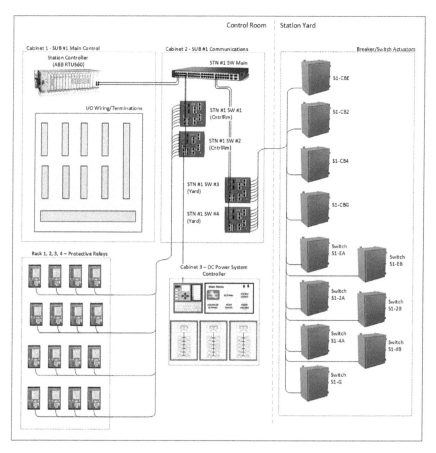

Figure A.12   Station Control via ABB RTU560 Direct to Breaker Actuators.

Substation dc Power System

The three critical transmission substations with connectivity to the EU market have been equipped with a new auxiliary dc power system. The dc system is comprised of a battery management system (controller, ac/dc rectifier electronics, on-board maintenance bypass and transfer capabilities), dc power distribution infrastructure (breakers, panels, wiring, etc.), a battery bank, and a resistive load bank. The dc system is a redundant system with multiple taps used to provide power to all substation control and protective devices, communications infrastructure, breaker, and switch actuators.

If the dc power system is incapacitated (battery failure, controller failure, loss of ac power supply and charging, etc.), the ability to automatically and/or remotely control and monitor the substation is lost. The battery management system provides control and monitoring of the dc system, a configuration interface, communications capabilities, and battery bank charging functions. Battery health/charge is critical—from a degraded charge state it can take up to 24 hours to restore batteries to a usable voltage level.

PHASE 3: CONSEQUENCE-BASED TARGETING

The summary of the HCE-relevant information collected in Phase 2 is drafted into a System Description, which forms the basis of Phase 3, consequence-based targeting. The goal of Phase 3 is to develop *plausible* **Attack Scenarios**. The CCE Team uses an adversary perspective to identify different ways to achieve the HCE, analyzing the data from Phase 2 and collecting additional details as required. The **System Targeting Description** is used to summarize and reference all the key details that are required for the Attack Scenarios. It should be noted that the findings in Phase 3 are not all inclusive; they represent a set of possible approaches (**Technical Approaches**) to disrupting critical systems or functions. At the same time, these identified attack scenarios may be limited or informed by the Boundary Conditions defined in Phase 1. The **Target Details** describe each location where manipulation or compromise occurs in an Attack Scenario to make the HCE possible and includes all the technical details an adversary would need.

Phase 3 is a targeting effort at its core, during which organizations systematically identify the necessary steps for adversary success—all from the adversary's perspective. A key component to this approach is identifying the critical information needs and targets, as well as access and actions required for the adversary to achieve the desired effect. These **Critical Needs** are tied to accomplishing the HCE, such as the technical requirements for the implant (**Development**), or the access required to deliver an implant (**Deployment**). Critical Needs can and will be identified outside of an entity's network boundary or direct control (vendors, suppliers, subcontractors, regulatory, or financial filings), as well as publicly available, open-source information found in various places. An entity's ability to identify what these Critical Needs are, where they reside, and who has access to them is a crucial step in understanding and ultimately mitigating risk.

For the CCE Team, the definition of critical information should extend well beyond documentation. An adversary will need to understand precisely how a process or piece of equipment operates in order to achieve a desired effect. To gain this type of knowledge, the adversary may need to acquire equipment, software, configuration files, or even access somewhere in the supply chain.

System Targeting Description

High-consequence event: Adversary gains access to the substation network and manipulates configuration of the battery management system. Modifications reduce battery bank recharging capability, as well as dc power availability. The dc system capacity is degraded to a level insufficient for sustained support of substation SCADA, protection, and operations infrastructure. Attack ensures that no indications are presented to system operators while the charging system is at reduced capacity. Adversary triggers station isolation and de-energization by opening breakers on the three transmission-level interconnects.

System Description Parsing
Baltavia transmission system grid location and substation identification (subsystem and station IDs):

Transmission System: Power delivery to the European market is delivered via the western Baltavian transmission grid. The five substations that comprise the western portion of the transmission system are arranged roughly in a ring structure to provide redundant pathways for power delivery (see Figure A.13). The ring structure ensures that if a single substation is taken completely out of service by a disruption, the remainder of the substations on the loop will still be able to provide connectivity.

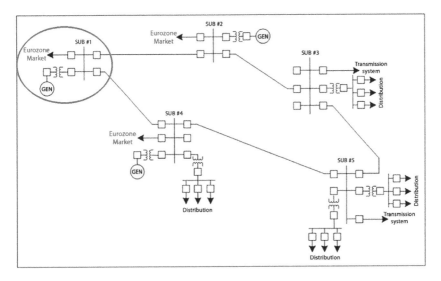

Figure A.13   Five Substations that Comprise the Western Portion in a Ring Structure.

Power delivery to the European markets is provided via substations #1, #2, and #4. All three substations need to be online for maximum stability and power delivery capacity.

Critical substation bus/power delivery infrastructure (station isolation, breaker identification):

Critical Substations: Each critical substation shares similar general topology. Dual transmission feeds provide the connectivity to the greater loop, and a third line provides connectivity to the target European market systems. Transmission voltage at each is established at 220kV. The bus structure of each substation is shown in Figure A.14. As mentioned earlier, each of the substations also provides some generation capacity to offset internal (Baltavian) and external power demands.

Critical substation control (controller capabilities, communications, circuit breaker operation):

Substation Control: Local monitoring and control capabilities are provided via a dedicated station controller platform. At the western grid critical substations, this critical device is an ABB RTU560. The station controller provides capabilities for: SCADA communications, field device (e.g., breaker and switch actuator) operations, power system protection task/sequence logic processing, physical and logical I/O tagging, dc

229

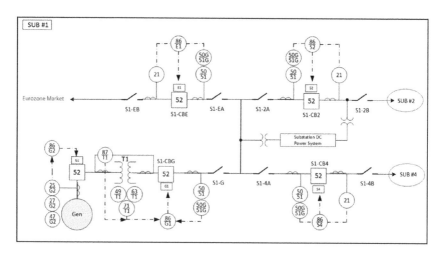

Figure A.14   Substation 1's Bus Structure.

power system communications, station events analysis, alarming, and protocol concentration. See Figure A.15 on the next page for substation major functional grouping and group relationship to station control.

Critical substation equipment power (dc power system—ID, capabilities, comms, restoration limitations):

Substation dc Power System: The three critical transmission substations with connectivity to the EU Market have been equipped with a new auxiliary dc power system. The dc system is comprised of a battery management system (controller, ac/dc rectifier electronics, on-board maintenance bypass and transfer capabilities), dc power distribution infrastructure (breakers, panels, wiring, etc.), a battery bank, and a resistive load bank. The dc system is a redundant system with multiple taps used to provide power to all substation control and protective devices, communications infrastructure, breaker, and switch actuators. If the dc power system is incapacitated (battery failure, controller failure, loss of ac power supply and charging, etc.), the ability to automatically and/or remotely control and monitor the substation is lost. The battery management system provides control and monitoring of the dc system, a configuration interface, communications capabilities, and battery bank charging functions. Battery health/charge is critical—from a degraded charge state it can take up to 24 hours to restore batteries to a usable voltage level.

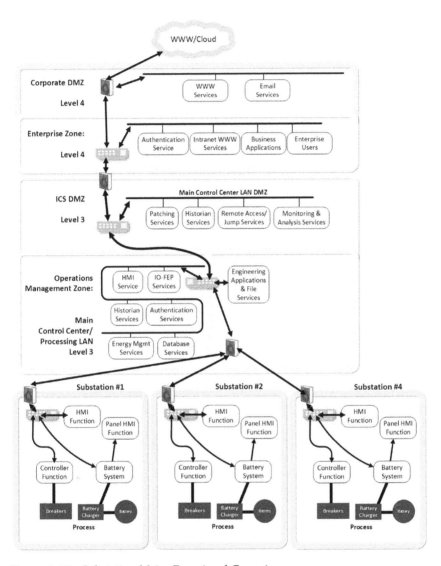

Figure A.15   Substation Major Functional Grouping.

Critical substation communications (network connectivity, key components, data flow):

System Communications: SCADA and individual substation operational environments reside on separate dedicated subnets within the corporate private network address space. SCADA functionality is communicated to each substation controller (ABB RTU560) over Ethernet on the SCADA subnet. The ABB RTU560 provides communications to local devices on the substation control subnet via separate on-board Ethernet interface.

Critical systems operations (control hierarchy, control capabilities, incident response limitations):

System Operations: Centralized transmission system operations, as well as generation dispatch, are performed remotely from a control center at the utility headquarters. Transmission operations (control/monitoring of the transmission system infrastructure) are implemented via a COTS SCADA platform, while generation dispatch uses an AGC module within the utility EMS. Each of the five transmission substations in the western ring has been recently commissioned with full SCADA capabilities via new front-end servers located at the HQ control center. The other transmission substations have active telemetry and metering; however, because necessary upgrades have not been made, they do not have supervisory control capability from the control center. Communications and control engineering staff have access to the SCADA system network for station device configuration and troubleshooting activities. Although individual substation control and protection devices function independently from the SCADA system, without SCADA operability, automated remote management of stations and the greater transmission system is reduced to manual operations via radio. Because of staffing "cost optimization" measures, there are only enough linemen available to handle manual local response duties at a limited number of substations at any given time. Travel and staging time for a site visit averages 3 hours or more.

System Analysis for Targeting
Additional analysis of key systems, components, people, processes, digital connectivity, data flows, etc. that "fill in the gaps" and enables an adversary to assemble a relationally contiguous system targeting description for attack.

Key additional targeting information and steps (reconnaissance—open source and target environment)

Remote Connectivity: Targeted Substation and dc Power System Controllers:

With creation of a free online account at each controller vendor website (substation—ABB, dc power system—BMT), "anonymous" review of technical documentation reveals a software application platform feature common to automation products—caching previously configured network communication paths. The communication paths are created by the support personnel as part of remote online controller engagement. The feature is utilized out of convenience by system technical support staff because it eliminates the need to remember and reconfigure complex network location/IP specifics associated with each of potentially dozens/hundreds of supported controllers in a large asset environment.

Technical Support Personnel:

Engineering/Operations On-Call Support schedule on the SCADA/Ops data/file server identifies a utility substation engineer by name. Online research provides member profile on LinkedIn. Open-source research produces the employee's home address. Social engineering confirms employee's ISP and further reconnaissance provides the employee's home router Wi-Fi network ID. Continued investigation of available documentation on the SCADA/Ops data/file server produces a "remote access procedure" for engineering/operations on-call personnel.

Engineering Laptop

The details of an engineering laptop used for backshift support are described in the "remote access procedure" found on the SCADA/Ops data/file server. This includes the specifics of the hardware and the remote access software, as well as the engineering applications (BMT ADV1 Configurator, ABB RTUtil 560 Configurator, and ABB MultiprogWT Configuration Software).

Technical Approach

Target 1 (T1): Utility Substation Engineer's Laptop

Access

Compromised home Wi-Fi router and substation engineer's laptop connected to home Wi-Fi network during on-call support.

Timing/Triggering

Immediately upon substation engineer's laptop connection to home Wi-Fi network.

233

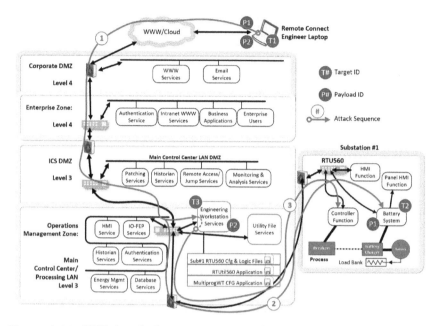

Figure A.16   HCE Attack Communications Path via SCADA to Sub#1 Battery System and RTU560 Station.

Action/Payload

Two separate malware payloads (P1 and P2) are installed on the laptop, reference Figure A.16. When the laptop is subsequently connected to the Utility SCADA Network, malware payload P1 will target and compromise the Substation #1 Battery Management Control System, and the malware payload P2 will be dropped on the SCADA Engineering Workstation and executed to target and manipulate the critical power delivery substation (Substation #1) infrastructure control.

Target 2 (T2): Substation #1 Battery Management Control System Access

The substation engineer's laptop certificate-based authentication and VPN server configuration for remote access through the company firewall to the utility SCADA network.

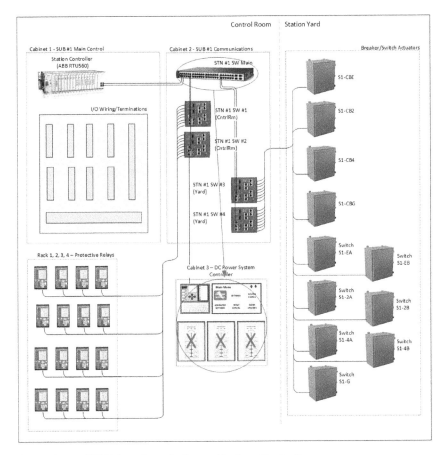

Figure A.17   HCE Attack on dc Power System Controller.

Timing/Triggering (Malware P1 BMT Battery Management System Drop)
Immediately upon the substation engineer's laptop VPN connection to
SCADA network.

Action/Payload
Leveraging the substation engineer's escalated privileges, the malware
deployment control on the laptop downloads the malware payload
P1 to the Substation #1 BMT dc power system controller for malicious
modifications to the BMT battery management software, see Figures A.17

235

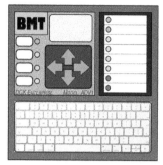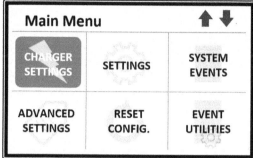

Figure A.18   (Left) Battery Management System Controller and (Right) Battery Management System Application.

and A.18. The modification will target the battery charging control function to degrade its operation resulting in the battery electrical potential being discharged through the station load bank. The software modifications also ensure that both Ethernet-dependent and local Human-Machine Interface (HMI) alarming are suppressed. System operators remain unaware that the charging system is at reduced capacity and after 12 hours, available stored battery power is insufficient to support critical substation loads: SCADA infrastructure, protective relays, and breaker actuators.

Target 3 (T3): SCADA Engineering Workstation
Access
The substation engineer's laptop certificate-based authentication and VPN server configuration for remote access through the company firewall to the Utility SCADA network.

Timing/Triggering (Malware P2 SCADA Engineering Workstation Drop)
Immediately upon the substation engineer's laptop VPN connection to SCADA network.

Action/Payload
Leveraging the substation engineer's escalated privileges, the malware deployment control on the laptop downloads the malware payload P2 to the SCADA Engineering Workstation. This malware will target the Substation #1 power system infrastructure.

Timing/Triggering (Malware P2 Execution)

Malware P2 payload will execute and take actions on the Substation #1 power system control after a 12-hour time delay as measured from drop time on the SCADA Engineering Workstation located within the Engineering Applications and File Services functional area.

Action/Payload

With the dc power system impacted and using the ABB MultiProg PRO RTU560 configuration software and Substation #1 project file on the local SCADA engineering workstation host, the malware establishes communication natively to the Substation #1 RTU560 (see Figure A.19).

From here, leveraging engineered functionality provided by the ABB MultiProg PRO RTU560 Application and based on the breaker "trip" logic (see Figure A.20), the attacker initiates station breaker operations on substation transmission circuit breakers S1-CBE, S1-CB2, S1-CB4, and S1-CBG (Figures A.21 and A.22).

The loss of bus connectivity from the transmission system isolates the substation and removes the substation ac supply to the station BMT battery management system. The ac and dc power sources at the

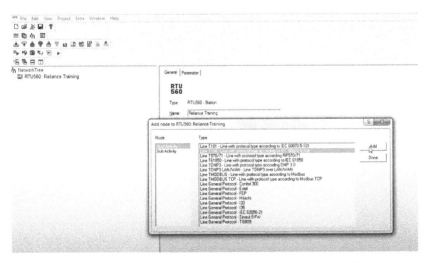

Figure A.19 ABB RTUtil 560 Application from Engineering Workstation to Configure RTU560 System.

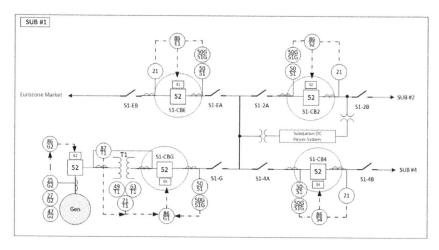

Figure A.20   Power System Control Trip Logic Used During the HCE Attack.

substation are lost. Adequate battery-stored dc power is unavailable from the battery system. Attempts from the utility control room SCADA operator to exercise breaker actuation causes excessive demand and damage on individual battery cells.

Target Details

The critical components involved in the HCE provide power system control, monitoring, and protection operability for Substation #1. A utility SCADA engineer laptop or workstation provides a familiar operating environment from which to stage the attack, but malicious modifications need only take place in the Substation #1 dc power BMT battery management system and at the Engineering Workstation that contains the ABB MultiProg PRO RTU560 application.

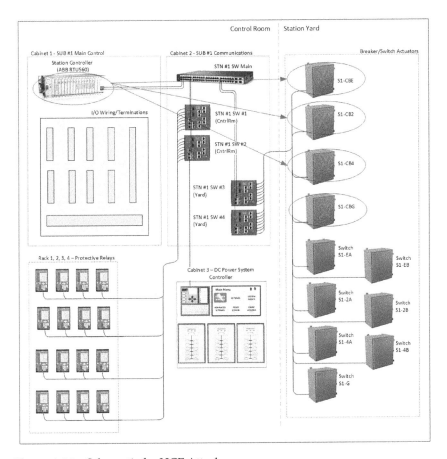

Figure A.21 Schematic for HCE Attack.

The preliminary HCE diagram can then be updated, as shown in Figure A.23, to represent the complete sequence of events and components involved in the HCE attack. The engineer's laptop was the first target, T1, where the attacker payloads, P1 and P2, were installed. When the engineer connected remotely, the P1 payload was transmitted, installed, and initiated in the T2 BMT Battery Charger Management System, and the P2 payload was transmitted and installed in the T3 Engineering Workstation, which will initiate a 12-hour timer. When the timer expires,

239

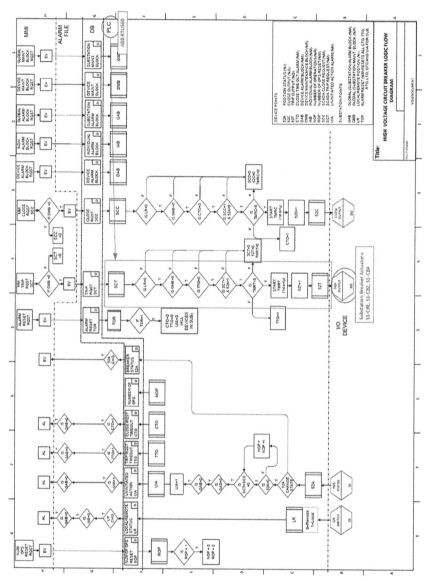

Figure A.22   Station Functional Groups and Control Used During HCE Attack.

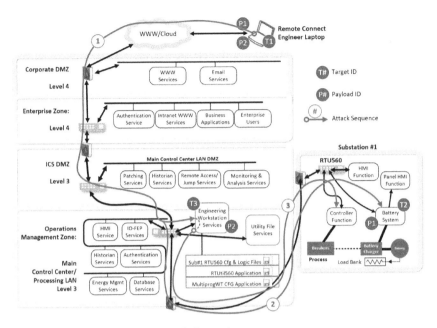

Figure A.23   Updated HCE Attack Scenario.

the breaker and switch operations will be transmitted directly to the substation #1 RTU560 via the ABB MultiProg PRO RTU560 Configuration Application.

Adversary efforts to expand understanding of the critical systems and devices would likely involve development of a critical component list (see Table A.2), which is a subset of Phase 2 taxonomy line items, and with details available via open-source vendor literature (where not provided already on the compromised workstation or file server).

Critical Needs—Development

In order to develop the attack that delivers the HCE, an adversary would need to understand the detailed functionality of each critical component, as well as the operational context for use of the technologies. Documentation providing these function and context details would be part of the adversary's critical needs. Table A.3 on the next page provides an example list of Critical Needs, including likely artifact location.

241

Table A.2 Critical Components

	Name	**Dell Laptop**
Utility SCADA Engineer Laptop	Function	SCADA Engineer Portable App/Data Host
	Vendor	Dell
	Model	Precision 7540
	OS/Misc	x64, Windows 10 Enterprise
	Protocols	TCP/IP/Ethernet, SSH, SNMP, HTTPS, HTTP, Telnet, DNP3, SEL Fast Message
Utility SCADA Engineering Workstation	Function	SCADA Engineer App/Data Host
	Vendor	Dell
	Model	Precision 3630 Tower
	OS/Misc	x64, Windows 10 Enterprise
	Protocols	TCP/IP/Ethernet, SSH, SNMP, HTTPS, HTTP, Telnet, DNP3, SEL Fast Message
Utility SCADA File Server	Function	SCADA Utility File Server
	Vendor	Dell
	Model	Precision 3630 Tower
	OS/Misc	x64, Windows 10 Enterprise
	Protocols	TCP/IP/Ethernet, SSH, SNMP, HTTPS, HTTP, Telnet, DNP3, SEL Fast Message
	Name	ABB RTU560
Substation Controller	Function	Substation Control
	Vendor	ABB
	Model	RTU560
	Protocols	Ethernet, IEC 61850 MMS, IEC 60870-101/104, Modbus TCP, IEEE C37.118, LG 8979, CP2179, Telnet, DNP3, EtherCAT
	Name	BMT Battery Management Controller
ADV1 Battery Management Controller	Function	Substation DC Battery Management System
	Vendor	DGK Enterprise
	Model	ADV1
	Protocols	Ethernet, Modbus, DNP3
	Name	RTUtil 560

Table A.2 (Cont.)

	Name	Dell Laptop
ABB RTUtil 560 Configuration Software	Function	RTU560 system configuration
	Vendor	ABB
	Model	RTUtil 560
	Name	MultiprogWT RTU Logic Configurator
ABB MultiprogWT Configuration Software	Function	Logic configuration for RTU560 Controller
	Vendor	ABB
	Model	MultiProg-wt
	Name	ADV1 Configurator
BMT Battery Management system application	Function	Battery Management System configuration
	Vendor	DGK Enterprises
	Model	ADV1

Critical Needs—Deployment

The only additional element required to deploy the payload is access to the engineer's home Wi-Fi network (see Technical Support Personnel, System Analysis for Targeting, earlier in Phase 3). Everything else required for Deployment is in the payload already.

Table A.3 Component Critical Needs—Development

Component	Critical Needs for Development	Location/Availability
Substation Engineer Dell Precision 7540 Laptop	Operating system	On board, available at initial compromise
	VPN	Utility/Networking Data/ app server
	Certificate-based authentication	Utility/Networking Data/ app server
	Security/Monitoring Software and Configuration	Utility/Security Data/app server

(*continued*)

243

Table A.3 (Cont.)

Component	Critical Needs for Development	Location/Availability
SCADA	Operating system	Open source
Engineering Workstation	VPN	Utility/Networking Data/ app server
Dell Precision 3630 PC	Certificate-based authentication	Utility/Security Data/app server
Tower	ABB RTUtil 560 Configurator	On board—SCADA Engineering Workstation
	ABB MultiprogWT Configuration Software	On board—SCADA Engineering Workstation
Utility	Operating system	Open source
SCADA/Ops File Server	Diagram—Sub#1 Bus/Breaker Schematic	On board—Utility/SCADA Ops File Server
Dell Precision 3630 PC	Diagram—Sub#1 Breaker Control Diagram	On board—Utility/SCADA Ops File Server
Tower	Diagram—Sub #1 Breaker Control Logic Diagram	On board—Utility/SCADA Ops File Server
	Diagram—Sub #1 Communications Schematic	On board—Utility/SCADA Ops File Server
	Diagram—SCADA Systems Network Topology Diagram	On board—Utility/SCADA Ops File Server
	Document—SCADA User Manual	On board—Utility/SCADA Ops File Server
	Document—Operating Procedure: Station Isolation	On board—Utility/SCADA Ops File Server
	Document—Operations Schedule/On-Call Duty List	On board—Utility/SCADA Ops File Server
	Document—Remote Access Authorized Users List	On board—Utility/SCADA Ops File Server
	Document—Remote Access Policy and Procedures	On board—Utility/SCADA Ops File Server
BMT ADV1	Product specs/manuals	Open source
Battery Management	Battery system one-line diagram	Utility SCADA/Ops File Server
Controller	Battery charger failure (alarm) operations procedures	Utility SCADA/Ops File Server
	Utility maintenance procedures	Utility SCADA/Ops File Server
	Files—ADV1 Sub#1 Configuration File	Utility/Sub#1Cfg/Battery

244

Table A.3 (Cont.)

Component	Critical Needs for Development	Location/Availability
BMT ADV1 Battery Management System Configurator	Software and associated documentation	(Purchase)
	Utility software update procedures	Utility SCADA/Ops File Server
ABB RTU560 Controller	Product specs/manuals	Open source
	Diagram—Sub#1 Bus/Breaker Schematic	Utility/SCADA Ops File Server
	Diagram—Sub#1 Breaker Control Diagram	Utility/SCADA Ops File Server
	Diagram—Sub #1 Breaker Control Logic Diagram	Utility/SCADA Ops File Server
	Sub#1 Comms Gateway specs / configurations	Utility SCADA/Ops File Server
	RTU560 wiring diagram	Utility SCADA/Ops File Server
	Files—RTU560 Sub#1 Configuration File	Utility/Sub#1Cfg/RTU
ABB RTUtil 560 Configurator	Software and associated documentation	(Purchase)
	Utility software update procedures	Utility SCADA/Ops File Server
ABB MultiprogWT Configuration Software	Software and associated documentation	(Purchase)
	Utility software update procedures	Utility SCADA/Ops File Server

PHASE 4: MITIGATIONS AND PROTECTIONS

Phase 4 "Mitigations and Protections" covers exactly that—mitigation and protection strategies. Using the CCE framework for Phase 4 in Figure A.24, we will attempt to come up with recommendations around protections and mitigations for the power system operator in anticipation of the HCE scenario.

245

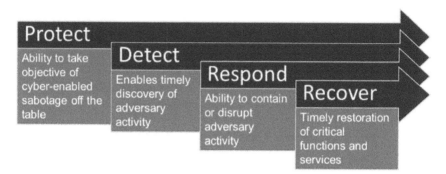

Figure A.24 Mitigation and Protection Framework.

Protect

Engineering: Battery Management System Network
Isolation and Hardwired I/O
- Remove capabilities for remote network access to the Battery Management System device. Maintain SCADA and local monitoring/alarming capabilities via physical aux contacts and/or dedicated "out-of-band" networking that is isolated from the general station network.

Operations: Station dc Power System Health/Availability Verification
- Separate, non-networked device-level dc battery system monitoring that provides alarming for under/over voltage, as well as other critical dc system parameters. Validation occurs visually via local HMI and/or transducer display. Operator verifies that dc power system parameters are within (+/- X%) of desired ranges (and local control setpoint) on a fixed time basis by procedure (such as, "check setpoint hourly as part of rounds"). This would also require the operator to have a response procedure (detailed in section below).

If these measures are not implemented, please consider the following. With digital access (remote via utility networks or locally via laptop), because the substation power system and battery management systems are programmable/configurable (for the purpose of improved operational efficacy and efficiency—automated fault/anomaly response), complete mitigation of the attacks in this HCE is not likely, short of replacing automated controllers with purely electromechanical devices. However, the substation dc power system ac tap location, Battery Management System

246

network connectivity, and the general substation attack surface presented in this scenario can be greatly reduced through several design, device, and network security improvements. A few of these are identified in the following.

Substation dc Power System ac Tap

- Although the existing dual supply approach provides excellent operational resiliency, in order to also eliminate complete dependence on the substation transmission feed to the substation, at least one of the ac taps should be located on the transmission system—but "upstream" of the switches controllable from the subject substation controller. This engineered, physical change maintains dual ac sourcing for the critical dc Power System, but it also eliminates impact capabilities from a single digital component and system (Substation HMI vs. SCADA Server).

Substation Network Architecture

- Network segmentation, access control, and monitoring: Small-scale industrial firewall (industrial protocol-aware) for establishing dedicated substation subnet, access control, and traffic Deep Packet Inspection (DPI) analytics for IDS/IPS. Effectiveness requires out-of-band management for support. Segmentation should include separating the cyber-enabled devices by voltage class and function.
- Implement an ICS-aware perimeter device at the field substations, if possible, or at the control center to ensure only the function codes used by the utility are allowed with a protocol.
- Configure the substation perimeter communications devices (e.g., communications gateway) to only accept control commands from the SCADA control center I/O server.
- Eliminate remote access to substation, except for specific devices/accounts in the SCADA zone.
- No direct internet access.
- If appropriate for the operation size, consider implementing area of responsibility control logic to limit the scope of what a single operator workstation can impact.

Remote Terminal Unit (RTU)

- Disallow remote device configuration of RTUs.
  - Single dedicated serial port for SCADA I/O

247

- No direct communications with SCADA servers. Configure SCADA data export/push/write via serial comms to substation ABB RTU560 for secure delivery outside of substation network environment. SCADA writes should be limited to operating parameters only, with hard-coded range limiters.

- If remote device configuration is required from substation network environment:
  - Single network comm interfaces plus single dedicated serial port for SCADA I/O.
  - No direct communications with SCADA servers, same limitations as above.
  - Substation Communications Gateway provides dedicated authentication/access control.

- If remote device configuration is required from SCADA zone, same as above with implementation of additional substation zone access control and monitoring requirements, such as dedicated MFA at substation firewall, out-of-band communications, permissive from the utility control center, session limitations, secondary device-authentication at Substation Communications Gateway, etc.

- Disable remote firmware upload capability administratively on the field devices. Ensure it is not being performed out of band through a directly attached device in the field.

- Local device configuration (vendor-specific to our example scenario)—if possible, disable the webserver diagnostics service to prevent remote modifications.

- Local device configuration (vendor-specific to our example scenario)—disable "parameter loading" capability.

Substation Engineer Data/App Server, Workstation, and/or Laptop

- Access control includes multifactor authentication to SCADA zone authentication server.
- Endpoint protection that includes malware, script control, and application whitelisting.
- All data-at-rest file storage uses encryption (production-critical, business-critical, etc.).

Additional security improvements (greater environment)—these can certainly make an attack more difficult to execute and will impose additional costs on an adversary.

All Network Environments

- Firewall-enforced zone segmentation, access control, and network traffic DPI analytics for IDS/IPS at zone boundaries.
- Controlled use of administrative privileges in all zones.

Detect

Device Event Monitoring and Analysis

- Deploy and/or configure device-level dc battery system supply monitoring that provides alarming for under/over voltage, as well as other critical dc system conditions. Alarming should be hard-wired to station notification controller and communicated out-of-band (dedicated SCADA network) to control center. Distributed monitoring at the individual device improves overall reliability and reduces risk of adversarial "masking" a more centralized approach.
- Enable automated logging on communications gateways.
- Enable automated logging on protective relays.
- Enable automated logging on RTUs.

Network Monitoring and Analysis

- Provide capture and DPI of all ingress/egress network traffic at SCADA zone interface router.
- Provide capture and DPI of all ingress/egress network traffic at each substation local gateway.
- Dedicated network IDS/IPS at SCADA and substation zone interfaces.
- Employ anomaly detection, network whitelisting monitoring, or behavioral analytic detection.
- Implement communications baselines.

Improved Endpoint Malware Detection

- Deploy malware signature detection at host and network level.

Account Monitoring and Control

- Endpoints.
- Implement directory level detection of abnormal logins to detect credential theft and pivot.

For Your Consideration
- Detection activities can be resource intensive. There are constant changes and alerts that need attention and proper staffing to be effective.
- What detection capabilities does your organization have currently?
- Does your organization belong to any communities to help share information about possible or actual attacks?

Respond

Operations: Station dc Power System Health/Availability Verification (Reference Protect from Above)
- Operator takes immediate actions per: Station dc Power System Failure response procedure. Steps include immediate SCADA control center notification, network isolation of battery management system, configuration validation/correction at local battery management system interface, dc power system voltage verification (manual spot measurements using hand-held meter), and continuous local monitoring of dc power system health restoration. Operator also initiates cybersecurity response and troubleshooting protocol.

Incident Response and Management—General
- Fully developed Incident Response (IR) and Management Plan for Operations and Business Environments
- Annual hands-on practice of IR and Management Plan
- Operations personnel on staff to support manual operations for widely distributed, multi-station event
- Out-of-band communications infrastructure, operable and available 24/7 to support Ops staff
- Establish chain of command in advance of emergencies
- Open communication channels between OT and IT (and corporate)

For Your Consideration
- Does your organization have a clear communication and action plan for an attack?
- Do you have checklists to follow (to avoid missing steps)?
- Has someone been given authority to make emergency decisions (i.e., shut down functions or systems)?
- Who will speak for the company if the press gets involved?
- How will information sharing be managed?

Recover

Operations: Station dc Power System Functional Restoration (Reference Respond from Above)

- Depending on conditions discovered during response activities, possibly disconnect existing dc system supply at distribution and provide temporary/mobile dc supply (battery units, diesel/gas generator with dc rectifiers, etc.) in its place until the permanent system can be restored and validated.

Incident Recovery—General

- Fully developed Recovery Plan for Operations and Business Environments
- Annual hands-on practice of Recovery Plan
- Operations personnel on staff to support manual operations for widely distributed, multi-station event.
- Out-of-band communications infrastructure, operable and available 24/7 to support Ops staff
- Maintain local manual control capabilities for substation components
- Ensure configuration data backups
- Tested recovery (dry run)
- Encrypted storage for sensitive files

For Your Consideration:

- A clear roadmap and a realistic timeline for recovery are key for getting back to full operation.
- Does your organization have a plan?
- Recovery plans often involve using backups and restoring a system to its pre-attack condition—Is this enough?
- This stage can become an opportunity to strengthen areas that were previously neglected—Are there systems that need to be updated (software, hardware, training materials, etc.)?

CASE STUDY: KEY TERMS

Electricity

A secondary power source harvested from the mechanical work that is exerted from a turbine to a coupled, rotary magnet that spins around copper coils within a generator. The purpose of the primary fuel's energy is to create mechanical power that can be transformed into electrical power.

Electrical Power

The instantaneous flow of electrical charges, or currents, which serve as the means to perform work. Currents are driven by an electromotive force, or voltage, which represents the driving potential for performing work. Electrical power flow is instantaneous and finite. Commercially viable storage options do not currently exist. The flow of electricity is governed by electromagnetic properties of the materials that make up the electric grid. Circuits are constructed to establish a path for power to flow, and flow can be controlled in a system using protective elements such as fuses, breakers, relays, and capacitors.

The structure of *electricity delivery* can be categorized into three functions: generation, transmission, and distribution, all of which are linked through key assets known as substations as represented in Figure A.24.

The Grid

Layout of the electrical transmission system; a network of transmission lines and the associated substations and other equipment required to move power. In the United States, the combined transmission and distribution network is often referred to as the "power grid" or simply "the grid." In the United States, there is no single grid, rather three distinct interconnections (the Eastern Interconnection, Western Interconnection, and the Texas Interconnection). Power demand fluctuates throughout the day and across regions with varying population densities because utility-scale electricity storage does not exist. To keep the electrical systems always balanced, generation operators must dispatch enough power required to supply demand. Power dispatch is coordinated by the plant operator and a transmission system operator making communications critical at generation facilities.

Figure A.25   Electricity Delivery Process.

Transmission

Power transmission lines facilitate the bulk transfer of electricity from a generating station to a local distribution network. These transmission lines are designed to transport energy over long distances with minimal power losses, which is made possible by stepping up or increasing voltages at specific points along the electric system. The components of transmission lines consist of structural frames, conductor lines, cables, transformers, circuit breakers, switches, and substations. Transmission lines that interconnect with each other to connect various regions and demand centers become transmission networks and are distinct from local distribution lines. Typical transmission lines operate at 765, 500, 345, 230, and 138 kV; higher voltage classes require larger support structures and span lengths.

Power Distribution

The power distribution system is the final stage in the delivery of electric power, carrying electricity out of the transmission system to individual customers. Distribution systems can link directly into high-voltage transmission networks or be fed by sub-transmission networks. Distribution substations reduce high voltages to medium-range voltages and route low voltages over distribution power lines to commercial and residential customers.

Substations

Equipment that switches, steps down, or regulates voltage of electricity. Also serves as a control and transfer point on a transmission system. Substations not only provide crucial links for generation, but they also serve as key nodes for linking transmission and distribution networks to end-use customers. While a substation can provide several distinct system functions, most utilize transformers to adjust voltage along the electric system. A substation may be designed initially for the purpose of bulk power transmission but may also incorporate an additional transformer to distribute power locally at a lower voltage. Power lines are classified by their operational voltage levels, and transmission lines are designed to handle the higher voltage ranges (typically > 100 kV). Transformer equipment at substations facilitates energy transfer over networks that operate at varying voltage levels. A substation generally contains transformers, protective equipment (relays and circuit breakers), switches for controlling high-voltage connections, electronic instrumentation to monitor system performance and record data, and fire-fighting equipment in the event of an emergency. Some important functions that are carried out at substations are voltage control, monitoring the flow of electricity, monitoring reactive power flow, reactive power compensation, and improving power factors.

Transformer

Electrical device that changes the voltage in ac circuits. Transformers are critical equipment in delivering electricity to customers, but many are in isolated areas and are vulnerable to weather events, acts of terrorism, and sabotage. The loss of transformers at substations represents a significant concern for energy security in the electricity supply chain due to shortages in inventory and manufacturing materials, increased global demand in grid developing countries, and limited domestic manufacturing capabilities. Substations are highly specific to the systems they serve, which also limits the interchangeability of transformers. Replacing a transformer is associated with a long delivery lead time because they are generally difficult to transport due to their size and weight, and larger, more sophisticated models are manufactured abroad. Failure of even a single unit could result in temporary service interruption. Although power transformers come in a wide variety of sizes and configurations, they consist of two main components: the core, made of high-permeability, grain-oriented, silicon electrical steel, layered in pieces; and windings, made of copper conductors wound around the core, providing electrical input and output.

Electrical Energy

The generation or use of electric power over a period, usually expressed in megawatt hours (MWh), kilowatt hours (KWh), or gigawatt hours (GWh), as opposed to electric capacity, which is measured in kilowatts (KW).
(see also: DOE/OE-0017.)

Protective Relays

Detect abnormal or unsafe conditions by comparing real-time operating parameters with pre-programmed thresholds. When those threshold values are met or exceeded, the relay will initiate an action—such as opening a circuit breaker—to isolate the components under fault condition (abnormal current) and prevent potential equipment damage. Relays were originally electromechanical, but today they are typically microprocessor based due to the increased functionality such devices provide.

Auxiliary dc Control Power System

Consists of batteries, battery management system (rectifier/charger/monitoring/config), and the dc power distribution to dependent loads: SCADA infrastructure (server, workstation, HMI, network devices), protective relays, and substation RTUs that monitor and operate circuit breakers and switches, and actuators. Under normal operation, power availability is managed to recover the battery voltage after a discharge and to maintain the float voltage while supporting any self-discharge losses in the battery system. The aux dc system is sized and operated to meet the demand of continuous, intermittent, medium-rate, and momentary high-rate loads (trip coils and dc motors). Upon failure of the battery charger or loss of its ac supply, the battery bank must support the station continuous loads along with the intermittent and momentary loads that may occur before the battery charger is repaired or the ac supply is restored.

Supervisory Control and Data Acquisition (SCADA) Systems

Highly distributed systems used to control geographically dispersed assets, often scattered over thousands of square kilometers, where centralized data acquisition and control are critical to system operation. They are used in distribution systems such as water distribution and wastewater collection systems, oil and gas pipelines, electrical power grids, and railway transportation systems. A SCADA control center performs centralized monitoring and control for field sites over long-distance communications networks, including monitoring alarms and processing status data. Based on information received from remote stations, automated or operator-driven supervisory commands can be pushed to remote station control devices, which are often referred to as field devices. Field devices control local operations, such as opening and closing valves and breakers, collecting data from sensor systems, and monitoring the local environment for alarm conditions.

Common major control components include the following:

- Control Server: A control server hosts the DCS or supervisory control software that is designed to communicate with lower-level control devices. The control server accesses subordinate control modules over an ICS network.

- SCADA Server: The SCADA server is the device that acts as the "master" in a SCADA system. Remote terminal units and Programmable Logic Controller (PLC) devices (as described below) located at remote field sites usually act as "slaves."
- Remote Terminal Unit (RTU): The RTU, also called a remote telemetry unit, is a special-purpose data acquisition and control device designed to support SCADA "remote" deployments. RTUs are field devices that often support a variety of communications mediums. Sometimes PLCs are implemented as field devices to serve as RTUs; in this case, the PLC is then referred to as an RTU.
- Programmable Logic Controller (PLC): The PLC is a small industrial computer originally designed to perform the logic functions executed by electrical hardware (relays, drum switches, and mechanical timer/counters). PLCs have evolved into controllers with the capability of controlling complex processes, and they are used substantially in SCADA systems and DCSs. Other controllers used at the field level are process controllers and RTUs; they provide the same control as PLCs but are designed for specific control applications. In SCADA environments, PLCs are often used as field devices because they are more economical, versatile, flexible, and configurable than special-purpose RTUs.
- Intelligent Electronic Devices (IED): An IED is a "smart" sensor/actuator containing the intelligence required to acquire data, communicate to other devices, and perform local processing and control. An IED could combine an analog input sensor, analog output, low-level control capabilities, a communication system, and program memory in one device. The use of IEDs in SCADA and DCS systems allows for automatic control at the local level.
- Engineering Workstation: A desktop or laptop PC-scale cyber asset where engineers and technicians utilize the appropriate software and design tools to perform system and device troubleshooting, configuration, tuning, and maintenance tasks.
- Human-Machine Interface (HMI): The HMI is software and hardware that allows human operators to monitor the state of a process under control, modify/configure some control set points within engineered limits, and may provide manually overriding of automatic control functions in the event of an emergency. The HMI typically displays process parameter and status information,

process alarming, and historical process data points for operators, administrators, managers, business partners, and other authorized users. The location, platform, and interface may vary a great deal. For example, an HMI could be a dedicated platform in the control center or a laptop on a protected LAN in the process environment.

- Data Historian: The data historian is a centralized database for logging all process information within an ICS. Information stored in this database can be accessed to support various analyses, from statistical process control to enterprise level planning. The trending application generally resides on the Historian server.
- Input/Output or Front-End Processor (IO or FEP) Server: The IO/ FEP server is a control component responsible for collecting, buffering, and providing access to process information from control sub-components such as PLCs, RTUs, and IEDs. An IO server can reside on the control server or on a separate computer platform. IO/FEP servers are also used for interfacing third-party control components, such as an HMI and an EWS.

(See also NIST 800–882.)

Appendix B: CCE Phase Checklists

ACCELERATE PHASE CHECKLIST

CCE Phase 1— Consequence Prioritization

☐ **Have you defined your company's critical functions and services? List them below.**
*These functions and services inform the entire CCE process about what is at stake.

    ☐ _____
    ☐ _____
    ☐ _____
    ☐ _____

☐ **Have you established Boundary Conditions by defining the Objective and the Scope?**
Briefly describe these concepts for your organization's CCE.

    ☐ **Objective** (Describe the extent or nature of a destructive, disruptive, or degrading act taken against critical functions or services)
        ☐ _____
        ☐ _____

    ☐ **Scope** (Identify key systems or processes that impact critical functions and services)
        ☐ _____
        ☐ _____

☐ **Have you identified adverse Events that could impact critical functions and/ or services? Make a list by brainstorming for any possible events that could lead to a "bad day."**

    ☐ Consider the following targeting concepts for each Event:
        ☐ Physical Infrastructure and Interdependency
        ☐ Horizontal Application of Technology
        ☐ Reliance on Automation and Control Capabilities

☐ **Have you screened the list to develop cyber-events to be evaluated?**

    ☐ Consider the following aspects of a cyber-event:
        ☐ Is this event actionable by cyber means (high-level description)?
        ☐ What additional assumptions need to be made about the event? (e.g., during the summer when the grid is fully loaded)

□ Have you developed criteria severity definitions and established weighting? Fill in the criteria and scoring elements on the cyber-event Prioritization Worksheet provided.

□ Consider the following questions:
  □ What criteria are most important to your company?
    □ Safety
    □ Cost
    □ Duration
    □ Other
  □ Which criteria would have the highest negative impact?
  □ Which criteria would have the lowest negative impact?

□ Have you determined a threshold for how many HCEs will be considered in the CCE engagement? We recommend focusing on fewer than six. List your HCEs below.

HCE #1 _____

HCE #2 _____

HCE #3 _____

HCE #4 _____

HCE #5 _____

HCE #6 _____

□ Choose one HCE from your list to carry throughout the remaining CCE phases. Each HCE above will need to be fully investigated separately. Write down the selected HCE.

_____
_____

261

CCE Phase 2—System-of-Systems Analysis

☐ **Has a data protection plan been established (complying with business rules and laws?)**

☐ Discuss the importance of security for your sensitive documents.
☐ Ensure that access to any aggregated data is strictly enforced.
☐ Draft a plan and begin implementing it immediately.

☐ **Have the following topics been considered and documented?**

☐ Do you have a detailed description of system infrastructure components?
☐ How is the system networked?
☐ What data exchanges occur and between what components?
☐ How is operational data stored?
☐ What communications are used?
☐ What ICS equipment is deployed in this/these system(s)?
☐ How are system components and functions controlled?
☐ What are normal operating procedures?
☐ How is the supply chain managed?
☐ Is any maintenance performed by outside entities?
☐ How is/are the system(s) accessed (by whom)?
☐ How is information about the system managed?
☐ Where (on the network) is information stored?

☐ **Have you created a high-level HCE block diagram that depicts the system of interest?**

☐ Does it identify the critical components?
☐ Does it show the dependencies?
☐ Does it explain the system's process from beginning to end?

☐ **Have you identified all the documents needed to understand the systems involved? Record key locations and identify who is needed to retrieve these documents.**

☐ Notes: (Refer to the diagram and record their relationship)
☐ _____
☐ _____
☐ _____

☐ **Have you identified where information resides inside your company? And information that resides elsewhere (subcontractors, open-source, vendors, etc.)? It is important to be aware of the data that is outside of your organization's control.**

☐ Notes: (Key data may exist in configuration files, cloud services, and at external entities)

☐ _____

☐ _____

☐ _____

☐ **Have all the required documents been gathered/requested and obtained?**

☐ List any critical documents that are still missing or are difficult to acquire:

☐ _____

☐ _____

☐ _____

☐ **Have you created a current or "as-is" functional knowledge base?**

☐ Consider the key features of a knowledge base:

☐ Able to baseline of the functional architecture of the system(s) involved.

☐ The information gathered should answers questions about functionality.

☐ **Have you researched all of your system-related ICS equipment?**

☐ Consider the following topics to research:

☐ Vendor

☐ Make/Model

☐ Firmware version

☐ Last date of device/component patch/firmware upgrade

☐ Age of the equipment

☐ Physical location(s) and accessibility of the equipment

☐ Network/connectivity location of the equipment

☐ **Have you created detailed system diagrams based upon the information gathered?**

☐ The following are possible types of diagrams that will be useful:

- Logic diagram
- ICS interconnect diagram
- Data flow diagram
- Network diagram (wired/wireless)
- Equipment Physical Address List

□ **Have you reviewed all diagrams for accuracy?**

- □ Do diagrams provide relevant information for each HCE?
- □ Has any missing information been properly identified (and requested)?
- □ Are any modifications needed to the diagrams (SME validation)?
- □ Are additional diagrams or charts needed to represent the ICS equipment?

□ **Has the gathered information been summarized into a System Description?**

- □ Have personnel, safety, engineering, and equipment documents been included?
- □ Is the description free of irrelevant data?
- □ Is the description easy to understand for non-technical individuals?

CCE Phase 3—Consequence-Based Targeting

☐ **Maintain records of critical information related to each HCE.**
Note: Refer to your data protection plan during Phase 3 to ensure this information is secure.

☐ For each HCE, describe the Objective that the adversary is trying to achieve.
☐ For traceability, link critical documents and data (identified during Phase 2) to the key aspects of your system(s).

☐ **Ensure the key aspects of a cyber-enabled sabotage are understood:**

☐ What: Technical Approach
 ☐ What does the adversary need to do to achieve the HCE?
 ☐ How is it achieved through misuse?
 ☐ What are the requirements of each Attack Scenario?
☐ Where: Target Details
 ☐ Where does the adversary have to be located within the organization's network to achieve the desired effect?
 ☐ What are the technical details of the specific elements identified from the Technical Approach?
 ☐ Where does digital meet analog or other choke points?
☐ How: Access
 ☐ What access is required to achieve the desired effect?
 ☐ What access methods are possible?
  ■ Network-based
  ■ Human-enabled
  ■ Supply chain

☐ **What system or component could store the payload?**

☐ Consider the following questions:
 ☐ What systems have direct/indirect access to the target?
 ☐ What (if any) existing functionality is being changed?
 ☐ What methods of storing the payload may be employed?
  ■ Where is the payload? Embedded on a chip, FPGA, EPROM, etc.?

☐ **Ensure that possible delivery methods are well-documented.**

☐ Consider the following questions:
 ☐ Are there multiple accesses to deliver the payload to the target?
 ☐ Is the target accessible from outside the network?
 ☐ Is the target susceptible to supply chain attacks?
 ☐ Is the programming encrypted (if so, by whom?), and is there a hash?

□ **Where do components, systems, and technical information reside that the adversary must acquire to design a Technical Approach?**

  □ Consider the adversary's Critical Needs:
    □ Hardware and software details.
    □ Critical or technical information (must obtain and be understood).
    □ Vulnerabilities must be identified.
    □ Sufficient expertise must be attained.
  □ Discuss credential gathering, capturing communications, and lateral movement.

□ **Have all possible methods of establishing and maintaining access to the network(s) been considered?**

  □ Identify systems that would provide advantages to an adversary:
    □ Locations that provide a broad view of network topology for internal discovery
    □ Privileged access for database or service manipulation
    □ Secondary locations to restore control

□ **Have the initial methods of intrusion been fully discussed?**

  □ Consider the steps used during the initial intrusion:
    □ Installation/Modification—Consider plausible malware implementations.
    □ Exploit—Identify system vulnerabilities on corporate or public-facing networks.
    □ Delivery—Study the possible delivery of weaponized and targeted exploits.

□ **What sensitive or useful information is accessible to an adversary?**

  □ Consider the following items of concern:
    □ Widely published information about your organization
    □ Your public-facing digital footprint
    □ Forums, blogs, or other third-party websites that discuss your organization
    □ ICS devices visible from the internet
    □ External sources of personnel data, vendor lists, component purchases, etc.

□ **Describe the following targeting concepts for each identified target.**

  □ Access: Steps, movements, and actions used to reach a target.
  □ Actions: Conditions or steps necessary to cause the end effect.
  □ Timing: The order in which steps must occur during an attack.
  □ Triggering: The activation of the payload based on conditions or timing requirement.

☐ **Prepare a summary of your findings to present to your C-Suite.**

☐ Introduce the HCE and describe how it can be achieved by cyber means.
☐ Explain the different Attack Scenario(s) that an adversary could use to cause the HCE.
☐ Describe the target(s) and access pathways an adversary could use to cause cyber-enabled sabotage.
☐ Describe any discovered chokepoints that provide opportunities for the adversary.
☐ Explain the steps an adversary would take to successfully complete the attack.

CCE Phase 4—Mitigations and Protections

☐ **Have you reviewed the HCE Attack Scenarios for details about the adversary's path?**

    ☐ Ensure that **Actions** taken by an adversary are understood.
    ☐ Ensure that functional **choke points** are accurately depicted.
    ☐ Notes:

    _____
    _____

☐ **Have protections (preferred option) and other mitigation options been considered?**

    ☐ Discuss various options for each category of mitigation:
        ☐ **Protect**—Limit or remove the impact before it happens (engineer it out).
        ☐ **Detect**—Timely discovery of cybersecurity events.
        ☐ **Respond**—Contain the impact after the attack begins.
        ☐ **Recover**—Return to normal operations in a timely manner.
    ☐ Notes:

    _____
    _____

☐ **What protection-based mitigations are available based on the HCE Attack Scenarios?**

    ☐ Discuss the following types of protection measures:
        ☐ Remove the Impact/Engineering or Technology Options
        ☐ Inventory of authorized/unauthorized devices and software
        ☐ Awareness and Training
        ☐ Data Security/Information Protection Processes
    ☐ Brainstorm to identify protections that could be implemented.
    ☐ Notes:

    _____
    _____

☐ **What detection-based mitigations are available based on the HCE Attack Scenarios?**

    ☐ Discuss the following aspects of detection:
        ☐ Anomalies and Events
        ☐ Security/Continuous Monitoring
        ☐ Intrusion Detection Processes
    ☐ Brainstorm to identify detection methods that could be implemented.
    ☐ Notes:

    _____
    _____

☐ **What response-based mitigations are available based on the HCE Attack Scenarios?**

- ☐ Discuss the following aspects of responding to an attack:
  - ☐ Response Planning
  - ☐ Event/Failure Analysis
  - ☐ Process Improvements
  - ☐ Eliminating unnecessary network segments
- ☐ Brainstorm to identify response strategies that could be implemented.
- ☐ Notes:

_____

_____

☐ **What recovery-based mitigations are available based on the HCE Attack Scenarios?**

- ☐ Discuss the following aspects of responding to an attack:
  - ☐ Root Cause Analysis
  - ☐ Base Configurations for Critical Service State
  - ☐ Utilize ISACs, Intel Agencies, and Peer Utilities
- ☐ Brainstorm to identify recovery efforts that could be implemented.
- ☐ Notes:

_____

_____

☐ **Have the previously identified mitigations been prioritized?**

- ☐ Consider the following while prioritizing:
  - ☐ Protections are the preferred course of action
  - ☐ If true protection cannot be achieved, focus on Detect, Respond, and Recover
  - ☐ Discuss cost, time, likelihood/complexity of attack, and confidence
  - ☐ Helps to have a "fresh set" of eyes
- ☐ Identify the most effective mitigations for each step of the **HCE Attack Scenarios** (fortify barriers).
- ☐ Notes:

_____

_____

☐ **Have the top mitigations been presented for implementation?**

- ☐ Schedule a meeting with business leaders to present mitigations for each HCE.
- ☐ Present mitigation benefits, timelines, and cost estimates.
- ☐ Follow up regularly with the decision-makers to ensure the mitigations take place.
- ☐ Notes:

_____

_____

INDEX

Note: Locators in *italics* refer to figures and those in **bold** to tables.

For Product Safety Concerns and Information please contact our EU
representative GPSR@taylorandfrancis.com
Taylor & Francis Verlag GmbH, Kaufingerstraße 24, 80331 München, Germany

www.ingramcontent.com/pod-product-compliance
Ingram Content Group UK Ltd.
Pitfield, Milton Keynes, MK11 3LW, UK
UKHW021055080625
459435UK00001B/4